The Aesthetic Ground of
Critical Theory

Founding Critical Theory

Series Editors: Owen Hulatt, Teaching Fellow, Department of Philosophy, University of York

Darrow Schecter, Reader in History amd Social and Political Thought, University of Sussex

This series publishes original research on prominent figures, texts and topics in, and associated with, the first generation of Frankfurt School Critical Theory. The series comprises specialized treatments of topics and thinkers together with new translations of key texts from the period. Emphasis is lent to Critical Theory as an on-going research project, and both its original research and historical scholarship is articulated in these terms. Critical Theory contains an intrinsic commitment to inter-disciplinary research, and this series attempts to honour this commitment where possible.

Titles in the Series

The Aesthetic Ground of Critical Theory

New Readings of Benjamin and Adorno

Nathan Ross

ROWMAN & LITTLEFIELD
Lanham • Boulder • New York • London

Published by Rowman & Littlefield
A wholly owned subsidiary of The Rowman & Littlefield Publishing Group, Inc.
4501 Forbes Boulevard, Suite 200, Lanham, Maryland 20706
www.rowman.com

Unit A, Whitacre Mews, 26-34 Stannary Street, London SE11 4AB

A catalogue record for this book is available from the British Library
ISBN: HB 978-1-7834-8292-4
PB 978-1-7834-8293-1

Library of Congress Cataloging-in-Publication Data

The aesthetic ground of critical theory : new readings of Benjamin and Adorno / [edited by] Nathan Ross.
p. cm.
Includes bibliographical references and index.
ISBN 978-1-78348-292-4 (cloth : alk. paper) -- ISBN 978-1-78348-293-1 (pbk. : alk. paper) -- ISBN 978-1-78348-294-8 (electronic)
1. Aesthetics. 2. Critical theory. 3. Benjamin, Walter, 1892-1940. 4. Adorno, Theodor W., 1903-1969. 5. Experience.
BH39.A2854 2015
111'.850922--dc23

2015029369

Printed in the United States of America

Contents

Contents   vii

Acknowledgments

The concept for this volume was born at the Society for Phenomenology and Existential Philosophy conference in 2013 thanks to an opportune conversation with Sarah Cambell from Rowman and Littlefield. Work on an edited volume seemed like a way to delay the completion of my own work of several years on the subject of aesthetic experience in German philosophy. The delay has been fruitful. I have to thank all of the contributors for their work, which has enriched my own understanding of two of my favorite philosophers.

One of the inevitable challenges in editing a work of such an international scope is the need to establish stylistic conformity across a wide range of different styles of writing and citation. This would not have been possible without the tireless work of my editorial assistant, Danielle Kutner, who spent many hours ensuring conformity and uniformity. I also owe great thanks on this note to Sinéad Murphy from Rowman and Littlefield for her patience in working with me and the contributors.

The work on this book was made possible by a sabbatical in 2014 and by many conference trips funded by the committee for faculty scholarship at Oklahoma City University. Conference travel, as well as a longer research stay in Berlin, made it possible for me to get to know the work of the scholars found here and to forge the connections that made this book possible.

One of the most often cited maxims in this book is Benjamin's famous, "Truth is the death of intention." The most felicitous moments of agreement, tension, and support to emerge between the various essays in this book are not a result of my planning, and rarely a result of interaction between the contributors. These unintentional moments of coordination are perhaps the best sign that the spirit animating these two thinkers still remains alive in many places.

Introduction

The Aesthetic Ground of Critical Theory

Nathan Ross

In the Prologue to *The Origin of German Tragic Drama*, Walter Benjamin articulates a relation between aesthetic presentation and philosophy that is central to this collection: "It is characteristic of philosophical writing that it must continually confront the question of representation."[1] Philosophy is dependent on language not merely as a means of communication, but as a medium of expression and representation. While science seeks freedom from the complexities of language through a set of unambiguous symbols, philosophy, like art, reveals the dependence of thought on its medium of expression. He argues that it is precisely this aesthetic experience of its own activity within the medium of expression that makes philosophy a pursuit of truth: "If philosophy is to be true to the law of its own form, as the representation of truth and not as a guide to the acquisition of knowledge, then the exercise of this form must . . . be accorded its due importance."[2] He articulates the truth content that inspires philosophy as an elusive phenomenon that flashes forth in the moments when reality does not accord with our intention. "Truth, bodied forth in the dance of represented ideas, resists being projected by whatever means, into the realm of knowledge."[3] And more strikingly yet: "Truth is the death of intention."[4] Philosophy has need of art and aesthetic experience in order to be more than the guarantor of scientific knowledge, to understand the ideal of truth that guides it. At the same time, this text articulates a revolution for philosophical aesthetics: art as truth content.

This articulation of the relation between philosophy, aesthetic presentation, and truth plays a pivotal role in the development of critical theory. It would have a deep and lasting impact on Benjamin's "only disciple," Theodor W. Adorno.[5] As a young private lecturer at Frankfurt University during

the 1930s, Adorno taught one of his first seminars on this text, and incorporated many of its themes into his inaugural lecture, "On the Actuality of
Philosophy." The true depth of the influence this text exerted on Adorno can
be felt most of all in his late work *Aesthetic Theory*. Despite the enigmatic
and fragmentary quality of Adorno's posthumous masterpiece, the work constantly circles around the problem of how to understand art as a form of truth.
"All aesthetic questions terminate in those of the truth content of the works:
is the spirit that a specific work objectively bears in its form true?"[6] Aesthetic philosophy has to understand art in relation to the *telos* of philosophy,
truth. This does not mean translating the results of aesthetic experience into
the form of propositional knowledge. Rather, it is because philosophy is in
some way blocked from fulfilling its own *telos* (according to the thesis of the
Dialectic of Enlightenment) that it must look to aesthetic experience as a
distinctive, non-propositional occurrence of truth. This concept of aesthetic
truth is central to Adorno's thoughts on art, as it provides a reprieve from
what might seem to be the overwhelming cultural and cognitive pessimism
of Adorno's work, and yet in contemporary approaches to Adorno it has
proven to be one of the most difficult thoughts to digest. This ideal of aesthetic truth that Adorno inherits from Benjamin seems to place their critical
theories in tension both with the ideal of communicative rationality, and with
the post-modern view that aesthetic experience is a purely negative process, a
disintegration of meaning.[7] It would thus be rewarding, not only for scholarship of Adorno, but for aesthetic philosophy and critical theory more generally, to seek a deeper understanding of the dynamic tension that unites the
thinking of Adorno and Benjamin.

In taking up the aesthetic as the theme that structures the relationship
between Benjamin and Adorno, this book seeks to return to the roots of
critical theory. If we want to understand the significance of *early* critical
theory in distinction from its later incarnations in Habermas and others, we
would do well to make the aesthetic into the primary object of inquiry:[8] For
Adorno and Benjamin, language consists not just of the communication of
knowledge, but also the expression of the subject's somatic experience. That
is, along with communication, there is also a mimetic function to language,
which is increasingly suppressed in modern society because of our reliance
on rationalized forms of cognition. Art is the inheritor of this mimetic comportment for Adorno and Benjamin, and so in this sense it brings philosophy
in touch with a set of problems that would be missing in an account of reason
focused on communication. Art thus raises deep methodological and philosophical questions for the early critical theorists: How does philosophy learn
from art a critical method? Is the aesthetic merely a field of passive enjoyment, or irrational mysticism, or does it offer thought distinctive resources
for establishing a critical engagement with the world? What irreplaceable
resources does aesthetic experience grant to a critical theory of society? How

can we conceptualize art as a form of truth, and what does aesthetic truth teach us about the limitations of conceptual knowledge? And how does the specific terrain of modern art, with its experiments in dissonance, abstraction, and absurdity, call for a new account of meaning and experience?

THE RELATIONSHIP

The relationship between Benjamin and Adorno is dialectical in the most complex sense[9]: On the one hand, if we examine any point of apparent agreement between the two thinkers, such as the commonplace that both share a mimetic conception of aesthetic experience, we find upon closer examination that the common theme actually leads each thinker to fundamentally divergent prescriptions on how mimesis can chart a critical direction for modern art. On the other hand, if we look at any point of disagreement between the two thinkers, such as their famous divergence about the political meaning of new forms of mass art from the 1930s, we find that their disagreements take such an incisive form because the two thinkers share a shorthand that allows them to articulate their divergence, that is, that they share a set of methodological presuppositions even in their debates that bind them even more closely together than those who seek to replicate their thinking in a purely scholarly manner. This book is as much about presenting the debate and divergence of the two thinkers, from both points of view, as it is about unpacking the shorthand that bound them.

The relationship between Benjamin and Adorno goes through three crucial phases, each of which suggests a different interpretative challenge that the works in this volume will confront in various ways.

Phase One—Frankfurt in the 1920s

The two first met in Frankfurt through their common acquaintance Siegfried Kracuaer. Adorno would reminisce: "It is scarcely an illusion of memory when I say that from the very first moment on, I had the impression of Benjamin as one of the most significant human beings that ever confronted me."[10] Benjamin was in a difficult process of writing his post-doctoral thesis *On the Origin of German Tragic Drama*. Even though the philosophical and philological faculties rejected Benjamin's text on German baroque drama, it went on to exert a pivotal influence on Adorno's philosophy, especially because of its "Epistemo-Critical Prologue." Benjamin thus failed in this last attempt to attain an academic career, and he came to regard the younger Adorno as his only disciple.[11] Adorno later taught his first seminar as a private adjunct on Benjamin's text at the very university that did not recognize the work, and he incorporated many of its themes in his inaugural lecture "On the Actuality of Philosophy," to such a degree that Benjamin bristled at being plagiarized. [12]

The importance of this early phase of interchange for the development of critical theory can hardly be overestimated. The prologue to Benjamin's *Origin* text defines a theme of pivotal importance to the thinking of Benjamin, and perhaps even greater significance to Adorno: the theme of aesthetic truth. We find the pivotal articulation of the notion of aesthetic truth first in the prologue: "The object of knowledge, determined as it is by the intention inherent in the concept, is not the truth. Truth is an intentionless state of being, made up of ideas. The proper approach to it is not therefore one of intention and knowledge, but rather a total immersion and disappearance in it. Truth is the death of intention." [13] This leads Benjamin and Adorno to a hermeneutics that focuses on the objective form of the artwork as well as its experiential content, rather than the psychological state or political intention of the creator. The work is true, and critical of society, in that it expresses structures of experience that stand in a complex relation to the forms of experience that support or undermine the society around it. As Susan Buck-Morss argues in her incisive study, it was Benjamin who lead Adorno beyond the hermeneutics of Dilthey, the phenomenology of Husserl, and the neo-Kantianism prevalent at the time by giving him a method for reading truth within the objective, unintentional expressions of culture. [14] As a culmination of this impetus, Adorno's *Aesthetic Theory* measures the function of art in terms of its ability to present truth content in its objective structure, that is, the truth is manifest in art's ability to induce an experience that transforms consciousness. However, both thinkers worked in subsequent years to gain a stronger conception of how this objective truth content of aesthetic experience could serve as a site of social critique.

Phase Two—1930s Exile

The Benjamin-Adorno relationship entered a new phase after 1933, with both philosophers living in exile from Nazi Germany. Adorno worked alongside Max Horkheimer in Oxford and New York to continue the work of the Institute of Social Research in exile. Benjamin, who had edged out a living as a journalist and freelance writer, lacked any stable position or even the opportunity to publish in Nazi Germany, and thus became almost completely dependent on the Institute to support him. As Benjamin labored away in Paris at research on Baudelaire and the Arcades project and developed the materialist theory of aesthetic experience for which he is best known today, he was constantly dependent on the approval of Adorno and Horkheimer. The fascinating letter exchanges between Benjamin and Adorno from these years involve deep theoretical debate, as well as expressions of mutual influence and respect. But this exchange is certainly marked by Benjamin's need for

Adorno's approval, as the latter engaged in extensive criticism of Benjamin's approach and Benjamin often felt compelled to revise his works in order to acknowledge the demands of the Institute. The revisions to his writings that Benjamin felt compelled to make by Adorno did not always lead to a clearer delineation of his philosophical insights.[15] A certain pattern crystallizes in these exchanges: Benjamin formulates a series of "dialectical images" in French culture from the nineteenth century, that is, he seeks concrete phenomena that would illustrate the entwinement of civilization and barbarity. Adorno constantly challenges Benjamin to think in a more systematic and speculative manner, and questions the immediacy with which Benjamin identifies political and philosophical themes in images. A particularly crushing blow, which illustrates the power structure of their relationship, came when Adorno wrote Benjamin a letter with a penetrating critique of his Baudelaire study, all but demanding revisions before it could be published in the Institute's journal.[16] The exchange reveals that the two thinkers have a somewhat different approach to politics and especially to the incorporation of Marxist themes in their philosophies: Benjamin tends to approach politics, and aesthetics from the perspective of class conflict, and seeks modes of aesthetic experience that would unlock revolutionary potential through solidarity with the working class. Adorno, by contrast, urges Benjamin to understand aesthetic phenomena in terms of the "total social process" and considers the perspective of the working class to be just as much a product of false consciousness as the ruling class.[17] This exchange, in which Benjamin was not fully free to resist the Institute's critique and defend his approach, has had an indelible impact on our reception of Benjamin: Adorno's influential critique has led others to adopt the view that Benjamin's conception of art is too affirmative, or that he naively overestimated the potential of popular art forms.[18]

It is my view that the famous letter exchange, with its somewhat one-sided power relation in favor of Adorno, does much to distort the proper relationship between their philosophies. Many of the critiques that Adorno articulates in these letters have burdened Benjamin's philosophy and kept it from getting a fair reading. Several of the chapters in this volume thus challenge us to pay attention to the aspects of Benjamin's thinking that are somewhat suppressed in the view that Adorno provides on it. The chapter by Stéphane Symons centers on a striking phrase that Benjamin possibly expunged from his work at the request of Adorno. The chapter by Georg Bertram defends Benjamin from the commonplace critique, first formulated by Adorno, that Benjamin's aesthetics is "too affirmative." And the chapter by Alison Ross argues for a view of Benjamin as highly skeptical of the category of aesthetic form, a central element of Adorno's aesthetic philosophy.

Phase Three—1960s

Despite Benjamin's tragic death in 1940, the intellectual relationship between Benjamin and Adorno entered its third, and perhaps most decisive phase during the 1960s, the last decade of Adorno's life. I argue this because of two factors: Adorno's absolutely crucial role in curating the first widespread reception of Benjamin's work, as well as Adorno's deep preoccupation with themes from Benjamin's writings in authoring his posthumous masterpiece *Aesthetic Theory*.

During his lifetime, Benjamin faced acute difficulties in publishing his works, especially during the era of Nazi control. He thus depended on the Institute's journal as a means to disseminate his writings, and the Institute often acted in way that forced Benjamin to alter significantly the course of his writings: we see this in the later version of the "Artwork" essay as well as the Baudelaire essay. During the 1960s, as Adorno and his assistant Rolf Tiedemann steered the first edition of Benjamin's works, they inevitably exerted a certain bias on which texts became available and established a narrative for how his works were to interpreted.

The last decade of Adorno's life was marked by a philosophical turn to aesthetics, that is, an attempt to complete a systematic view of his aesthetic thought, *Aesthetic Theory*. Having already published major works critiquing Western culture and epistemic practices, Adorno turned to art as the mode of experience that could serve to mitigate the limitations within "reified consciousness." It is striking today how much this work stands in dialogue with Benjamin. Throughout the work, Adorno returns often to the theme of truth content that he absorbed from Benjamin in the 1920s and develops an aesthetics in which the purpose of art is essentially bound up with its ability to expose structures of reified consciousness and question them. If his debate with Benjamin hinged on the question of how art could become a vehicle for social critique without becoming a simple voice for party politics, then *Aesthetic Theory* represents the most nuanced and complex effort to develop an alternative model of aesthetic experience to the one that he criticized in Benjamin. At many vital turns in his work, Adorno makes positive or critical usage of concepts that he first learned or came to appreciate through Benjamin: the dialectic of concentration and distraction within aesthetic experience, the mimetic mode of experience, the distinction between play and semblance as two modes of aesthetic comportment, the constellational form, and the way in which artistic production resembles rationalized labor.

* * *

The relationship between Benjamin and Adorno thus reveals three layers that will be reflected in the various approaches of the chapters in this volume: On the one hand, there is a need to pay attention to the influence of Benjamin on Adorno, especially via the *Origin* text. On the other hand, there is a need to investigate Benjamin's later, materialist aesthetics in a way that grants these works their proper role in Benjamin's development and frees them from the suppression and distortion that they might receive if we merely read them through Adorno. Finally, there is a need to re-evaluate Adorno's *Aesthetic Theory* as a work that stands in dialogue with Benjamin's conception of aesthetic truth.

THE CHAPTERS

The book begins with a section of five chapters that examine the intellectual relationship between Benjamin and Adorno, before moving on to sections devoted to each thinker.

The opening chapter by Georg Bertram gives us a fresh understanding of how to think of art as a mode of social critique by working to distinguish and defend Benjamin's approach against Adorno's influential criticism. For Adorno, and those who follow in his footsteps, critique entails the ability to stand critically outside of social practice, a so-called aesthetics of negativity.[19] Bertram shows that Benjamin, by contrast, develops a model of aesthetic critique rooted in the capacity of art to transform perceptual practices. Art is critical for Benjamin to the extent that it engages with our socially trained and historically formed habits of perception in ways that transforms them and give us new modes of perceiving the world. Art entails an evolving assemblage of ways of sensing, interpreting, moving, and discussing that can reveal and transform the way in which we carry out these activities outside of the context of art.[20] Art is critical not merely when it gives a negative account, but even more in its power to engage with and transform social practices.

The subsequent chapters in this section explore the rich pattern of mutual influence between Benjamin and Adorno. Marcia Morgan gives an account of how both thinkers conceptualize the Bourgeois *intérieur* as a paradigmatic experience of "failed, inward subjectivity." Finding such a subjectivity in nineteenth-century thought and literature, they consider the way in which aesthetic experience has to replicate and unsettle this phenomenon in order to bring about a truly politicized form of subjectivity. While capitalism creates a volatile market characterized by dispossession, this very volatility leads to fetishizing a safe, interior space. The aesthetic phenomenon of the bourgeois living room reflects the epistemology of the idealistic system, which seeks truth in a flight from volatility into inwardness. The Bourgeois *intérieur* seems to protect the subject against the volatile dispossession at the heart of modern capitalism, but it results in a mere illusion of control, a speculative urge to dominate the real while actually fleeing from it. Social critique thus begins with the Benjaminian impulse to find truth not in a system, but in an "intentionless state of being."[21] The chapter brilliantly culminates in a juxtaposition of two aesthetic figures from the nineteenth century: The Kierkegaardian aesthete falling back into the speculative idealism he sought to repudiate stands in dialectical opposition to the *flâneur* who finds "modern beauty" in the unsettling masses of the mega-city. Her work demonstrates that the transition to politicized subjectivity comes about through an aesthetic experience of the contradiction within closed forms of subjectivity and through the willingness to embrace the "death of intention." Aesthetic experience does not become political consciousness when art can be harnessed for political intentions, but rather when this experience by its own dynamic reaches that state of hopelessness that gives it the courage to embrace the intentionless expression of suffering.

The chapter by Natalia Baeza deepens this analysis of how Adorno adopts Benjamin's thesis that truth is an intentionless state of being, and focuses particularly on the ways in which Adorno's philosophical epistemology reflects insights acquired from Benjamin. In *Negative Dialectics*, Adorno seeks to redefine philosophical knowledge as a capacity for experiencing the "non-identical." Baeza demonstrates that this project is not merely a reaction to Hegel, but owes an essential debt to methodological innovations that Adorno acquired from Benjamin. In particular, she develops the concepts of *constellation* and *mimesis* as two Benjaminian moments that Adorno employs in order to overcome the limitations that he found in idealistic metaphysics. As several of the other chapters will demonstrate, these two methodological innovations are central to defining aesthetic experience as a unique comportment. Baeza argues that they are essential to the effort to think truth as an unreserved effort to give expression to suffering.

The chapter by Eduardo Mendieta focuses on the way in which language gives an aesthetic shape to philosophizing in early critical theory. For Adorno, thinking has need of language's aesthetic materiality in order to give form to its experience. Mendietta demonstrates how he absorbs this insight from Benjamin's philosophy of language, which argues that "philosophy must continually confront the question of representation."[22] For Benjamin, the act of philosophical critique stands in an essential analogy to translation. In translating a foreign text into our own language, we make our own language grow through an encounter with a foreign way of thinking. Analogously, Mendieta demonstrates that for Adorno the language of philosophy is not so much a "house of being," but an incessant foray into foreign language to find resources for critical thought. While Heidegger seeks the privileged original language of philosophy, Adorno sees philosophy as a pursuit of truth through constellations of foreign terms. The foreign language reminds us that our words do not correspond to reality in a simple way by showing us that our way of conceptualizing the world stands in tension with other ways, and at the same time, foreign language ensures us that experience remains open to the pursuit of truth. We might claim that critical theory has need of art in much the same way that thought has need of foreign languages, as a reminder of the limits in our concepts as well as of the purpose that animates thinking.

In my own chapter, I explore the concept of mimesis in more detail and reveal a divergence in how Benjamin and Adorno articulate the critical form of this concept. Adorno and Benjamin share a mimetic concept of aesthetic experience, and both diagnose the decline in the mimetic capacity as a result of modern, rationalized subjectivity. However, I demonstrate that the two thinkers had very different conceptions of how mimesis could actually render a true, or socially critical experience. In his late aesthetics, Benjamin wrote of a dialectical "polarity informing mimesis": art can create a semblance of reality, or enable an interplay. He sought to drive this polarity to an opposi-tional extreme in his "Artwork" essay so as to show that the liquidation of semblance from art would make possible an aesthetic interplay with nature. Benjamin saw a new political function for art in its ability to transform experience into a mode of perception characterized by provisionality and reciprocity with nature. By contrast, Adorno seeks to "rescue semblance" as a necessary function within art's critical mimesis of society. This means that Adorno finds aesthetic truth precisely in the ability of art to engage mimeti-cally with the fetishistic and illusion producing of society. Art becomes for Adorno a "double illusion" that transforms consciousness by making it aware of its dependence on mechanisms of projection and ideological justification.

The section of chapters on Benjamin begins with two chapters that offer highly complimentary readings of Benjamin's most influential work in aes-thetics, "The Artwork in the Age of its Technological Reproducibility." Ben-jamin's essay promises nothing less than a materialist aesthetic theory that would mobilize art to stem the tide of fascism. It makes especially bold claims regarding the political fruitfulness of film as a medium for promoting politically infused, collective modes of aesthetic experience. Since Benja-min's time, readers have been fascinated by the richness of his phenomeno-logical analyses and frustrated by their failure to give concrete form to its bold political claims. Both Alison Ross and Stéphane Symons develop read-ings of the "Artwork" essay that place it in continuity with Benjamin's earli-er writings, and thus provide us with a sense of how this provocative work stands within a larger epistemological and aesthetic context. Without under-mining the "contradictory and mobile" quality of Benjamin's thinking, they thus provide us with a way to take this essay's claims as suggestive of a deeper philosophy of aesthetic experience. As Ross demonstrates, the essay's insistence on liquidating the aura of artworks belongs to a larger critique of the category of aesthetic form, which she locates particularly in Benjamin's essay on Goethe's *Elective Affinities*. She argues that for Benjamin, our fascination with totalizing schemas of aesthetic appearance derives from the oppressive force of *myth* over human life. Myth continues its hold on modern life because capitalism is, at its root, based on a belief in progress that dooms us to repeat the archaic state of hopelessness, a view that informs Benjamin's "Capitalism as Religion." This insight into the complicity of aesthetic form with ideology leads Benjamin to a new model of social critique as aesthetic critique, which she succinctly calls a "shift away from the artwork towards aesthetic experience." In the "Artwork" essay, this focus on aesthetic experience as the site of liberation leads Benjamin to analyze the new form of aesthetic experience entailed by film: an experience that is collective, distracted, and tactile, and thus liberated from the reign of totalizing, hierarchical schemas of aesthetic appearance.

Symons focuses on the line of continuity between Benjamin's "Artwork" essay and his earlier theory of allegory in *Origin of German Tragic Drama*. His comparison departs from a highly fertile phenomenon that Benjamin finds in film: the way that film "alienates" the actor by absorbing her performance into an "apparatus."[23] The actor does not create the semblance of a character, but rather responds to a series of demands that must conform to the demands of the medium. For Benjamin, this alienation is "highly productive" because it gives us an experience of the relation between human life and the technology that controls our life. Symons demonstrates that Benjamin's diagnosis of this fruitful political experience has deep roots in Benjamin's thought. His *Origin* text speaks as well of the ability to respond to the immense melancholy of an age of war and civic strife through an aesthetic "depersonalization" that is "highly fruitful." The allegories of Baroque drama are not for Benjamin a unified aesthetic form, but an unsettling medium of understanding world events in terms of "the death of intention." In the works of both Alison Ross and Symons, we find that Benjamin's late aesthetics rests on a deeper philosophy of aesthetic criticism, which replaces the unified work with a mobile medium of experience that responds to the lack of transparency in our collective, historical existence.

Joseph Weiss' highly original chapter pursues Walter Benjamin's philosophy of aesthetic experience onto a terrain that is mostly reserved for Adorno: music aesthetics. The chapter demonstrates that some of Benjamin's most radical challenges to aesthetic theory can serve to illuminate the meaning of more recent compositional innovations in art music. As Weiss makes clear, music is a medium of experience that lends itself to the kind of materialist exposition at the heart of Benjamin's late aesthetics, because music mimes the vibrational energy of the industrially formed material world of our experience. The compositional practices of contemporary composers such as John Cage and Karlheinz Stockhausen acknowledge the materiality of sound as an accompaniment to our daily life, and Weiss demonstrates that Benjamin's aesthetic thinking gives us a much more generous paradigm for understanding the revolutionary meaning of these tendencies than Adorno's paradigm of preserving semblance. (His essay assiduously and strategically avoids mentioning the name of Adorno, through stylistic measures, even while establishing a dialogue between the two thinkers on a terrain where Adorno had far more to say.) The considerations informing the prior two chapters, Benjamin's liquidation of aura and his framing of a mode of tactile, distracted aesthetic experience, appear in this chapter as conditions for a philosophy of music that focuses on the materiality of sound rather than the autonomy of works as autonomous entities. Additionally, it seems helpful to read Weiss' chapter as an applied illustration of the thesis developed in Bertram's chapter about Benjamin's distinctive conception of art as a critical practice: Music is a critical practice to the extent that it engages with the other practices of perception that form the basis of our life and subtly challenges us to hear, and respond to the vibrations of the world, in a different way.

The first two chapters in the section on Adorno seek to understand his philosophy of aesthetic experience in terms of its practical, transformative effect. In this sense, they take up the challenge implicitly issued by Bertram's chapter on art as critical practice: to understand art in its capacity to transform practice. Both chapters demonstrate that for Adorno, the practical import of aesthetics has to do with the way in which having a truly aesthetic experience transforms consciousness. The first chapter, by Surti Singh, argues that the aesthetic involves an experience of shudder that alters the subject's practical relation to reality. She demonstrates that the true aesthetic experience (*Erfahrung*) is based on the experience of negativity within the self, and she argues that this experience of shudder has real possibilities to transform the historical comportment of the subject. She shows how Adorno appropriates Kant's notion of the sublime, as an experience that reveals the nullity of ego, in order to understand what kind of aesthetic experience could break through reified consciousness. In the next chapter, Rick Elmore reinforces this reading of aesthetic experience by relating it to ecology. He supports Singh's conception of aesthetic experience as one that shakes the subject and argues that this kind of experience has radical implications in transforming our relation to nature. Recent scholarship has acknowledged that Adorno's critique of the enlightenment subject's domination of nature offers valuable resources to ecological philosophy, but it has done little to acknowledge the importance of nature in Adorno's aesthetic thought. Returning to a theme from Kant, Adorno focuses on the ethical importance of the ability to have an aesthetic experience of nature. However, in Adorno, this theme leads not to a sentimentalizing view of natural beauty, but to anthropological considerations about the ways in which mimesis works against the limiting form that rationality takes in modern culture. Elmore demonstrates that Adorno's nature aesthetics articulates the imperative to respond to nature in a way that challenges the self to relinquish its control over nature's way of appearing.

Andrea Sakoparnig gives us a deeper account of the kind of negativity involved in Adorno's account of aesthetic experience by focusing on the concept of enigma (*Rätsel*, which might also be translated as riddle). To have an experience of an artwork as an artwork means to experience an enigma. An enigma is a structure that calls for conceptual understanding and definition, while at the same time undermining the possibility to arrive at a definitive understanding. She shows that this peculiar kind of negativity rests not merely on the attitude of the subject, but the formal structures of the artwork. By creating this kind of experience, the work speaks to us as rational subjects and challenges us to think about the world in a new way. She argues that there is more to Adorno's notion of enigma than some accounts of aesthetic negativity would have us believe.[24] The artwork is not merely a meaningless object that negates our ordinary ways of creating meaning, but a structure that dialectically plays with and challenges these structures of meaning. She demonstrates that Adorno conceived of this enigmatic mode of experience as a way of correcting some of the deficiencies that he diagnosed in practices of conceptual knowing. She also draws a fruitful connection between Benjamin's conception of constellation, where meaning emerges dynamically from the unintentional juxtaposition of elements, and Adorno's thesis on the enigmatic quality of art.

The final chapter, by Tom Huhn, makes an important contribution to scholarship on Adorno's conception of aesthetic experience by arguing for the vital influence of Friedrich Schiller on Adorno's thinking. Although Adorno does not refer to Schiller nearly as often as Kant or Hegel, Huhn demonstrates that Schiller's way of defining the aesthetic reveals deep affinities to Adorno's project. Reading Adorno in terms of Schiller can serve as a corrective to views of Schiller as a utopian, apolitical aesthete, while also deepening our understanding of the way in which we have to think Adorno's aesthetics as political. Schiller, more than any thinker in the German tradition, defines the approach to aesthetics as fundamentally an issue of philosophical anthropology. Art matters as a subject for philosophical speculation because it serves as an index for the relation between sensibility and intellect in human life. As Huhn demonstrates, this kind of anthropological concern for the development of the human capacities marks out the horizon in which Adorno thematizes the aesthetic.

Huhn's work can also play a vital role in our understanding of the relationship between Benjamin and Adorno. One of the most persistent themes of debate between Adorno and Benjamin was the issue of aesthetic semblance (*Schein*). The program of Benjamin's late aesthetics rests on the imperative that modern art must liquidate art's quality as semblance in order to make way for a form of aesthetic experience that enables interaction and engagement. Adorno, on the other hand, seeks to "rescue semblance" and argues that the feeling of distance and aura is central to art's ability to shake the subject out of its complacency.[25] This vital and yet highly abstract debate between Benjamin and Adorno about the fate of aesthetic experience and its political relevance will make more sense if we can read it as happening in a shorthand for concepts that they inherit from the period of classical German aesthetics. Huhn shows us the richness of the conception of aesthetic semblance in Schiller: the capacity of human beings to relate to the way things seem, without reducing them to concepts or consuming them, represents a vital capacity that indicates the freedom of the subject *within* nature. This aspect of aesthetic experience also plays a central role in Adorno's thought and guides his resistance to Benjamin's critique of the auratic arts. For Adorno, as for Schiller, the capacity of art to represent a realm of autonomous semblance is precisely what makes it a radical critique of the domain of instrumental rationality and reified consciousness.

In this sense, I propose reading the first and last chapters, those of Bertram and Huhn, as chapters that give us the clearest sense of the space between Benjamin and Adorno, the diverging directions of their aesthetic philosophies. Each of these chapters seeks to give an account of the way in which these two thinkers with deeply intertwined aesthetic theories develop divergent prescriptions for the direction and value of aesthetic experience in the modern age. For Benjamin, the fate of art in the modern age has much to do with the question of whether it can challenge the way aesthetic appearance has reinforced hierarchical schemas and political distance. For Adorno, on the other hand, the critical fate of art in the modern world is bound up with its ability to preserve this aesthetic sensation of distance as a force for undermining the illusion of necessity and order in modern life. Articulating this divergence should not, however, undermine our ability to perceive the common cause and many shared insights that bound together the two philosophers.

NOTES

1. Walter Benjamin, *The Origin of German Tragic Drama*, transl. John Osborne (London: Verso, 2009), 27.
2. Ibid., 28.
3. Ibid., 29.
4. Ibid., 36.
5. Benjamin is reported to have said this to his cousin Egon Wissing. Eiland and Jennings write: "Adorno's early academic career was shaped by a knowing appropriation of Benjamin's work." Howard Eiland and Michael Jennings, *Walter Benjamin: A Critical Life* (Cambridge: Harvard University Press, 2014), 359.
6. Theodor Adorno, *Ästhetische Theorie* (Frankfurt: Suhrkamp, 2003), 498.
7. "Neither the truth nor truthfulness can be ascribed to the artwork in a non-metaphorical sense if we are understanding 'truth' and 'truthfulness' in terms of a pragmatically differentiat-

ed everyday concept of truth." Albrecht Wellmer, *Persistence of Modernity: Essays on Aesthetics, Ethics and Post-modernity* (Cambridge: MIT Press, 1993), 23. For interesting positive readings of the theme of aesthetic truth in Adorno, see Lambert Zuidervaart, *Adorno's Aesthetic Theory: The Redemption of Illusion* (Cambrdige: MIT Press, 1993), 178–213. Also see Andrew Bowie, *From Romanticism to Critical Theory* (New York: Routledge, 1996). What seems apparent in the readings of scholars such as Wellmer and Christoph Menke is that the notion of aesthetic truth places Adorno's philosophy at odds both with contemporary critical theory and deconstructive accounts of aesthetic experience.

8. For a survey of the way in which contemporary Frankfurt school theorists distance themselves from some themes in Adorno, see Jürgen Habermas, "The Entwinement of Myth and Enlightenment: Adorno and Horkheimer" in *The Philosophical Discourse of Modernity*, transl. Fredrick Lawrence (Cambridge: MIT Press, 1996), 106–30. Also for an account that criticizes Adorno's aesthetics in a way so as to bring into line with the theory of communicative rationality, see Albrecht Wellmer, *Persistence of Modernity: Essays on Aesthetics, Ethics and Post-modernity* (Cambridge: MIT Press, 1993). Finally, there is an interesting recent effort to show why critical theory needs something like the theory of aesthetic experience found in Benjamin and Adorno to compliment the emphasis on rationality: Gregg Daniel Miller, *Mimesis and Reason* (Albany: SUNY Press, 2011).

9. For works on the Benjamin Adorno relationship, see Susan Buck-Morss, *The Origin of Negative Dialectics* (New York: The Free Press, 1977); Eiland and Jennings, *Walter Benjamin*, 301, 332–33, 359–60, 562–66, 657. Also see Shierry Weber Nicholsen, "Aesthetic Theory's Mimesis of Walter Benjamin" in ed. Tom Huhn and Lambert Zuidervaart. *The Semblance of Subjectivity* (Cambridge: MIT Press, 1997), 55–91.

10. Theodor W. Adorno, *Über Walter Benjamin*, ed. Rolf Tiedeman (Frankfurt am Main: Suhrkamp, 1970), 70.

11. Eiland and Jennings, *Walter Benjamin*, 359.

12. Ibid., 385.

13. Benjamin, *Origin*, 36.

14. Susan Buck-Morss, *The Origin of Negative Dialectics* (New York: The Free Press, 1977), 21.

15. This will become apparent for example in Symons chapter, which is devoted to understanding a phrase in Benjamin's "Artwork" essay that was possibly eliminated at Adorno's behest.

16. Eiland and Jennings, *Walter Benjamin*, 493–95.

17. This contrast represents a central thesis of Buck-Morss, *The Origin of Negative Dialectics*. See especially pages 151–63. She writes of Adorno as a "Marxist without the Proletariat."

18. For the prevalence of Adorno's interpretation in later readings, see for example Jürgen Habermas, "Consciousness-Raising or Rescuing Critique," in *Philosophical-Political Profiles*, transl. F. Lawrence (Cambridge, MA: MIT Press, 1983). Such a view of Benjamin also permeates the latter chapters of Buck-Morss' *The Origin of Negative Dialectics*.

19. This interpretation of Adorno is best illustrated in Christoph Menke, *The Sovereignty of Art* (Cambridge: MIT Press, 1999).

20. For a more detailed account of art as critical practice, see Georg W. Bertram, *Kunst als menschliche Praxis* (Suhrkamp: Berlin, 2015).

21. Benjamin, *Origin*, 36.

22. Benjamin, *Origin*, 27.

23. Benjamin, *Selected Writings Vol. 3*, ed. Howard Eiland and Michael Jennings (Cambridge: Harvard University Press, 2002), 113.

24. Her thesis on enigma represents a subtle challenge to the well known account of negativity by Christoph Menke in *The Sovereignty of Art*.

25. See Adorno, *Theorie*, 154. For what is at stake in Adorno's conception of semblance see also Tom Huhn and Lambert Zuidervaart, eds. *The Semblance of Subjectivity* (Cambridge, MA: MIT Press, 1997), especially J. M. Bernstein, "Why Rescue Semblance?"177–212.

Chapter One

Benjamin and Adorno on Art as Critical Practice

Georg W. Bertram

To what extent is art critical? How can we understand the critical character of art under the aspect of its sensuousness? A debate took place between Adorno and Benjamin about these questions, the result of which has become familiar to us as follows: Adorno gave a powerful critique of Benjamin's position and thereby contributed to bringing about the fact that this position played and to this day continues to play a rather marginal role in systematically determining the concept of art. Adorno has made many philosophers— among others, Jürgen Habermas and those whom he influenced such as Albrecht Wellmer and his students—think that Benjamin's conception of art is too affirmative. On this view, Benjamin fails to appropriately articulate the critical aspect of art because he does not conceive the form of art in terms of the resistance of this form. By contrast, Adorno's position of negative aesthetics claims precisely to do justice to and appropriately understand the critical potential of art.

It is my view, however, that Adorno is not completely right about this point and that his position has thoroughly problematic consequences for the philosophy of art. It has set many more recent positions, especially in so-called continental philosophy of art, in the direction of a negative understanding of art. Such an understanding is based, however, on a one-sided conception of critique. As I will argue in what follows, it is precisely this one-sided conception of critique that Benjamin's position challenges. It is thus my view that Adorno's interpretation of what is actually in dispute between his and Benjamin's positions is mistaken. It is my aim, then, to frame this dispute appropriately. An appropriate conception of this dispute is helpful in my view for arriving at an understanding of art as critical practice.

1

It is important for this purpose to emphasize that Benjamin works with an understanding of art as critical practice that differs in some significant ways from Adorno's. It is precisely this different understanding of critique on Benjamin's part that can be made systematically fruitful for the concept of art.

The question of how art can be understood as critical practice is connected with that of how one understands the sensuous aspect of art. To what extent do the sensuous aspects of art provide a critical impetus to the latter? Does art in its sensuousness bring about a disturbance of other practices? Does art in this way provide a basis for a form of critique that it initiates? Or is it rather the case that this form of critique can be conceptualized independently of the sensuous aspects of art? These are also questions that figure in the debate between Benjamin and Adorno.

In what follows, I will take up this debate by first examining Adorno's critique of Benjamin. I will then turn to Benjamin's essay on the artwork in the age of its technical reproducibility and lay out the extent to which Adorno inadequately conceives Benjamin's concern in its central points. This will then, in the subsequent section, put me in position to analyze the divergent understandings of critique that guide Adorno and Benjamin as the issue that is actually in dispute between them. In a concluding section, I will sketch a Benjaminian perspective on art as critical practice that emerges by returning to Hegel's aesthetics as the common basis on which Adorno's and Benjamin's views diverge.

ADORNO'S CRITIQUE OF BENJAMIN

Adorno shares with Benjamin the project of formulating a materialistic aesthetics. He aims to ascribe a potential to art as a resource for criticizing society. Art should be conceived as a critique of existing relations of domination. For Adorno, this means that art should breach the cycle of subjectivity that dominates members of a community and is dominated by the same members of a community. We are thus confronted with an essentially dialectical task according to Adorno: to make intelligible the extent to which existing relations of domination turn against their own goal of realizing freedom. On this view, the practice of freedom turns against itself into a mythology to which subjects succumb and which causes their oppression. Adorno considers this account of the dialectic of liberating practice as a concern that fundamentally connects him with Benjamin.

Nevertheless, he sees Benjamin's philosophy of art as retrograde in light of this concern. From his perspective, Benjamin abandons a dialectical conception of art in favor of the goal of effecting the politicization of art. His objection that Benjamin goes wrong by failing to conceive art in a sufficiently dialectical fashion is directed above all against the concept of *aura*. According to Adorno, Benjamin understands aura as an "illusion [of] autonomy"[1] that art emanates in the course of being set out within ritualistic contexts. Since the Renaissance, artworks have been created as objects that realize such an illusion of autonomy. This illusion comes about when artworks in practice are brought into a position of uniqueness. Artworks are treated as objects that stand out from the historical flux and historical contexts in which they are situated. This "auratic" way for artworks to stand out is reflected in the distantiated stance that their recipients maintain in relation to them. Recipients in this distantiated stance are individual subjects who stand on their own in their experience of art. They are extricated from their societal contexts.

Benjamin did not elaborate this concept of aura directly in relation to art. He illustrates it solely by way of considering the aura of natural objects. He defines the aura of the latter as "the unique phenomenon of a distance, however close it may be."[2] Our encounters with "auratic" art bring about such a distance. Now, with the onset of technically reproducible arts (or so Benjamin tries to shows), this aspect of distance and uniqueness is overcome. Art is produced now in such a way that it directly involves its recipients. This "post-auratic" art is thus an art that does away with the illusion of autonomy, thereby revealing the way in which art is embedded in society. Such an art breaches the subjectivity of auratic art and renders art into a medium through which the masses are mobilized.

From Adorno's perspective, this is a brief way of summarizing Benjamin's line of thought in the latter's essay on the nature of the artwork. For Adorno, Benjamin's analysis is insufficiently dialectical because it does not make the dialectic of illusion of autonomy intelligible. In his representative letter to Benjamin from March 18, 1936, Adorno formulates his objection to it (among other things) as follows:

> Though your essay is dialectical, it falls below this in the case of the autonomous work of art itself; for it neglects a fundamental experience which daily becomes increasingly evident to me in my musical works, that precisely the uttermost consistency in the pursuit of the technical laws of autonomous art actually transforms this art itself and, instead of turning it into a fetish or taboo, brings it that much closer to a state of freedom, to something that can be consciously produced and made.[3]

From Adorno's perspective, what Benjamin fails to grasp can be summarized as follows: The extent to which art produces the illusion of autonomy does not only bring its recipients into a distantiated stance. Rather, it brings its recipients at the same time into a stance that is affected by how an object asserts itself over against a subject. Artworks are objects that confront subjects with unique forms. For this reason, they do not allow themselves to be

classified by subjects. Subjects can only confront artworks by letting themselves be guided by them. A certain liberation from domination occurs precisely when this happens. The subject is liberated from the structures that the
subject established for the sake of his or her domination of nature and of him-
or herself. The artwork that is thoroughly formed in a technical sense, which
realizes an illusion of autonomy, by means of this thoroughly technical formation, stands opposed to the recipients as something that cannot be simply
grasped in established structures. Adorno's analysis means, then, to show
how the dominating technology in art attains a new aspect: On the basis of
this technology, recipients are dominated by an artwork in a way that they
cannot control. In this case, domination does not turn against itself.

Adorno insists, therefore, that the illusion of autonomy is not connected
with a reversal of domination against itself. Rather, that which dominates,
namely, the subject, is cut loose from the structures that dominate and are
dominated by him or her. The subject thereby undergoes an experience that
points a way to freedom: to a state in which the subject makes something out
of him- or herself, but not in a way such that what gets made shapes the
subject in accordance with the subjective structures. The "primacy of the
object"[4] that realizes itself in the aesthetic illusion of autonomy thus
breaches the mythologizing of practices that dominate: The object asserts
itself over against the subject and the structures that the latter has established.
Its primacy consists in the fact that it is able to assert itself in this way.

Adorno's objection to Benjamin is that his concept of aura fails to have
this dialectic of aesthetic autonomy in view. This failure is connected with a
second one in Adorno's view. The latter has to do with the determination of
various modern tendencies in art, through which aura comes to an end from
Benjamin's point of view. Adorno fundamentally agrees with Benjamin in
this diagnosis. The production of art at the threshold of the transition from
the nineteenth to the twentieth century arrives at a juncture where the illusion
of autonomy increasingly diminishes. Here, Adorno is in basic agreement
with Benjamin. But this agreement ends with regard to their respective explanations of this transition. For Adorno, the techniques of reproduction in the
arts are not the essential cause of this process. Instead, this process goes back
in his view to a dialectic of aesthetic autonomy itself. Adorno conceives this
dialectic of aesthetic autonomy as follows: With the increasing development
of art, society—and to this extent the autonomy of art is also an illusion for
Adorno[5] —makes the techniques established in art consistently available for
itself. This drives art towards the unending development of the techniques
realized in artworks. Art thus follows a "law of movement" (*Bewegungsge-
setz*)[6] that leads for Adorno to a necessary point of culmination where the
technological development of art is spurred on to such an extent that the
illusion of autonomy can no longer be produced. Art becomes at this point a
paradoxical operation in order to salvage this illusion: It renounces its own

autonomy. Adorno understands the emblematic works of aesthetic modernity and postmodernity precisely as the results of a "rebellion against semblance."[7] This rebellion, which one can also characterize with Benjamin in terms of the loss of the aura of art (as its "de-auratization" [*Entauratisierung*]), results from the development of aesthetic autonomy itself. Adorno speaks here of a "deaestheticization [*Entkunstung*] of art."[8] For Adorno, in this state of "deaetheticization," art can no longer be conceived as entering a new stage. It is rather a question here of how the illusion of autonomy is essential for art's development as a practice. According to Adorno, Benjamin fails to have just this aspect of art in view in his juxtaposition of auratic and post-auratic art. For this reason, Benjamin fails not only to conceptualize aura in a sufficiently dialectical way; he also fails to do so regarding the nexus between auratic and post-auratic art.

BENJAMIN'S CONCEPTION OF ART

It is decisive in my view to raise the question of whether Adorno adequately grasps the critical direction of Benjamin's position in his critique. Toward this end, it is first important to clarify once again, independently of Adorno's perspective, what Benjamin is concerned with in general. What does Benjamin aim at with his novel justification of aesthetics for the sake of a politicizing of art? What is the significance of his concept of aura in this context?

Benjamin introduces the concept of aura in a context in which he comes to speak about questions of perception. The above-cited passage where he discusses the determination of the aura of natural objects begins as follows: *"During long periods of history, the mode of human sensuous perception changes with the whole of human existence."*[9] It is thus necessary, so argues Benjamin, to conceive sensuous perception as historically determined. This is the central point of departure for Benjamin's reflections. What does this point of departure imply for the concept of aura? It implies that with this concept Benjamin works out a determinate, historically established mode of perception. It concerns a mode of perception that Benjamin characterizes in terms of the concepts of distance and uniqueness. When objects acquire aura, sensuous perception becomes shaped in such a way that perceivers stand in a distantiated relation to the objects of their perception. Within the framework of an auratic practice, subjects are set at a distance from what they perceive. The auratic objects are thus perceived uniquely in this sense, since they filter through a determinate historical development and stand at a determinate moment in complex contexts of tradition (in Benjamin's term: in "the whole of human existence" [*menschliche Kollektiva*]). Individual subjects are powerless in relation to such historical developments and contexts of tradition. Auratic objects are in this sense objects that have a primacy in relation to subjects who perceive them. This primacy, however, cannot be understood for Benjamin apart from the perceptual practices that society has shaped. This primacy does not result from the particular constitution of the objects themselves. For this reason Benjamin speaks of how "the unique value of the 'authentic' work of art" has "*its basis in ritual [Fundierung im Ritual], the location of its original use value.*"[10] He also speaks of how art is "*based on ritual [Fundierungaufs Ritual].*"[11] The concept of being "based on ritual" expresses and indicates a determinate alignment of practices. I designate such a determinate alignment of practices as an *assemblage (Dispositiv)*. I resort here to the familiar concept of assemblage that Foucault elaborates because Benjamin's reflections exhibit aspects that fit well with this concept.[12] According to Benjamin, the structures of perception that are established in communal practices ("being based on ritual") determine the particular perceptual practices of subjects. This is characteristic of a certain constellation of communal practices: The practices of particular subjects are constrained by forms that are realized by many subjects and to which these subjects are bound. "Being based on ritual" thus results in the sensuous perception of all individuals being directed and shaped in a certain way.

Now, it is this context that makes the "decay of aura" comprehensible.[13] Benjamin argues that a transformation takes place in the assemblage of sensuous perception with the onset of technically reproducible arts. One can articulate this transformation in Benjamin's sense by speaking of a new assemblage of sensuous perception. What is characteristic for this new assemblage are modes of perception in which there is no distance between objects and those who view them. It is in this sense that a viewer *penetrates* the objects under observation. Benjamin understands the perception involved in this new assemblage to that of a surgeon: "The surgeon greatly diminishes the distance between himself and the patient by penetrating into the patient's body, and increases it only a little bit by the caution with which his hand moves among the organs."[14] According to Benjamin, technically reproducible arts make such a mode of perception feasible. The undistantiated perception that arises in this way enables viewers to undertake "optical tests"[15] of the objects in question. Photographs and films isolate different moments from movements; they open up viewpoints from positions from which no viewpoints are possible in everyday perception. Objects are optically tested in this sense. These tests take for granted that viewers are not confronted with a uniqueness that overwhelms them. The post-auratic or non-auratic perceptual situation is thus in this way bound up with the possibility of viewing objects in arbitrarily close ways.

Benjamin elaborates technically reproducible arts in this sense as instruments for exercising a new assemblage of sensuous perception: "*Reception in a state of distraction, which is increasing noticeably in all fields of art and is symptomatic of profound changes in apperception, finds in film its true in-*

strument of exercise."[16] Artworks are means of exercise insofar as they initiate an altered perceptual comportment and activities in their recipients. But
Benjamin makes it clear that this result is not created by art itself. Art and the
practices that flow from it instead form a "symptom" for Benjamin. The
"profound changes of apperception" that this symptom makes manifest are
constituted in an assemblage. I can distill Benjamin's position by attributing
two theses to him:

1. Art can be determined only by recourse to assemblages of sensuous
   perception that determine communal practices.
2. Post-auratic art, which is brought about in a special way by technically
   reproduced arts, is constitutively connected with a change of modes of
   sensuous perception within communal practices.

These theses make intelligible the extent to which Adorno's critique of Benjamin's position misses its target. Adorno assumes that Benjamin's reflections seek to assert the end of an aesthetic autonomy that has always been
illusory. In the spirit of Adorno, Habermas has thus read Benjamin as tracing
the "dissolution of autonomous art."[17] But Benjamin is not concerned with
such a dissolution. He insists rather that all aesthetic autonomy remains
constitutively illusory. It follows that there can be no talk of a substantial end
of aesthetic autonomy in Benjamin's sense. Furthermore, it follows that there
is no fundamental difficulty in ascribing an aspect of autonomy to art in
Benjamin's way of thinking, insofar as one understands this aspect as illusory in the sense of thesis (1). Benjamin could be seen as agreeing with Adorno
that artworks are objects with a distinctive language or a distinctive law of
form[18] —insofar as one does not (as Adorno himself does) infer that artworks are sealed off from communicating with other practices. There can
thus be significant agreement between Benjamin and Adorno on this point.

This implies, however, that the point that Benjamin is concerned to make
here cannot generally be made in terms of concepts revolving around aesthetic autonomy. Benjamin aims to clarify the nexus between art and certain
forms of sensuous perception that are established in communal practices.
This is the reason why he draws attention to the arts in the age of their
technical reproducibility. In these arts, he sees an exemplary realization of
the change of modes of sensuous perception.[19] For Benjamin, artworks are
thus measured with respect to their capacity to open up new fields of action
(*Spielräume*). He speaks to this extent of an "immense and unexpected field
of action"[20] that is opened up by arts that are technically reproducible. The
concept of autonomy is uninformative in considering this field of action.
Rather, the latter must be conceived in terms of a change of modes of perception. The idea of the "decay of aura" highlights precisely such a change.
Accordingly, contrary to what Adorno has in mind, the concept of aura is not

primarily a concept concerned with the illusion of autonomy, and post-auratic arts cannot be characterized by means of a possible supersession (*Aufhebung*) of this illusion. The concept of aura applies rather to a certain assemblage of sensuous perception; the rise of "de-auratized" arts indicates the
genesis of a new assemblage for Benjamin.

Adorno also errs by taking Benjamin to be concerned with the explanation of a dialectical development. He attributes to Benjamin (as shown above
in the previous section) the aim of working out a dialectic of aesthetic autonomy, understood as a dialectic of the supersession of the illusion of aesthetic
autonomy. Adorno thus arrives at the diagnosis that Benjamin conceives this
dialectic inadequately. But to the extent that Benjamin is uninterested in
aesthetic autonomy, he is also understandably unconcerned with this dialectic. Rather, his concern above all is with *critique*. His interest lies in clarify-
ing the way in which art is capable of disclosing a critical impetus. What
stands in the foreground for Benjamin is the goal of conceptualizing art as
critical practice. He already alludes to this in the Preface of his essay when he
writes: *"The concepts that are introduced into the theory of art in what
follows . . . are . . . useful for the formulation of revolutionary demands in the
politics of art."*[21] He makes this point even clearer when he sees films in
general as promoting "a revolutionary criticism of traditional concepts of
art."[22] These customary conceptions of art ascribe certain perceptual assemblages to art and nourish the conception that perceptual assemblages and the
installations bound to them are natural. By contrast, Benjamin seeks to justify a conception of art that connects it with critique in a fundamental way.
For this reason, he finds it necessary that we make sense of how modes of
perception are historically conditioned. Technically reproducible arts provide
Benjamin with an essential impetus for just this purpose. These arts make
clear how art in general is capable of giving a critical impetus in the development of modes of perception.

Sensuous perception therefore attains a central place in Benjamin's determination of art. Nevertheless, he does not conceive sensuousness as the basis
for the critical impetus from which art takes its point of departure. This is
precisely what distinguishes him from Adorno. For Adorno, the sensuousness of art is one of the aspects that assure art's capability to resist existing
practices of domination. Where the sensuousness of art steps into the foreground, it is an aspect of the dialectic of art that struggles for its negating
potential.[23] For Benjamin, sensuousness is not in this way attached to the
capability of art to resist existing practices of domination. It is rather a
dimension of societal reality. Art can shape this dimension in different ways.
Benjamin introduces (among others) two concepts that apply in this context:
the concepts of "concentration" and "distraction."[24] Attending to this distinction, auratic art produces modes of perceiving characterized by how subjects
are overwhelmed by objects. This is the sense in which a subject concentrates

on an object in his or her perceptions. By contrast, post-auratic art produces modes of perceiving that are shaped by an aimless openness. The subject is neither overwhelmed by the object, nor does he or she guide his or her perceptions on the basis of his or her own attentiveness. This results instead in distracted perceptions. Benjamin additionally characterizes these perceptions as tactile, and thereby notes that sensuousness consists here in the way in which these perceptions penetrate various objects without any distance. Thus, sensuousness is not for Benjamin simply an aspect that characterizes art, for example, in its distinctiveness. Rather, sensuousness is the connecting point by which art produces its connection with societal practices.

ART AS CRITICAL PRACTICE

As shown above, the concern of Benjamin's analysis of the nexus between art and societal practices has to do essentially with critique, not with sensuousness. From his perspective, this is the actual topic of the debate between him and Adorno. Accordingly, this debate does not revolve around the dialectic of aesthetic autonomy, but rather around the question of how art can be conceived as critical practice. Benjamin's answer to this question is different from that of Adorno. It is thus helpful at this point to consider the extent to which Adorno's and Benjamin's understandings of critique differ from each other.

Adorno's understanding of critique derives from his analysis of modern societies. He holds that comprehensive nexuses of communication in modern societies are established, which in turn encompass all expressions of their subjects. This is the reason why he assumes that every functioning communication within the framework of a modern society is by its nature affirmative. Each communication must help itself to an established language. In so doing, it (re)affirms societal nexuses, even when, as a matter of content, it goes against certain aspects of societal practice. Adorno for this reason thinks that communication cannot bring about critique. His reflections on the affirmative character of all communication in modern societies lead him to formulate a demanding condition for the realization of critique: Critique can only be carried out through *noncommunication*. Critique is bound to the condition of being constitutively negative in relation to the rest of society. This conception of critique informs Adorno's negative dialectics as well as his aesthetics. Accordingly, the communicative nature of artworks is explained as follows: "The communication of artworks with what is external to them, with the world from which they blissfully or unhappily seal themselves off, occurs through non-communication."[25] According to Adorno's understanding, art can only succeed as critical practice in this way. This is how the space is fixed for the possibility of art that is politically engaged: An engagement of art can only come to exist through its non-communication.[26] Adorno conceives this non-communication dialectically: The non-communication of artworks has to gauge itself in relation to the current state of societal practices; artworks refuse in certain ways to play along communicatively in relation to a certain practice. This characterization at the same time hints at how critique can succeed. For Adorno, critique can only do so through the *negativity of form*: Critique is actualized by being incommensurate, as a matter of form, with the modes of communication of a societal practice.[27] In short, critique is a negative practice through its form. This negativity has in turn a decisive consequence. Non-communication necessarily implies the renunciation of engaging in practice (this is the final step of the dialectic that Adorno has in view).[28] This means, however, that everything remains the same when critical non-communication is at work. By refusing to communicate and hence succeeding on its own terms, critique in this sense tips over ironically into affirmation.

Benjamin works out a different model of critique. For him, critique starts with the *change of a practice*. A critique that is structurally affirmative is not a critique from Benjamin's perspective. A practice is only conceived as critical when it is related to a change of practice. Benjamin sees precisely such a change of practice taking place with respect to arts in the age of their technical reproducibility. It is a question of those arts through which modes of perception change. For Benjamin, the thesis is crucial that the practices of art that have been customary in the past are no longer suitable for the specific demands of a new societal situation. These specific demands come to the fore in terms of politics. This point stands at the center of Benjamin's text: "*Instead of being based on ritual, it* [i.e., art—GWB] *begins to be based on another practice—politics*."[29] With this new foundation, art turns out to be a critical practice.[30] This practice is critical because it provokes a change of practice. As discussed in the previous section, Benjamin conceives this change in terms of a change within sensuous perception. It also becomes intelligible now how Benjamin's idea of "politicizing art"[31] does not mean that art is related to specific political contents. Because Benjamin understands this change in turn as one that must suit the new societal situation in each case, his position can also quite easily be conceived (*pace* Adorno) as dialectical. In this sense, Benjamin is concerned with a new foundation for societal practice. Critique is constituted for him by the impetus for such a new foundation.

Critique, then, is for Benjamin not connected with the aim of raising consciousness or with that of negation. Nor is it connected clearly with the aim of rescue, as Habermas asserts in his eye-opening interpretation of Benjamin.[32] Rather, there are two aspects of Benjamin's concept of critique that are capable of complementing but also conflicting with each other. On the one hand, Benjamin connects the concept of critique with the *emphatic aim of rescue*. Benjamin clarifies this aim in his theses on the philosophy of history (among other places). He argues there against the belief in progress and in favor of an understanding that enables the realization of justice by meeting the need for redeeming the past. For this purpose, he requires a practice that is redemptive. A certain mode of experience in turn guides such a practice, as Benjamin already formulated this earlier in his thinking (among other places in "On the Program of the Philosophy to Come"): an experience that is not undermined by the one-sidedness in the relation between the subject and the object.[33] It concerns in this sense a sort of "metaphysical experience,"[34] as a form of experience through which the fundamental tension between the subject and the object is superseded. Critique is to this extent connected with the aspect of rescue for Benjamin, such that it leads to the occurrence of this sort of experience.

On the other hand, however, the *aspect of change* is also relevant for Benjamin's conception of critique. This aspect comes to the fore especially in his later texts in which the metaphysical impetus of the earlier texts is in a certain respect transcended. Critique is supposed to provoke a change. In this sense, Benjamin is concerned in his "Theses on the Developmental Tendencies of Art under Present Conditions of Production"[35] with the question of which changes art can provoke. When Benjamin analyzes the new assemblage of perception that technically reproducible arts bring about, an essential change of the modes of perception involved in societal practices is connected with this new assemblage. It is not a matter here of the emergence of metaphysical experiences, but rather of the change of societal modes of perception. Critique is oriented towards factual changes. It is not oriented (as is the case with the aim of rescue) towards the task of making a historical happening in its need for redemption be equal to all other historical happenings.

One can suspect, following Habermas, that Benjamin articulates here a "conservative-revolutionary understanding of critique."[36] This assessment does not do justice, however, to Benjamin's understanding of critique as practice that effects change. To be sure, Benjamin's understanding can fit with the moment of redemption, to the extent that metaphysical experiences are capable of resulting from change. Nevertheless, change is not attached to the emergence of such experiences. In the artwork essay, Benjamin claims to develop an understanding of art that does justice to the specifically modern demands on perception. These demands have a historical nature. Because they have a concrete, historical-societal character, they cannot be solely determined from a metaphysical standpoint. To this extent, Benjamin's conception of critique as effecting change, which his conception of art aims to achieve, outruns that of critique as redemption. His conception of art does not aim at the occurrence of a certain experience, but at the distinctive way in which art can intervene in societal practices.

In light of this consideration of the two aspects of Benjamin's conception of critique, the extent to which it differs from Adorno's conception now becomes even more evident. The distinction that Habermas makes between consciousness-raising and rescuing critique does not suffice in defining this difference. Rather, the idea of a critique that effects change in Benjamin's sense must be put forward as a third option to be considered. Adorno's understanding of critique as negativity realized by form rests on the thought that possibilities of change imply *eo ipso* an affirmative stance. Put paradoxically, possibilities of change are given only where there can be no change in the full sense of this word. For this reason, critique cannot be related for Adorno to possibilities of change. This is precisely the conclusion that Benjamin rejects.[37] For him, critique is essentially related to the realization of states and conditions that change. It is not affirmative to the extent that it does justice to new impetus or new demands. The basis of this position lies in the thought that a historical practice is connected essentially with the possibility of change. New assemblages can always be realized within a historical practice. For Benjamin, this thought is essential for a conception of critique.[38] Even when he appeals to the idea of rescue, he also develops an understanding of critique that essentially has to do with the aspect of change. This conception of critique opposes Adorno's understanding of critique as a practice that is negative in virtue of its form. In a different way from what Adorno himself thinks, herein lies the core of the divergences between his aesthetics and that of Benjamin.

ART AS CRITIQUE THAT EFFECTS CHANGE

Benjamin sketches in his artwork essay, then, a position in the philosophy of art that can distinguish itself in comparison with Adorno's negative aesthetics. He does not conceive the function of art primarily on the basis of its autonomy. For this reason, neither does he develop an aesthetics of the supersession of autonomy. He seeks rather to advance the revolutionary potential of art by considering art as critique that effects change. This consideration is revealing precisely in the context of critical theory by enabling us to see the possible limitations of Adorno's position. According to Adorno, art is committed to the structurally ever-present but powerless reflection of societal practices that run up against the subject.[39] By contrast, Benjamin upholds a conception of art that does not put up with such a form of powerlessness, but rather connects the potential of change with art.

Nevertheless, this conception of art still remains too abstract in Benjamin. Many questions remain open in his elaboration of it. Among others are the following: How can we differentiate between a change that simply happens from one that results decisively from a critical impetus? How do the developments in the arts relate to changes that take place in societal practices? Is art the expression of these changes? Can it contribute to provoking such changes or is it rather solely their impetus? Is the critical potential of art attached solely to the perceptual assemblages or can art also initiate changes in other respects? Benjamin does not give answers to these and other questions in his essay on the nature of the artwork. Thus, it remains unclear in Benjamin how precisely art carries out the critical practice in terms of which he proposes to understand art.

I cannot attempt in this chapter to present in any way a satisfactory elaboration of art as critical practice. At most, I can only indicate here the direction that such an elaboration could take. Toward this end, I can rely on a position in which both Benjamin's and Adorno's positions in the philosophy of art are rooted: namely, Hegel's aesthetics. Hegel also dedicates reflection in his aesthetics to the question of how art can attain a critical potential. Even if Hegel thinks that the realization of this potential is connected with the fact that art does not achieve its highest determination anymore, he nevertheless conceives this realization as an important stage in the development of art. According to Hegel, a transformation of the function of art is connected to this development in such a way that a critical practice results from this transformation. He elaborates this practice in referring to art after the end of the Romantic form of art.

Two aspects are relevant for this account. First, art is to be understood as the articulation of various ways of determining what it means to be a human being. Hegel finds a handy formulation for this aspect when he writes that post-Romantic art "makes *Humanus* its new holy of holies."[40] Second, art develops multiple articulations of these determinations. The determinations of the human being are articulated from the particular perspectives of individual artworks. If art essentially brings these particular perspectives to expression, however, then art must be conceived as an agonistic practice. Artworks quarrel about how best to present plausible articulations of the determinations of the human being; they are engaged in contests with one another about this issue. They are at odds—as one can say with regard to Benjamin's reflections—about, for example, the determination of perceptual practices, about how best to make certain colors or features of surfaces conspicuous, etc. The quarrel of art is not just restricted, however, to disputes concerning sensuous perception. Artworks also dispute over understandings of love, of human failure, or one's relationship to transcendence. And they also have disputes about rhythms and emotions. Art is concerned with what it is to be a human being in the entire multiplicity of its determinations. The critique that effects change initiated by art cannot be restricted simply to sensuous perception.

The articulations of various artworks are bound up with one another within the practice of art as a whole. An artwork cannot by itself constitute the agonistic practice that allows us to make sense of art as critical practice. For this purpose, it needs the competition between different particular perspectives. Insofar as such a competition is realized, different perspectives come to relate critically to one another. They wrestle over the most suitable determinations. In so doing, these determinations can also complement one another. Artworks standing in competition are not only up against one another. They also engage in interplay in manifold ways. Paintings by Paul Cézanne and Francis Bacon can affect the activity of seeing in wholly different ways, and something similar can happen when we consider musical works by Johannes Brahms and Alban Berg. The different determinations of these artworks can combine to affect human practices. Artworks open up in this way, in interplay and through partial juxtaposition, different determinations that are relevant for human practices. Insofar as these determinations make an impact in societal practices, artworks can bring a critical impetus into the latter. This impetus can be understood entirely in Benjamin's sense. Artworks time and again open up an "immense and unexpected field of action." Through them, structurally time and again, revolutionary interventions in societal practices come into play.

These considerations in relation to Hegel's conception of post-Romantic arts indirectly highlight how Benjamin's conception of art not only focuses too narrowly on sensuous perception, but also conceives art in a way that is too unitary. Benjamin considers the changing demands made on the human perceptual system as a unitary movement. Even when he is not committed to understanding art as a unitary practice, he nonetheless does not sufficiently exclude the possibility of such an understanding. In this context, an agonistic understanding of art, like the one that one may develop out of Hegel, is instructive: Changes that art provokes bring about critique when they are based on a dispute about the appropriate determination of practice. It is necessary to conceive art in terms of such a dispute. But the explanation of such a dispute is very much in Benjamin's spirit. It offers a way of understanding art as critical practice. Benjamin gestures in this direction with his conception of art and thereby leads us beyond certain one-sided characteristics of Adorno's aesthetics. If one overcomes these characteristics, art is conceptualized as a critical practice that is capable of provoking changes in the determinations of human practices.[41]

Translation: Jo-Jo Koo

NOTES

1. Walter Benjamin, "The Work of Art in the Age of Mechanical Reproduction," reprinted in *Illuminations*, trans. H. Zohn (New York: Schocken Books, 1968), 226.
2. Ibid., 222.

3. Theodor Adorno, "Letter to Walter Benjamin on 18 March, 1936," in *The Complete Correspondence 1928-1940*, ed. H. Lonitz and trans. N. Walker (Cambridge, MA: Harvard University Press, 1999), 128f.

4. Theodor Adorno, *Aesthetic Theory*, trans. R.Hullot-Kentor (Minneapolis: University of Minnesota Press, 1997), 109.

5. The illusory quality of autonomy of art becomes clear in Adorno's thesis: "No artwork is an undiminished unity; each must simulate it, and thus collides with itself" (Adorno, *Aesthetic Theory*, op. cit., 105).

6. Ibid., 3.

7. Ibid., 110.

8. Ibid., 16.

9. Walter Benjamin, "The Artwork in the Age of Mechanical Reproduction," op. cit., 222, translation modified, emphasis in the original German.

10. Ibid., 224, emphasis in the original German.

11. Ibid., 224, emphasis in the original German.

12. As I use the concept of assemblage, it refers to the abstract structure the forms of which constrain and constitute subjects and their practices, as these forms are realized within a configuration of communal practices.

13. Ibid., 222.

14. Ibid., 233.

15. Ibid., 228.

16. Ibid., 240, translation slightly altered, emphasis in the original German.

17. Jurgen Habermas, "Consciousness-Raising or Rescuing Critique," in *Philosophical-Political Profiles*, trans. F. Lawrence (Cambridge: MIT Press, 1983), 136, translation slightly altered.

18. Cf. Adorno, *Aesthetic Theory*, 5, 78.

19. Joel Snyder also emphasizes in a different way that Benjamin is concerned with such a change; see his "Benjamin on Reproducibility and Aura: A Reading of 'The Work of Art in the Age of Technical Reproducibility," in *Benjamin: Philosophy, Aesthetics, History*, ed. G. Smith (Chicago: University of Chicago Press, 1989), 158–74, especially 159.

20. Benjamin, "The Artwork in the Age of Mechanical Reproduction," op. cit., 236.

21. Ibid., 218, translation slightly altered, emphasis in the original German.

22. Ibid., 231.

23. Christoph Menke's interpretation of Adorno has especially worked this out; see Christoph Menke, *The Sovereignty of Art: Aesthetic Negativity in Adorno and Derrida*, trans. N. Solomon (Cambridge, MA: MIT Press, 1998), 22ff.

24. Benjamin, "The Artwork in the Age of Mechanical Reproduction," op. cit., 239.

25. Adorno, *Aesthetic Theory*, 5.

26. Theodor Adorno, "Commitment," in *Notes to Literature*, vol. 2, trans. S. Weber Nicholson (New York: Columbia University Press, 1992), 76–94.

27. Cf. Adorno, "The Essay as Form," in *Notes to Literature*, vol. 1, transl. S. Weber Nicholson (New York: Columbia University Press, 1991), 3–23.

28. Adorno puts this (among other things): "By virtue of its [i.e., art's—GWB] rejection of the empirical world . . . art sanctions the primacy of reality" (Adorno, *Aesthetic Theory*, op. cit., 2).

29. Benjamin, "The Artwork in the Age of Mechanical Reproduction," op. cit., 224, emphasis in the original German.

30. This aim is misunderstood when one reads Benjamin as pleading for a direct political efficacy of art in a determinate historical situation. For such a reading, see Richard Wolin, *Walter Benjamin: An Aesthetic of Redemption* (Berkeley: University of California Press, 1994), 184.

31. Benjamin, "The Artwork in the Age of Mechanical Reproduction," op. cit., 242.

32. Habermas, "Consciousness-Raising or Rescuing Critique," op. cit.

33. Benjamin, "On the Program of the Coming Philosophy," in *Benjamin: Philosophy. Aesthetics, History*, ed. G. Smith (Chicago: University of Chicago Press, 1989), 1–12, especially 5.

34. Ibid, 8.

35. Benjamin, "The Artwork in the Age of Mechanical Reproduction," op. cit., 218.

36. Habermas, "Consciousness-Raising or Rescuing Critique," op. cit., 153, translation slightly modified.

37. I argue elsewhere that Adorno's commitment to the thesis of the unchangeability of a conceptual practice of identification, as with Derrida, could be criticized; see G. W. Bertram, "Metaphysik und Metaphysikkritik", in *Adorno-Handbuch*, eds. R. Klein et al. (Stuttgart: Metzler Verlag, 2011), 405–14.

38. Without a doubt, the meaning of this thought is not obvious. It really deserves its own proper discussion, which is something that I cannot carry out here. There would be at least three positions in such a discussion that could be compared and contrasted: Adorno's conception of historical practice as a unitary context, the thesis developed (among others) by Foucault (which in my view has become orthodox in the context under consideration for the interpretation of Benjamin) that different assemblages can become detached in this practice, and the Gadamerian understanding (among others) of historical practice as a context that is not unitary because it is always undergoing change.

39. I show elsewhere that Adorno's position can be further developed in an immanent way above and beyond such an understanding of art; see G. W. Bertram, "Das utopische Potential der Kunstnach Theodor W. Adorno: EineReaktualiseriung," in *Äesthetik – Religion – Säkularisierung II: Die klassischeModerne*, eds. S. Prombka and S. Vietta (Munich: Fink Verlag, 2009), 247–63.

40. G. W. F. Hegel, *Lectures on Fine Art*, vol. 1, trans. T. M. Knox (Oxford: Oxford University Press, 1988), 607.

41. The reflections of this text trace back to a seminar that I held together with Karen Feldman in the winter semester of 2010/2011 at the Free University of Berlin. I thank her and its students for intensive discussions about the nexus between art and critical theory in Benjamin and Adorno, as well as the participants of my research colloquium for many helpful comments about an earlier version of this paper. I would also like to thank my translator Jo-Jo Koo for helpful suggestions.

Chapter Two

The Benjaminian Moment in Adorno's Aesthetic Theory: Spaciality and the Topos of the Bourgeois *Intérieur*

Marcia Morgan

Topos can signify a common place, a *locus communis*, a topic or line of argument, a literary meme. In the aesthetic writings of Benjamin and Adorno, the topos of the bourgeois *intérieur* constitutes all of these things. I will examine the literary motif of the bourgeois *intérieur* in Adorno's aesthetics as a collapsed space of failed inward subjectivity, which Adorno reinscribes into the space for the appearance of the non-identical and as the *locus communis* of the experience of the emancipatory artwork. The topos of the nineteenth-century domestic interior is therefore both problematic and productive in the philosophical thought constellations of Benjamin and Adorno. I will argue that for Benjamin and Adorno there is a tension between the problematic destructiveness and imaginative productivity entailed by the interior place of the bourgeois living room—a tension that is mirrored in the correspondence between the two philosophers about this specific topos—and that this tension marks a significant motif that brings the two thinkers together in formulating a newly constructed notion of the space of aesthetic emancipation. In order to make this clear, my chapter will carry out the following moves: I will present a brief archaeology of the concept of the bourgeois *intérieur* in the writings of Benjamin and Adorno, as well as an archaeology of the space of subjectivity. The latter bifurcates into two spaces according to both authors: the social and the private, which interrupt and interpolate each other. The social colonizes the private, and the private reacts through imaginative freedom. In response to the intervening structure between the social and the private, Adorno turns to the emancipation enacted via the aesthetic. Seyla Benhabib has recently advocated for the political efficacy of Adorno's aesthetic theory through what she has called "the Benjaminian moment," Adorno's emphasis on the non-identical, an element which, I will argue, opens up a radical spatiality for aesthetic experience of "the new." I therefore begin with Benhabib's notion of "the Benjaminian moment" as the initiating spark that creates space for a renewed conception of ethico-political subjectivity in Adorno's aesthetics via the topos of the bourgeois *intérieur*. It is furthermore my claim that since the notion of the domestic interior represents the transcription of subjectivity into a collapsed space, the collapse of subjectivity makes way for the appearance of the non-identical, which subsequently and provocatively influences Adorno's *Aesthetic Theory* of 1969, and thus culminates in Adorno's profoundly new understanding of the space of aesthetic emancipation in his magnum opus.

* * *

In her essay, "Arendt and Adorno: The Elusiveness of the Particular and the Benjaminian Moment," Seyla Benhabib notes that both Arendt and Adorno focus on the task of "thinking anew"—"beyond the traditional schools of philosophy and methodology"—and this is what she calls the "Benjaminian moment" shared by Arendt and Adorno.[1] This moment is crucial, according to Benhabib, because it opens up thinking to being an adventure involving ever new possibilities of thought constellations, which enable a robust foundation for the political efficacy of aesthetic experience and its link to "thinking anew." Benhabib draws on this common thrust in the thinking of Arendt and Adorno to free themselves from "false universals." Benhabib writes: "This means not only refuting historical teleologies but, at a much deeper level, it involves a categorical critique of all philosophical attempts at totalizing and system building."[2] Such an approach facilitates political efficacy on the part of the subject by taking a critical stance towards all such totalizing and system building because it attempts to situate thinking from the perspective of exile. Thinking anew is positioned in the topos of the margin, of that which has been excluded, striving to experience what has not yet been permitted to appear. This perspective provides a crucial challenge to authoritarian and oppressive social-political structures by establishing an aesthetic openness for that which has never existed. This openness relates directly to what Adorno calls "the non-identical." For Adorno, an experience of the non-identical is most compellingly made manifest through specific, emancipatory forms of aesthetic experience.

We can see a most compelling exemplar of the above-described attempt to think anew, vigorously opposing any totalizing and system building, in the shared inspiration that Arendt and Adorno take from the literary aesthetics of Walter Benjamin. Foremost in consideration on this point stands Benjamin's *The Origin of German Tragic Drama*, published in Berlin in 1928, of which the "Epistemo-Critical Prologue" is particularly relevant. In the Prologue, Benjamin articulates the way in which his method intends to cite pieces of writing out of context as a means to fragment the coherent and systematized whole of a text, thus allowing its elements of truth to arise in the act of tearing the whole to shreds.[3] Benjamin's technique is intended for a kind of object that comprises a unified and coherent, systematic whole, a text which idealistically closes itself off from transient and unassimilatable phenomena, as well as from unique, unrepeatable, individual experience. Benjamin makes clear that such is the target of method in his negative reference to the nineteenth century and its concept of system, exemplified in the following passage in the "Prologue":

> The methodological element in philosophical projects is not simply part of their didactic mechanism. This means quite simply that they possess a certain esoteric quality which they are unable to discard, forbidden to deny, and which they vaunt at their own peril. The alternative philosophical forms represented by the concepts of the doctrine and the esoteric essay are precisely those things which were ignored by the nineteenth century, with its concept of system. Inasmuch as it is determined by this concept of a system, philosophy is in danger of accommodating itself to a syncretism which weaves a spider's web between separate kinds of knowledge in an attempt to ensnare the truth as if it were something which came flying in from outside.[4]

Benjamin here criticizes the systematic philosophical forms of the nineteenth century, which attempt to weave together incongruent kinds of knowledge in order to set a trap for that truth which lies external to this web. Benjamin's method is to work in the opposite direction: to take texts apart through fragmentation instead of assembling them into coherent wholes. He models his writing on the form of a tractate, which "may be didactic [*lehrhaft*] in tone," but is devoid of "the conclusiveness of an instruction which could be asserted, like doctrine, by virtue of its own authority."[5] He most clearly explains his usage of fragmentation, and its reliance on quoting out of context, in the following passage, which needs to be quoted in full:

> In the canonic form of the treatise the only element of an intention—and it is an educative rather than a didactic intention—is the authoritative quotation. Representation is the epitome of its method. Method is detour. Representation as detour—such is the methodological nature of the tractate. The absence of an uninterrupted course of intention is its primary characteristic. Tirelessly the process of thinking makes new beginnings, returning in a roundabout way to the thing itself. This continual pausing for breath is the form of existence of contemplation. For by pursuing different levels of meaning in its examination of one single object it receives both the incentive to begin again and the justification for its irregular rhythm. Just as mosaics preserve their majesty despite their fragmentation into capricious particles, so philosophical contem-

plation is not lacking in momentum. From the individual and disparate they come together; and nothing could bear more powerful testimony to the transcendent force of the sacred image and the truth itself. The value of fragments of thought is all the greater the less direct their relationship to the underlying idea, and the brilliance of the representation depends as much on this value as the brilliance of the mosaic does on the quality of the glass paste. The relationship between the minute precision of the work and the proportions of the sculptural or intellectual whole demonstrates that truth-content is only to be grasped through immersion in the most minute details of subject-matter. In their supreme, western, form the mosaic and the treatise are products of the Middle Ages; it is their very real affinity which makes comparison possible.[6]

The most crucial line in this passage claims: "The value of fragments of thought is all the greater the less direct their relationship to the underlying idea, and the brilliance of the representation depends as much on this value as the brilliance of the mosaic does on the quality of the glass paste." The *lack* of relation of the thought fragments to the underlying idea is here metaphorically equivalent to that which holds a mosaic together. The absence of a relationship to any referential idea, which would serve to unify the pieces, is itself—ironically, in an ungrounded manner—the glue, if you will, of Benjamin's method. Also crucial is the subsequent line in which Benjamin claims that "the truth-content is only to be grasped through immersion in the most minute details of subject-matter," with these minute details optimally having the least possible relation to the whole from which they have been extracted. Benjamin's method is therefore one of detour, as he himself describes it: "Representation [*Darstellung*] is the epitome of its method. Method is detour. Representation [*Darstellung*] as detour—such is the methodological character of the tractate. Renunciation of an uninterrupted course of intention is its primary characteristic."[7]

We can now take this outlay of Benjamin's method and discern its relevance for Adorno's early work, *Kierkegaard: Construction of the Aesthetic*, written between the years 1929 and 1933 and published in 1933. For in this text, Adorno critiques the model of philosophical writing that attempts to construct a whole out of an accumulation of knowledge, through which the reader is led by means of the writing to such an accumulation. This is likewise what Benjamin was attacking in *The Origin* text, where he distinguishes such a philosophical doctrine of knowledge accumulation from one that aims to evoke a truth that, even though whole, only appears as an essence that cannot be possessed by any concrete form of knowledge. In *The Origin*, Benjamin writes:

> If representation is to stake its claim as the real methodology of the philosophical treatise, then it must be the representation of ideas. Truth, bodied forth in the dance of represented ideas, resists being projected, by whatever means, into the realm of knowledge. Knowledge is possession. Its very object is

determined by the fact that it must be taken possession of—even if in a transcendental sense—in the consciousness. The quality of possession remains. For the thing possessed, representation is secondary; it does not have prior existence as something representing itself. But the opposite holds good of truth. For knowledge, method is a way of acquiring its object—even by creating it in the consciousness; for truth it is self-representation, and is therefore immanent in it as form. Unlike the methodology of knowledge, this form does not derive from a coherence established in the consciousness, but from an essence. [8]

In his early work of 1933, *Kierkegaard: Construction of the Aesthetic*, Adorno appropriates Benjamin's method in the service of a literary-philosophical critique of Kierkegaard, through which Kierkegaard's alleged coherent whole—in the style of the nineteenth-century reinscription of Hegelian system—is devolved upon itself. Adorno's aim is to allow the essence of a coherent truth content—embodied in Kierkegaard's Hegelianism, according to Adorno—to arise through what has been destroyed. As I have argued elsewhere, Kierkegaard's writings—both pseudonymous and signed—never had such a model of knowledge accumulation or systematic idealism as its goal. [9] Nor did Kierkegaard's project manage such ends *unintentionally*, as Adorno has claimed. [10] However, important for the purposes of the present chapter is the evidence that Adorno is utilizing a Benjaminian notion of truth from the *The Origin*'s "Prologue," where Benjamin elaborated the following: "The object of knowledge, determined as it is by the intention inherent in the concept, is not the truth. Truth is an intentionless state of being, made up of ideas. The proper approach to it is not therefore one of intention and knowledge, but rather a total immersion and disappearance in it. Truth is the death of intention." [11] The last sentence from this just-quoted passage is perhaps among the most famous, and arguably most significant, dicta to arise out of Benjamin's corpus. Adorno appropriates this most significant dictum that "[t]ruth is the death of intention" in a twofold manner in relation to Kierkegaard. First, Adorno claims that the truth for which Kierkegaard was striving is one that he could not access via his intentions; and second, that the truth which unfolds from the ashes of a Kierkegaard critique is one that Kierkegaard never intended to find. This is, of course, according to Adorno the truth that marks the failure of Kierkegaard's philosophical undertakings. In *Melancholy Dialectics*, Max Pensky explains the details of Adorno's use of Benjamin's method as follows:

> passages removed from Kierkegaard's own works are constructed into constellations of tension between isolated fragment and conceptual context. Recovered textual fragments, cited against themselves, reveal the truth content dwelling within Kierkegaard's own text, a truth content that becomes legible only when referred to the mediated social totality in which the text is embedded. [12]

Crucial to my own analysis in the present chapter is the way in which Adorno brings out the truth content "dwelling within Kierkegaard's own text," which "becomes legible only when referred to the mediated social totality in which the text is embedded," by following Adorno's employment of the image of the bourgeois *intérieur*. In *Kierkegaard: Construction of the Aesthetic*, in the section titled "Intérieur," Adorno writes:

> The fitting name of the "situation," as the powerless-momentary indifferentia-
> tion of subject and object, is . . . to be found in the imagery of the apartment
> interior, which, while it discloses itself only to interpretation, demands inter-
> pretation by its striking independence. It is the bourgeois *intérieur* of the
> nineteenth century, before which all talk of subject, object, indifferentiation,
> and situation pales to an abstract metaphor, even though for Kierkegaard the
> image of the *intérieur* itself serves only as a metaphor for the nexus of his
> fundamental concepts. The relation is reversed as soon as interpretation gives
> up the compulsion of identity that is exerted even by Kierkegaard's idea of
> situation, which indeed exclusively occurs as the actual site of inward deci-
> siveness. [13]

From Adorno, as well as Pensky's analysis of the Kierkegaard text, we can see the interpolation of the social space into the private domain of subjective space, for the social space both colonizes and reifies the private domain. The private space retreats into Kierkegaardian "inward decisiveness," only to invert its own situation—against its intention and self-interpretation—thus making explicit its embeddedness in the social "situation." Because of the failed space of inward subjectivity, Adorno necessitates the turn to the aesthetic, which facilitates moments—albeit transitory, fleeting ones—of emancipation from the oppression of social norms.

The image of the bourgeois *intérieur* has been thematized and comment-ed upon by several distinguished scholars in the tradition of critical theory. For example, Susan Buck-Morss has written in regard to Adorno's reliance on Benjamin's method and the notion of the bourgeois *intérieur* in her semi-nal work, *The Origins of Negative Dialectics*:

> The philosophical "unriddling" of Kierkegaard did not involve giving an an-
> swer to the apparent meaninglessness of life, but demonstrating the meaning-
> lessness of the existential question. . . . Attacking Kierkegaard from within,
> using his own words against their intent, Adorno needed to demonstrate that
> the "configuration of inwardness" which appeared at all points of contradiction
> in Kierkegaard's philosophy was permeated by the external world. Existential
> inwardness had to be translated out of conceptual abstraction into sociohistori-
> cal concreteness. To achieve this, Adorno constructed a "historical image"
> using the elements of a metaphor supplied by Kierkegaard himself: the interior
> of a bourgeois flat of the mid-nineteenth century. [14]

Furthermore, through the image of the bourgeois *intérieur*, according to Pensky, Adorno has caused one facet of Kierkegaard's writing to explode the static emptiness that Adorno indicts as the final product of Kierkegaard's inwardness. In explaining the consequences of this explosion as Adorno has conducted it, Pensky concludes:

> In this way, Kierkegaard's supposed liquidation of Hegelian idealism, by shunning any vital, mediated relationship with the realm of the objective and plunging itself ever deeper into subjective inwardness, in effect recapitulates the very idealism it set out to overcome, falling into an objectively false, mythical realm in which external reality is merely a shadowy reflection of inner emotional states, where historical processes are vague and ultimately unreal reflections of the inward path of the soul in its search for meaning.[15]

Buck-Morss synthesizes similarly:

> Adorno's historical image aimed at *de*mythification by transforming the symbolic relationships established by Kierkegaard's words into dialectical ones. By bringing Kierkegaard's philosophical contents into *critical* juxtaposition with symbols from the historical reality which had been their source, Adorno transformed Kierkegaard's eternally fixed images (which ruled over the individual with the fatalism of an astrological sign) into dynamic, *historical* constellations: he set their elements in motion so that they negated the very concepts they were intended to symbolize.[16]

It is precisely the explosion of static emptiness in Kierkegaard's notion of inwardness, which creates "dynamic, *historical* constellations" by provoking thought that I wish to explore in more detail on its own and through its impact upon Adorno's later aesthetic theory. One way to accomplish this is to further elaborate the mutual influence between Adorno and Benjamin evident in their joint engagement with the concept of the bourgeois *intérieur*. In his personal correspondence with Adorno, Benjamin commented on the symbiotic intellectual relationship between the two of them. After having received a copy of the *Kierkegaard* manuscript from Adorno, Benjamin responded with the following: "Not since reading Breton's latest verse (in the 'Union libre') have I felt myself so drawn into my own domain as I have through your exploration of that land of inwardness from whose bourn your hero never returned. Thus it is true that there is still something like collaboration; that there are still sentences which allow one individual to stand in for and represent another."[17]

We can assert with confidence that Benjamin's influence on Adorno's *Kierkegaard* can be seen on a very large scale, since Adorno had used the technique laid out by Benjamin in the "Epistemo-Critical Prologue" to *The Origin* text as the method by which to carry out his analysis of Kierkegaard. An additional reference point for their continued, reciprocal influence stems from Benjamin's *Arcades Project*, which was conceived in 1927 in Paris and was still being developed when Benjamin fled the Occupation in 1940. Fragments quoted by Benjamin in the sections on "The Interior, The Trace" and "The Flâneur" evince in great nuance the role Kierkegaard played—but specifically, Adorno's *Kierkegaard*—in Benjamin's seminal *Arcades Project*. However, in this context it must be noted that while their collaboration included a great deal of mutual influence, it also allowed for disagreement, evidenced in Adorno's comments on Benjamin's *Arcades Project* in their personal correspondence. For Adorno claimed as a critique of the *Arcades Project*, "The interior should be rendered transparent as a social function and its apparently autarchic character revealed as an illusion—not vis-à-vis some hypostatized collective consciousness, but vis-à-vis the actual social process itself. The 'individual' is a dialectical instrument of transition which must not be mythicized away [as Adorno is accusing Benjamin of performing] but can only be superceded."[18] Nonetheless, it is my aim to show the harmony of their collaboration, against the intentions of Adorno's statements. Here I gain support from Georg Betram's essay in the present volume, which defends Benjamin against Adorno's criticism of not being dialectic enough in his thought images; hence Benjamin's literary aesthetic is indeed relevant to Adorno's own aesthetic theory.

Benjamin's construction of the interior is already one that begins to mimic the outside world. But it is likewise mimicked by the outside world in a manner that aims to frustrate, indeed mock, the static comfort of the enclosed domestic space. This external mimicry is an aesthetic mirroring that seeks to inject dialectical movement into the creaturely habitus of the domicile as a system, which all too easily comports itself—oppressively— in protecting one against the outside world. The bourgeois *intérieur* seeks to shelter itself from the visceral materiality of the conditions of late capital. Here we see again the interpolation of the social into the private domain of subjectivity, and the subject's response as a retreat to inward, imaginative subjectivity. Consider the following fragment cited by Benjamin in "The Interior, The Trace": "To render the image of those salons where the gaze was enveloped in billowing curtains and swollen cushions, where, before the eyes of the guests, full-length mirrors disclosed church doors and settees were gondolas upon which gaslight from a vitreous globe shone down like the moon."[19] The concrete reality of the middle-class living room constructs a soothing atmosphere through its own enclosed space. In a further passage, we see clearly Benjamin's critique of the disguise of comfort donned by the nineteenth-century domestic interior, about which he claims:

> The space disguises itself—puts on, like an alluring creature, the costumes of moods. . . . In the end, things are merely mannequins, and even the great moments of world history are only costumes beneath which they exchange

> glances of complicity with nothingness, with the petty and the banal . . . the nineteenth-century interior is itself a stimulus to intoxication and dream. . . . To live in these interiors was to have woven a dense fabric about oneself, to have secluded oneself within a spider's web, in whose toils world events hang loosely suspended like so many insect bodies sucked dry. From this cavern, one does not like to stir. [20]

Precisely because the inhabitant of this space "does not like to stir," both Benjamin and Adorno frustrate the seeming placidity of the topos of the bourgeois *intérieur* through fragmentation and implosion from within, or what Adorno calls his "immanent critique," which he executed for the first time aesthetically in his *Kierkegaard* text. The secret inwardness of the "indwelt spaces" analyzed in *The Arcades Project* and in Adorno's *Kierkegaard* is thereby exposed as "the frenetic topicality concealed in habitual behavior." For Benjamin, "[dwelling] has to do with fashioning a shell for ourselves."[21] Accordingly, in Benjamin's investigation, the plush material that comprises the interior of such shells is "the material in which traces are left especially easily."[22] Indeed, the traces of Kierkegaard's inwardness lay at the core of Benjamin's notion of interior in *The Arcades Project*. In the latter text, Benjamin often quotes Adorno, who is in turn citing Kierkegaard's "Diary of a Seducer." After having analyzed a passage from "The Diary," in which Kierkegaard's fictional aesthetic character, Johannes, pontificates on the role of environment and setting for memory and poetic recollection, constituting a specific variation of aesthetic reflection for Johannes that is grounded in romantic irony, Adorno writes: "Just as external history is 'reflected' in internal history, semblance, '*Schein*,' is in the *intérieur* space. Kierkegaard no more discerned the element of semblance in all merely reflected and reflecting intrasubjective reality than he sees through the semblance of the spatial in the image of the interior. But here he is exposed by the material."[23] By including this fragment in his *Arcades Project*, among other significant quotations from Kierkegaard's "Diary of a Seducer," Benjamin "exposes" Kierkegaard by transposing the latter's pseudonym, Johannes, into a *flâneur*, following Adorno's move in *Kierkegaard*—however, a *flâneur* trapped by imagination within the walls of the domestic interior. Adorno explicates the maneuver as follows:

> Thus the *flâneur* promenades in his room; the world only appears to him reflected by pure inwardness. Images of interiors are at the center of the early Kierkegaard's philosophical [aesthetic] constructions. These images are indeed produced by the philosophy, by the stratum of the subject-object relation in the work, but they point beyond this stratum by the strength of the things they record. Just as in the metaphorical *intérieur* the intentions of Kierkegaard's philosophy intertwine, so the *intérieur* is the real space that sets free the categories of the philosophy. [24]

Hence the entrapment within the interior that is caused by Johannes' father's forbidding him the concrete sense-experience of a walk through the city streets becomes the source of Johannes' imaginative freedom. In an ironic embrace of the limits to his individual freedom stemming from the authoritarian voice of the "the father," the romantic aesthete turns his small room into the pretend space of a stroll downtown during which he and his father "greeted other pedestrians; passing wagons made a din around them and drowned out his father's voice; the comfits in the pastry shop were more inviting than ever."[25] Johannes is able to "drown out" the presence of the father, whose restricted movement within the topos of the domestic living room goes nowhere. Johannes aesthetically and poetically transforms the room into the best possible "appearance" of freedom for himself as an aesthetic subject in the face of authoritarianism.

However, an important transformation takes place in Adorno's aesthetics: the *Schein*, the appearing quality of the room, the "seemingness" of the domestic interior becomes transmogrified through Adorno's critique into a horror chamber reiterating in the worst possible manner the idealism Kierkegaard is attempting to overcome. Kierkegaard's romantic aesthete must fail, as Adorno abides by Benjamin's methodology that "the truth is the death of intention." (Again, Kierkegaard would agree with the failure of this aesthetic position, although not with the ramifications Adorno claims for Kierkegaard's philosophy at large, but that is beyond the scope of the present essay.) Adorno's strenuous implementation of Benjaminian thwarting of intentionality brings Kierkegaard's nineteenth-century aesthetic interior—the heart of subjective inwardness at the aesthetic level of Kierkegaard's writings, according to Adorno—into a collapsed space of failed subjectivity. In fact, for Adorno, the interior space of Kierkegaardian subjectivity is no space at all. In *Kierkegaard*, Adorno writes: "the force of the material goes beyond the intention of the metaphor. The *intérieur* is accentuated in contrast to the horizon, not just as the finite self in contrast to the supposedly erotic-aesthetic infinitude, but rather as an objectless inwardness vis-à-vis space. Space does not enter the *intérieur*; it is only its boundary."[26] But the failure of this aesthetic space will be also its redemption, for it allows for a dialectic, that is, a dynamic to be infused into the void within which the position of the romantic aesthetic has been rendered into philosophical rubble. The latter is analogous to what Kierkegaard calls "philosophical crumbs"—indeed the most important part of any alleged or misfired philosophical "system."[27] Adorno uses the place of failed subjectivity in which subject and object have been forced into an empty and therefore static equation, as the best means to hope for the appearance of "the new." This I aim to make clear in and through a concluding examination of Adorno's *Aesthetic Theory*.

The dialectical movement infused into the shards of the remains of the domestic interior allows for the appearance of that which has not yet existed:

"the new" in Adorno's *Aesthetic Theory*. And it is thinking "the new" which facilitates the possibility of the experience of the non-identical. Consider some of the following thought provocations from the *Aesthetic Theory*: "Even the category of the new, which in the artwork represents what has yet to exist and that whereby the work transcends the given, bears the scar of the ever-same underneath the constantly new. Consciousness, fettered to this day, has not yet gained mastery over the new, not even in the image: Consciousness dreams *of* the new but is not able to dream the new itself."[28] Consciousness cannot master the new, indeed it cannot even grasp the new— hence Albrecht Wellmer's description of "the rationalistic fiction" at the heart of Adorno's thinking.[29] However, the striving for the new—as an ever infinite process of unraveling the ever-same and simultaneously constructing that which challenges the static—constitutes the dynamic as a praxis of nega- tive dialectic internal to artworks. This brings up their "situation," or what is referred to as their "*Ortsbestimmung*" in the German original of Adorno's *Aesthetic Theory*, and which was already constructed as a thematic in Ador- no's *Kierkegaard* (consider again the citation referenced above from Ador- no's *Kierkegaard* section titled the "Intérieur"). This is most relevant to my analysis, since *Ortsbestimmung* translates literally as the determination of their place, localization, or fixation of position. Here we are reminded of the self-shattering of the bourgeois *intérieur* through Adorno's appropriation of Benjamin's methodology. For Benjamin's frustration of intentionality decon- structs the inward space of the interior from within. The place from which to determine the artwork can then lie only in the margins, in exile. It belongs everywhere and nowhere contemporaneously, as a rationalistic fiction that dreams of the ever new without being able to seize it consciously. This is both its freedom and its limitation. The *Ortsbestimmung* of the emancipating aesthetic experience recognizes the double-bind of its fixedness in a place that has never been. This gives it an object-like character that is also its praxis: the non-identical must always be strived for and can never reside in any one space. Art must empty itself of content in order to make way for aesthetic emancipation, which entails the redemption of art through its own self-abnegation. As Adorno articulates succinctly: "[art's] content is dynamic in itself."[30] He engages this dynamic through a critique of bourgeois art: "The bourgeois want art voluptuous and life ascetic; the reverse would be better."[31] In order to enact this reversal, Adorno constructs a praxis of the artwork by emptying the voluptuous space of bourgeois art—embodied by the *locus communis* of the nineteenth-century domestic interior—and dis- placing the latter's voluptuousness into "life"—beyond the domain of private spaces and into the public sphere. Here we see perhaps the most significant connection to Seyla Benhabib's analysis of the "Benjaminian moment." For Benhabib, this moment is made manifest through an Arendtian attempt to secure "the inter-subjective quality of all judgment" while "elucidating the particular" epistemologically, which for Adorno is similar to a non-conscious striving for the non-identical in aesthetic judgment.[32] This becomes particularly ironic through the way that Adorno advocates for art that is most difficult to decipher: in refusing accessibility, difficult artworks become the most equitably constructed. They become available to all because they are little understood or not grasped consciously by anyone. Again, they belong everywhere and nowhere, hence their egalitarianism. The praxical comportment of difficult artworks for Adorno shifts the ownership of art from the bourgeoisie to an onus on each individual living subject to decipher any given artwork anew. The philistine is no longer excluded from the means of high art, and the aesthetic nobility no longer has claim to the comfort of the artwork as the material of their own private domain. Adorno's *Aesthetic Theory* can be quoted in this context provocatively and constructively:

> Socially implicated in the guilt of those who lay claim to aesthetic nobility, the philistine's disdain grants intellectual labor an immediately higher rank that manual labor. That art benefits from certain advantages becomes, for art's self-consciousness and for those who react aesthetically, something better-in-itself. This ideological element in art stands in need of permanent self-correction. Art is capable of this because, as the negation of practical life, it is itself praxis, and indeed not simply on the basis of its genesis and the fact that, like every artifact, it is the result of activity. Just as its content is dynamic in itself and does not remain self-identical, in the course, in the course of their history the objectivated artworks themselves once again become practical comportments and turn toward reality. In this, art and theory are allied. Art recapitulates praxis in itself, modified and in a sense neutralized, and by doing so it takes up positions toward reality.[33]

The Benjaminian moment explicated at the beginning of my essay returns through Adorno's late theory of the *Ortsbestimmung* of aesthetic emancipation. The Benjaminian "moment" in my analysis is a collapsed space inside the comfort of the middle-class living room, through which each living individual subsequently gains access to the striving of thinking "the new." However, because "the new" resists any administrative or oppressive grasp via consciousness, the moment of aesthetic emancipation facilitates a praxis that allows for political efficacy through the challenge of deciphering the difficult artwork. Adorno writes:

> The more deeply artworks are deciphered, the less their antithesis to praxis remains absolute; they themselves are something other than their origin, their fundament, that is, this very antithesis to praxis, and they unfold the mediation of this antithesis. They are less than praxis and more: less, because . . . they recoil before what must be done, perhaps even thwart it. . . . Their truth content cannot be separated from the concept of humanity. Through every mediation, through all negativity, they are images of a transformed humanity and are

unable to come to rest in themselves by an abstraction from this transformation. Art, however, is more than praxis because by its aversion to praxis it simultaneously denounces the narrow untruth of the practical world. Immediate praxis wants to know nothing of this as long as the practical organization of the world has yet to succeed. The critique exercised a priori by art is that of action as a cryptogram of domination.[34]

The topos of the bourgeois *intérieur* has served Adorno and Benjamin as a cryptogram for their shared project of aesthetic emancipation. Although the two critical theorists are frequently discussed in terms of divergences in their respective aesthetic theories, I have tried to show the *locus communis* of the nineteenth-century domestic interior as a constructive motif in both of their aesthetic positions. Through an understanding of Adorno's and Benjamin's shared critique of the bourgeois *intérieur*, we achieve a renewed understanding of aesthetic emancipation through "thinking anew"—within the imaginative parameters available in the face of oppressive, administrative regimes of appearances.

NOTES

1. Seyla Benhabib, "Arendt and Adorno: The Elusiveness of the Particular and the Benjaminian Moment," in *Arendt and Adorno: Political and Philosophical Investigations*, eds. Lars Rensmann and Samir Gandesha (Stanford: Stanford University Press, 2012), 33.
2. Ibid.
3. The following three paragraphs have been previously published in my monograph, *Kierkegaard and Critical Theory* (Lanham, MD: Lexington Books, 2012). I have modified the previously published material. I am grateful to Lexington Books for permission to reprint these paragraphs.
4. Walter Benjamin, *The Origin of German Tragic Drama*, trans. John Osborne (New York and London: Verso, 1998), 28. In German: in Benjamin, *Gesammelte Schriften*, vol. 1, part 1, eds. Rolf Tiedemann and Hermann Schweppenhäuser (Frankfurt am Main: Suhrkamp Publisher, 1974), 207 (hereafter GS 1-1).
5. Ibid., 28; GS 1-1, 208.
6. Ibid., 28–29; GS 1-1, 208–09.
7. Ibid., 28; GS 1-1, 208.
8. Ibid., 29–30; GS 1-1, 209.
9. See Morgan, *Kierkegaard and Critical Theory* (Lanham, MD: Rowman & Littlefield/Lexington Books, 2012), Chapters 1–3.
10. Ibid.
11. Benjamin, *The Origin*, 36; GS 1-1, 216.
12. Max Pensky, *Melancholy Dialectics* (Amherst, MA: University of Massachusetts Press, 1993), 141.
13. Theodor W. Adorno, *Kierkegaard: Construction of the Aesthetic*, trans. Robert Hullot-Kentor (Minneapolis: University of Minnesota, 1989), 40–41.
14. See Susan Buck-Morss, *The Origin of Negative Dialectics* (New York: The Free Press, 1977), 116. In this groundbreaking study, Buck-Morss clearly demonstrates Adorno's usage of Benjamin's early method in *The Origin* for Adorno's *Kierkegaard*. She writes, "In the same year [1929] Adorno began work on a second *Habilitationsschrift* [his first was rejected] with a totally new topic: it was an implementation of the cognitive method outlined in the introduction to Benjamin's *Trauerspiel* [*The Origin*] chapter for the purpose of providing a Marxist critique of the philosophy of Søren Kierkegaard," 23. Adorno himself made reference to the influence

of Benjamin's *Trauerspiel* book on his thinking at this time, in particular in Adorno's opening lecture into a university position. See "Die Aktualität der Philosophie" in Adorno, *Gesammelte Schriften* vol. 1, ed. Rolf Tiedemann (Frankfurt am Main: Suhrkamp Publisher, 1997), 335; in English: "The Actuality of Philosophy" in *The Adorno Reader*, ed. Brian O'Conner (Malden, MA: Blackwell Publishers, 2000), 32: "The task of philolsophy is not to search for concealed and manifest intentions of reality, but to interpret unintentional reality, in that, by the power of constructing figures, or images (*Bilder*), out of the isolated elements of reality it negates (*aufhebt*) questions, the exact articulation of which is the task of science, a task to which philosophy always remains boud, because its power of illumination is not able to catch fire otherwise than on these solid questions." Adorno here very specifically and closely binds his notion of the "project" or "task" [*Aufgabe*] of philosophy to the thinking of Benjamin, along with Benjamin's language usage, in *The Origin*.

15. Pensky, ibid., 141.

16. Buck-Morss, ibid., 121.

17. See Theodor W. Adorno and Walter Benjamin, *Adorno Benjamin Briefwechsel 1928-1940*, ed. Henri Lonitz (Frankfurt am Main: Suhrkamp, 2004), 32; in English, Adorno and Benjamin, *The Complete Correspondence 1928-1940* (Cambridge: Polity Press and Blackwell, 1999), 20–21. I have slightly modified the English translation.

18. Adorno and Benjamin, *The Complete Correspondence: 1928-1940*, 113; Adorno and Benjamin, *Adorno Benjamin Briefwechsel 1928-1940*, 149.

19. Benjamin, *The Arcades Project*, trans. Howard Eiland and Kevin LcLaughlin (Cambridge, MA: The Belknap Press of Harvard University Press, 1999), 213.

20. Ibid., 216.

21. Ibid., 221.

22. Ibid., 222.

23. Ibid., 220, citing Adorno, *Kierkegaard* (Tübingen, 1933), 46–48.

24. Adorno, *Kierkegaard: Construction of the Aesthetic*, 41.

25. Benjamin, *The Arcades Project*, 421.

26. Adorno, *Kierkegaard: Construction of the Aesthetic*, 43.

27. For a more sympathetic portrait of Kierkegaard than the one Adorno has provided, see Kierkegaard's own *Philosophical Fragments* (otherwise translated as *Philosophical Crumbs*) in Kierkegaard, *Philosophical Fragments/Johannes Climacus*, trans. Hong and Hong (Princeton: Princeton University Press, 1985). For a history of the reception of Kierkegaard by Adorno, including some of the problems of the translations available to Adorno at the time he was writing his *Habilitationsschrift*, see Morgan, "Adorno's Kierkegaard Reception: 1929-1933," in *Søren Kierkegaard Newsletter: A Publication of the Howard and Edna Hong Kierkegaard Library*, no. 46, 2003, St. Olaf College, Northfield, Minnesota; reprinted in Chapter 2 in Morgan, *Kierkegaard and Critical Theory* (Lanham, MD: Rowman & Littlefield/ Lexington Books, 2012), 15–28. For a partial defense of Adorno's reading of Kierkegaard, see Robert Wyllie, "Kierkegaard's Critique of the Public Sphere," *Telos*, vol. 2014, no. 166, 57–79.

28. Theodor W. Adorno, *Aesthetic Theory*, trans. Robert Hullot-Kentor (Minneapolis: University of Minnesota, 1997), 238–39; in German, Adorno, *Ästhetische Theorie* (Frankfurt am Main: Suhrkamp, 1970), 354–55.

29. Albrecht Wellmer, "Modernism and Postmodernism: The Critique of Reason Since Adorno," in *The Persistence of Modernity: Essays on Aesthetics, Ethics and Postmodernism*, trans. David Midgley (Malden, MA: Polity Press, 1991), 71; cited also in Benhabib, ibid., 54.

30. Adorno, *Aesthetic Theory*, 241.

31. Ibid., 13.

32. Benhabib, ibid. 34.

33. Ibid., 241.

34. Ibid.

Chapter Three

Adorno's Critical Theory at the Crossroads of Hegel and Benjamin

Natalia Baeza

Most interpreters of Adorno have tended to read him as a left-Hegelian. I call "left-Hegelian" any interpretation that upholds some version of the ideas (1) that Adorno rejects Hegel's "dogmatic" presupposition of the system in order to release the critical power of dialectics, and (2) that thus freed, Adorno takes the dialectic to undergo a turn to non-identity (understood specifically as the non-identity of the concept and the non-conceptual) that causes it to remain always incomplete and open, in contradistinction with the Hegelian dialectic's closure into the "absolute." I am intentionally defining these two characteristics in a very general way, so as to cast a wide net over a variety of interpretations that differ widely among themselves but nonetheless satisfy (1) and (2), and thus offer versions of what I am calling "the left-Hegelian reading." Most commentators on Adorno defend some version of this reading, though they disagree over whether Adorno's position is ultimately coherent and feasible.[1] The picture of Adorno that emerges from this reading is roughly that of Hegel without the absolute. However, this picture ignores key aspects of Adorno's philosophy that are decidedly *not* Hegelian but rather due to Benjamin, and which, when taken seriously into account, lead to a very different reading of Adorno.

My aims are to argue against the left-Hegelian reading and to go back to some key notions that Adorno takes from Benjamin in order to propose a new reading. The first section concentrates on the relation between the structure of dialectic in Adorno and the structure of dialectic in Hegel, with the aim to show, against thesis (1) of the left-Hegelian reading, that the concept and reality of the system is central to both. But most interpreters argue that Adorno "breaks through" the system with the notion of the non-identity. In

the following section, I argue that this view follows from a reading of Adorno's notions of non-identity and the non-conceptual that is unduly Hegelian
and does not give appropriate weight to the notions' endebtedness to Benjamin. Reading Adorno's notion of the non-conceptual through the lens of
Benjamin's concepts of nature, I argue against thesis (2) of the left-Hegelian
reading that non-identity precludes neither the completeness nor the closure
of the system, but rather renders possible an experience of damaged life
under the system. The conclusion argues that only by being deployed together do the Hegelian and Benjaminian elements of Adorno's philosophy
amount to a truly critical social theory, such that the Hegelian moment discloses the systematic structure of modern society under conditions of advanced capitalism, while the Benjaminian moment condemns the system for
its repression of, and violence against, the natural non-conceptual aspect of
life.

ADORNO'S HEGELIANISM: SYSTEM AND TOTALITY

Adorno's notion of the system is based on the idea that modern society is a
fully integrated whole in which all parts are interconnected and exhibit a
fundamental mode of operation determined by the capitalist relations of exchange.[2] Everything from the geopolitical order[3] to the private lives of individuals[4] and the structure of conceptual practices (and hence conceptual
relations in general)[5] exhibits an internal logic that reproduces the order of
exchange. In fact, Adorno refers to exchange as a *principle*: "*das Tauschprinzip*." But, according to Adorno, modern society produces systematic mis-
apprehensions that block cognitive access to the society's own mode of operation: the exchange principle operates "behind the back of consciousness"
and gives rise to illusions—beliefs and widespread forms of private and
public discourse—that actively conceal the primacy of exchange, where this
concealment is a functionally *necessary* component of the supremacy of
exchange.[6]

Hence in modern society there is an opposition between the appearance or
surface grammar of reality and its essence or deep logical structure, which
corresponds to exchange.[7] The form of thought appropriate to tracking and
illuminating the structure of this opposition is dialectical thought. Such
thought begins by considering an object of analysis as it presents itself in
appearance and then, through careful development of this appearance, derives materially incompatible views of society. These materially incompatible views are dialectical (as opposed to logical) contradictions. To resolve
the contradictions, dialectical thought then develops a new more encompass-
ing conception of the object, which is proposed as the essence or ground of
intelligibility behind the appearance. But this conception too proves proble-

matic and leads to contradictions, and hence falls back to the status of appearance. A new more essential conception is taken up, and the process is repeated by considering in ever more comprehensive steps the object's embeddedness in the social totality. Finally, dialectical thought reaches a conception of the object that shows *that* and *how* it exhibits the totality's principle of intelligibility, which is ascertained as the logic of exchange.

This insight does not cancel out the contradictions derived along the way, but renders intelligible whence they arise and how they are held together. Dialectical thought thus enables the critic to move from the analysis of any part of society as it is given in appearance to the articulation of the principle of intelligibility of society as a whole (i.e., exchange). This is why Adorno says that the object is a *monad*: its internal logic coincides with the logic of the totality (i.e., the logic of exchange) such that the particular can be seen as an "abbreviation" of the whole world. And the logic of the whole can *only* be ascertained *in the particular*, for the social totality cannot be apprehended or surveyed on its own right, as something independent from its instances in concrete phenomena.[8]

This understanding of the opposition between appearance and essence, and of how the opposition is taken up in dialectical thought, is fundamentally Hegelian. Like Hegel, Adorno holds that any particular element of reality is fully intelligible only in view of the structure of connections in which it is embedded, which structure also endows concepts with determinate content. This is why, starting with a finite set of concepts to characterize the object of thought, one can develop a structure of dialectical connections that reveals the structure of the whole world. This structure is systematic in that it exhibits a unified principle of intelligibility: for Hegel it is Absolute Reason, and for Adorno the exchange principle. Moreover, Adorno and Hegel both argue that systematicity is *discovered* (in the order of thought) through dialectics, but is *presupposed* (in the order of being) as a condition for the possibility of dialectics in the first place. It is *because* the real is systematically ordered by a principle that generates an opposition between appearance and essence that it is possible to derive dialectical contradictions that lead to ever more comprehensive views of the object until the principle of intelligibility of the totality is brought into view. Finally, in both Adorno and Hegel the whole is not something above and beyond the "contradictions" between appearance and essence that are discovered along the course of dialectical thought, but is constituted precisely by these contradictions in their systematic connectedness. The structure of dialectic (both as a structure that ontologically orders the real and as a structure of the form of thought most appropriate to disclose the real) and the conditions that make it possible are fundamentally the same in Adorno and Hegel. In particular, both accounts presuppose as a condition for the possibility of dialectics that reality is structured *as a system*, that is, as an interconnected whole that exhibits a single principle of order.

Of course, Adorno does say, in contraposition to Hegel, that "the whole is the untrue"[9] —a statement that has been used to support the idea that Adorno holds the system to be mere illusion.[10] This statement, however, does not point to Adorno's denial of the reality of the system, though it does point to a decisive difference in how Adorno and Hegel think of the system. Let us look at this difference and then come back to Adorno's statement. As I have said above, for both Adorno and Hegel dialectical analysis moves from an initial appearance of whatever object or part of society is under consideration to the concept of the totality and the articulation of its principle of intelligibility. Put succinctly, the main difference between Adorno and Hegel is that, while Hegel views this principle as the ultimate *essence* of the real and hence the most advanced point of the dialectic, Adorno views it as still susceptible to the derivation of a contradiction that makes it collapse into appearance. Recall that, for Adorno, the dialectic captures dynamics distinctive of *reification*,[11] a condition under which human beings are not *aware* of their agency in creating social reality but instead see the social as governed by natural, given, immutable laws. The social appears to be ruled by the invisible hand of reason rather than by brute exchange, and this appearance keeps the primacy of exchange hidden from consciousness. However, dialectical analysis brings the primacy of exchange to the foreground of consciousness, and in so doing transforms the initial consciousness of appearance into a consciousness whose object is the *contradiction* between appearance and essence. The culmination of dialectical development is a consciousness of the world as intrinsically contradictory. This contradiction causes the notion of the world as a totality systematically ordered by exchange to collapse into appearance. But there is no further essence to be found behind this overarching appearance.

The obvious candidate for an overarching conception of essence (i.e., of a final, most fundamental principle of intelligibility behind the world of appearances) would be exchange, which after all constitutes the principle of order of reality as a whole, and which connects and renders intelligible all lower-level contradictions. But positing exchange as the essence of the real leads to dialectical contradiction, for the exchange principle cannot live up to the role of "essence." Consider some of the most basic components (conceptual "marks" or *Merkmale*) of the concept of essence (i.e., rationality, necessity, and self-groundedness).[12] The exchange principle fails to exemplify any of these conceptual elements. First, the exchange principle is not intrinsically rational; in fact, its primacy has led to unprecedented humanitarian and ecological catastrophe and the failure to meet human needs that could be satisfied. Second, the primacy of exchange emerges from mere historical contingency, not rational or natural necessity. Third, the primacy of exchange is neither self-grounding nor self-justifying. Positing exchange as the essence of the real thus leads to dialectical contradiction. As a result, the exchange principle remains the material of appearance, which is to say that it becomes not an answer but a "riddle" in need of interpretation and resolution,[13] not a point of satisfaction for the philosophical spirit but a cause for intellectual (*geistig*) unrest. But the dialectic cannot qualm this unrest because it cannot go forward to a new concept of essence. Thus in Adorno the highest point of the dialectic is a vision of the real as an overarching appearance that contains the contradiction between appearance and essence, but that has no underlying essence.

For Hegel, on the other hand, the principle of order exhibited by the totality—the Absolute—connects and renders intelligible all lower-level contradictions (the contradictions of finite consciousness) but is itself beyond contradiction and non-contradiction.[14] Hence for Hegel the culmination of the dialectic (absolute knowledge) is consciousness of the final essence of reality and is beyond contradiction, while for Adorno its culmination is a consciousness precisely *of* contradiction. And whereas the exchange principle cannot satisfy the role of essence, Hegel's Absolute clearly satisfies the basic conceptual marks of the concept of essence: it is rational, necessary, self-grounded, and self-justifying. Its rationality literally cannot be questioned because it constitutes the standard by which anything can be evaluated as fulfilling or falling short of rationality. Additionally, the Absolute is the result of rational necessity, the very force that moves dialectical thought forward to absolute knowledge. Finally, since nothing external to the Absolute can *meaningfully* be *thought* at all, the question of "evaluating" or "justifying" the Absolute by anything that is not already contained within it cannot even be meaningfully formulated. The Absolute is the final *essence* of the real and marks the resting point for the philosophical spirit.

The main difference between Adorno and Hegel with respect to the "system" has then to do not with the system's reality, but with its status: how *fundamental* it is, ontologically speaking. For Adorno, the systematic structure woven by exchange is an overarching and internally contradictory appearance, while for Hegel the system is woven by Absolute Reason and is the ultimate essence of reality. Adorno and Hegel both express the point in terms of truth and untruth. For Hegel, the system *is* truth itself, and since Hegel deploys the concepts of truth and falsity as *ontological* categories, to say that the system is true is to say that it fully actualizes all its rational possibilities.[15] In fact, for Hegel *only* the system is fully true, for only reality considered as a totality actualizes the rational essence of Spirit. For Adorno, on the other hand, reality is a closed totality that has the status of an all-encompassing appearance with an internally contradictory structure. In other words, reality *is* ideology, and ideology is an *ontological* category: the world is structured as a system of contradictory appearance-essence relations, and there is nothing beyond this system to solve the contradictions or rationally justify their existence. When Adorno opposes Hegel to say that "the whole is the untrue," he also means the sentence in an ontological way: the social totality is untrue not because it is not real but because it fails to actualize its own rational possibilities; it fails to actualize itself as essence and exists only as a field of contradictions that reproduce the structure of ideology in every part of social life.

The concept of the systematic totality is as central to Adorno, to his view of society, and to his dialectical practice, as it is for Hegel. Adorno's critique of Hegel is not that the system is a chimera but that it is an all-too-real totality integrated by exchange (not by reason), whose existence is a brute contingency (not self-grounding or self-justifying) and whose meaning is a pressing puzzle (not a resting point) for the philosophical spirit.

> Satanically, the world as grasped by the Hegelian system has only now, a hundred and fifty years later, proved itself to be a system in the literal sense, namely that of a radically societalized society. . . . A world integrated through "production," through the exchange relationship, depends in all its moments on the social conditions of its production, and in that sense actually realizes the primacy of the whole over its parts; in this regard the desperate impotence of every single individual now verifies Hegel's extravagant conception of the system.[16]

However, some commentators have argued that Adorno deploys the concept of the totality only because it is necessary to make sense of society, but without affirming its actual existence as a whole—in fact, denying it. The concept of the system would then be a sort of Kantian regulative principle for thought, not a constitutive principle of the real. The idea is that the system is a conceptual necessity, and reality can be seen as tending toward it, but not as fully embodying it, because there is a basic non-identity between concepts and the non-conceptual, mirroring a non-identity between societal structure and non-conceptual nature. This fundamental non-identity allegedly shows the ultimate falsity of the system—in the sense that, although it may be a telos of conceptual thought, it is not fully actualized in reality.[17] Let us then look at Adorno's idea of "non-identity" and how it alters, if at all, his notion of the system.

ADORNO AND BENJAMIN: NON-IDENTITY AND THE NON-CONCEPTUAL

Adorno's thesis of non-identity—of the basic heterogeneity between concepts and the non-conceptual—is often interpreted as a result of the fact that conceptual determination is always confronted with a non-conceptual remainder, which can be further determined conceptually, but only in part; it cannot be exhausted. In this view, the non-conceptual is amenable to conceptual determination but can never become *fully* determined, and as a result, the dialectic never ends: no matter how refined the conceptual articulation of the object is, it always leaves something out, and the attempt to further articulate this remainder drives dialectical motion onwards. Non-identity thus allegedly renders Adorno's dialectic incomplete and open as opposed to Hegel's complete and closed system: The in-expungeability of the non-conceptual belies the system's claim to completeness because the non-conceptual is never fully captured by the system, and it belies the system's claim to closure because the non-conceptual constitutes an ever-present "remainder" apt for dialectical determination, in the course of which the new and unexpected may appear. [18]

The attribution of this notion of the non-conceptual to Adorno is very problematic. First, this reading renders Adorno's notion of the non-conceptual just as relative as Hegel's notion is: as not *absolutely* non-conceptual, but rather non-conceptual *relative* to the degree of conceptual determination achieved at any particular stage of dialectical development. The non-conceptual would then be *implicitly conceptual*, for it could always become further—even if not completely—determined conceptually. The only difference with Hegel (if there is any, and this depends on one's reading of Hegel) would then be that for Adorno the exercise of conceptual determination is never-ending, a regulative and infinite task that is always delayed and never "accomplished" in something like Hegel's Absolute. [19] Yet Adorno insists that the non-conceptual is inherently and in principle not conceptual, not even just implicitly so. For Adorno, it follows from the nature of the non-conceptual that its content cannot be expressed with the type of determination of concepts, that is, in terms of relations of material exclusion and implication with other concepts—the type of relations that drive dialectical development forward. Second, the left-Hegelian reading of the non-conceptual makes it seem as though the non-conceptual cannot be *expressed* adequately through any means, but Adorno explicitly says otherwise. [20] The non-conceptual cannot be expressed *in concepts*, but it can be expressed linguistically and in a manner that has a determinate meaning—only this meaning is made determinate in the affective and bodily experience that linguistic expression makes possible, rather than through propositional content.

But if the non-conceptual is not related to concepts by way of inferential relations, how then is it related to concepts and language in general? Importantly, Adorno views concepts and the non-conceptual as essentially related insofar as they jointly constitute objectivity. Like Hegel, Adorno conceives of any object apt for interpretation as having a self-reflexive structure; hence an object is for example a theory, a work of art, a philosophical position, a literary text, a product of the culture industry, or any other object in which a society and culture reflexively expresses itself. The object thus understood has both a conceptual component and a non-conceptual "nature." Adorno conceives of the conceptual component in a Hegelian way: this component involves the explicit or implicit conceptual content in the object (and the relations of material exclusion and implication that this content has to other concepts and theories), as well as the interpretations through which the object has been historically understood by a culture or tradition.

On the other hand, Adorno's notion of the non-conceptual is not based on Hegel, as the left-Hegeliean reading would have it, but on Benjamin's notion of "nature" and of how history becomes inscribed in nature.[21] The non-conceptual in this sense is a material repository of pre-reflective meanings that constitute the ground from which the object emerges, and in relation to which the object develops historically. The object's emergence (e.g., in the writing of a work of literature, the development of a philosophical theory, the invention of a new architectural form, etc.) involves, on the one hand, the conscious articulation of meaning and, on the other, the expression of the unconscious inclinations of the author or producer, the unreflective dreams of her historical epoch, and the affective life of her social life-world. These pre-reflective elements express the non-conceptual social-experiential life-world from which the object arises, and in the creative process this life-world is mimetically expressed[22] in certain material aspects of the object, such as the rhetorical language and recurrent imagery deployed in the articulation of a theory, the affects subtending a literary form (like melancholy in *Trauer-spiel*), or the economy of bodies presupposed by a text (like the masses in Baudelaire's poetry).

As the object develops historically, its content changes in a manner determined by changes in its reception, interpretation, and significance for a culture or tradition. These changes alter both the conceptual and non-conceptual contents of the object. For instance, the history of Kant interpretation and the debates alive in the literature today affect how we (and future generations) understand the concepts central to Kant's theory; hence, they affect the conceptual content of the theory, and, at the same time, they indicate a certain relation between Kant's theory and the pre-reflective social life-world of the present: the types of anxieties that this generation feels with relation to the text, the questions that are asked of the theory, the elements that interpretation highlights and suppresses, etc. The reception and interpretation of Kant is not extraneous to Kant's theory; to understand the theory, we need to understand the course of its relation to the cultural, historical, and social world in in which it exists as an object, both at the conceptual and the non-conceptual levels, from its emergence, through its historical development, and up to the present—hence Adorno's notion of the object as a "sedimented history."[23]

Importantly, the relation that the conceptual and non-conceptual levels have to each other as they constitute the object reflects the historical character of an epoch. Concepts always fail to capture the non-conceptual, but the qualitative character of this failure depends on how a particular historical period relates to the unconscious experiential ground of social life. For Adorno, modern society's relation to the non-conceptual substratum of life is specifically *repressive*, and this results in a relation of concepts to the non-conceptual that is similarly repressive: concepts repress the suffering of non-conceptual nature under the rule of the totality. Thus the interpretation of any object involves, on the one hand, the interpretation of the conceptual elements that express our culture's self-reflexive (explicit and implicit) historically developed understanding of the object, and, on the other hand, the interpretation of the non-conceptual, which expresses experiential contents repressed by our culture. The articulation of conceptual content proceeds in the familiar dialectical way inherited from Hegel: The critic develops "contradictions" on the basis of the explicit and implicit conceptual content of the object, and these contradictions are progressively developed into more comprehensive views of the object until the dialectical process deciphers the intelligibility of the totality. The non-conceptual, however, cannot be brought to expression with the same dialectical method, for it is not subject to conceptual determination at all. How, then, is the interpretation of the non-conceptual achieved?

Recall that the non-conceptual first becomes impressed in certain material aspects of the object through mimesis of the non-conceptual social-experiential ground of the object. This process makes the material *like* the original experience, giving rise to a similarity between the two. Similarity here is not a form of structural resemblance, but what Benjamin calls "non-representational similarity,"[24] an example of which would be the way in which patterns of handwriting express the unconscious of the writer,[25] or the way the tone or inflection of a voice gives away a particular meaning that can even contradict the explicit conceptual content of a statement. The interpretation of the non-conceptual searches for these non-representational similarities in order to trace its way back from the material aspects of the object (e.g., the patterns of handwriting or the tone of speech) to the experiential substance that first constituted these aspects. The interpretive role of the critic is not unlike that of a psychoanalyst who searches for linguistic cues in which repressed material expresses itself, and, just like in analytic interpretation, there is no algorithm for the critic to follow. The process requires a combination of receptivity and creativity: receptivity to grasp the non-representational similarities in the material, and creativity to express these similarities in a way that summons the experiential content sedimented in the object.

Importantly, the interpreter does not go back to a content that is already constituted, "present-at-hand," and ready to be communicated, but rather calls the experiential content forth in its expression: correspondences are gathered, set in relation to each other, and linguistically presented in such a way that they *evoke* or *summon* the experiential content in the object, instead of pointing to it. Hence the goal of interpretation is an event of disclosure.[26] To open up this event, the interpretation makes recourse to rhetoric, exagger-

ation, metaphor, and other expressive linguistic devices[27] to arrange correspondences in ways that are reciprocally illuminating and affectively suggestive. In a successful interpretation, the arrangement discloses a content that is
more than the sum of its parts, hence the aptness of calling the interpretation
a "constellation." "The perception of similarity," Benjamin writes, "is in
every case bound to a flashing up. It flits past, can possibly be won again, but
cannot really be held fast as can other perceptions. It offers itself to the eye as
fleetingly and transitorily as a constellation of stars."[28] Thus the construction
of a constellation requires the capacity not only to recognize non-representational similarities and draw correspondences, but also mimetically to reproduce the experiential content inscribed in the object in a new act of creative
repetition. The experience opened up by the constellation brings to life content that had been repressed in the object, and it does so in a transformative
way, in a manner similar to when a psychoanalytic patient brings back to life
the content of a traumatic experience and thereby transforms her response to
the original event. The culmination of the constellation is an experience in
which the interpreter mimetically expresses the repressed material and thereby recuperates the traumatic past sedimented in the object without simply
reiterating it.[29] The experience provides an affective "image" of the world by
retrieving the past and expressing the suffering it has wrought on the object,
and brings out the stakes of the present as a unique opportunity for radical
transformation.

Having looked in some detail at Adorno's notion of the non-conceptual,
we are now in a position to see why it is not the case—*pace* the left-Hegelian
reading—that the non-conceptual renders the system (1) incomplete and (2)
open. Incompleteness allegedly results from the fact that the non-conceptual
is never fully captured by the system. However, we have seen that the non-
conceptual is not a "remainder" left "outside" the system, but a standpoint
that *from within* the system allows us to experience *the system* as violent and
repressive. The non-conceptual is the repressed natural life of modern society
in conditions of total integration under the exchange principle; that is, under
the system. It is precisely because the non-conceptual has been shaped by the
system that its expression enables a recollection, recuperation, and transformative repetition of history under the system. So, the non-conceptual does
not "break" the system "open" by pointing to a "remainder" outside, but
rather allows us to *experience* the "inside" of total integration. On the other
hand, idea (2) that the non-conceptual makes the system *open* is based on the
view that the non-conceptual is an ever-present remainder the further determination of which may change the course of the dialectic. The possibility of
change then means that whatever seems to be the logic of the real may, upon
further dialectical determination, turn out to be otherwise. However, the non-
conceptual, and its theoretical expression in the constellation, do not alter the
structural dialectical analysis of modern society; they do not add to dialecti-

cal development. The interpretation of non-conceptual nature does not open up a more fundamental ontological or epistemological ground for the structure of the social order (which structure is illuminated dialectically, as shown in the first section), and hence does not relate to this order as essence to appearance. The dialectic remains "blocked" at the point of describing society as an overarching appearance with an internally contradictory structure, where this structure is systematically connected by the logic of exchange, and where the whole does not have any essence underlying it. Hence the interpretation of the non-conceptual does not "open" the dialectic to new developments, but rather complements it *externally*—"like a stepping out of dialectics"[30] —by expressing the experiential substance of the system.

Of course, Adorno does differ from Hegel in holding that there is an ineradicable non-identity between concepts and the non-conceptual, mirroring a basic non-identity between society and nature. But, as we have seen, non-identity is not a generalized failure by concepts to express reality simply because there is always a "remainder" left out. Such a generalized failure would be abstract; it would be a failure of the same type whether we are talking about how the concept of "red" exceeds its instantiation in a red flower or how the concept of "freedom" exceeds its instantiation in the actual condition of individuals under medieval serfdom or advanced capitalism. Instead, Adorno's notion of non-identity is determinate and historical. In modernity, it denotes a *repressive* relation between concepts and the non-conceptual. Non-identity does not call into question the reality of the system, but rather denotes the system's violence against nature and nature's damaged condition under the system.

CONCLUSION: ADORNO AT THE CROSSROADS OF HEGEL'S DIALECTIC AND BENJAMIN'S CONSTELLATIONS

In the preceding sections, I have argued against widespread left-Hegelian readings of Adorno's notions of the system, non-identity, and the non-conceptual, and I have proposed alternative interpretations. In concluding, I wish to outline how these interpretations come together into an overall reading of Adorno's critical method. I have argued that, for Adorno, the interpretation of any part of social life involves a twofold approach. On the one hand, there is a dialectical moment that shows how the phenomenon's intelligibility replicates the logic of the fully integrated system of modern society. On the other hand, there is the construction of a constellation, which expresses the experiential content repressed in the phenomenon, where this content corresponds to the suffering of natural life under the social totality. So, while the dialectic yields an understanding of whatever aspect of life is under scrutiny *as determined by the totality*, hence from the standpoint of the totality, the constellation triggers *an experience* of the effects that the totality has had on the unconscious inner life of human society, hence viewing the totality from the standpoint of non-conceptual nature. It is from this latter standpoint that philosophy passes judgment on the totality, showing it to be "wrong" and in need of urgent transformation.

Importantly, the two moments of philosophical interpretation are individually necessary but only jointly sufficient for critique. On the one hand, Adorno holds that an interpretation that does not give due weight to the systematic, dialectical moment of critique becomes ideological because it is unable to articulate the structure of the totality and the logic of its subversion of particularity under the order of exchange. A critique of the system that does not itself have a systematic moment helps to conceal the fact that the social order *is in fact ordered as a system*—"the diabolical system"[31] —and is therefore ideological.

> In the form of the barter principle, the bourgeois *ratio* really approximated to the systems whatever it would make commensurable with itself, would identify with itself—and it did so with increasing, if potentially homicidal, success. Less and less was left outside. What proved idle in theory was ironically borne out in practice. Hence the ideological popularity of talk about a "crisis of the system." . . . Reality is no longer to be construed, because it would be all too thoroughly construable. Pretexts are furnished by its irrationality, intensifying under the pressure of particular rationality: there is disintegration by way of integration. If society could be seen through as a closed system, a system accordingly unreconciled to the subjects, it would become too embarrassing for the subjects as long as they remain subjects in any sense.[32]

But, on the other hand, systematic dialectical thought *on its own* remains ideological because it is unable to see the system as pathological, violent, and repressive. Only through the experience opened up by the constellation are we able to see dialectics as "the ontology of the wrong state of things,"[33] and only together can the dialectical moment and the constellation garner the power of the system in order to oppose the system.[34]

Reading Adorno's critical method as bringing together the two distinct philosophical approaches of Hegel's dialectic and Benjamin's constellations helps account for the formal structure of Adorno's thought. Adorno's philosophical reflections are always conducted under the structure of fragments[35] that have a tight internal dialectical structure with virtually no gaps, where, however, there seems to be a leap between one fragment and the next. The connection between fragments is not tightly dialectical but rather associative and creative, and it follows an unconstricted, free-flowing process of thought. We can read it as the result of drawing together the "correspondences" that ultimately give rise to the constellation. Additionally, even within fragments, there are moments where the tone or force of dialectical development is altered with the evocation of feelings, fantasy, wishful thinking, and other rhetorical or interpretive devices that interrupt and alter the meaning of the dialectic without themselves being the result of dialectical development. These interruptions, leaps, sudden twists of focus, and rhetorical moves rouse the characteristically "negative," affectively rich but intellectually vertiginous experiences that accompany Adorno's texts. These elements can also be read as belonging to the interpretation of the non-conceptual through the construction of the constellation. The formal structure of Adorno's reflections can thus be read as a combination of tightly woven dialectical fragments and the construction of constellations, which accounts for the gaps and leaps that sometimes interrupt his fragments and of the macrostructure that connects the fragments into a mosaic of mutually illuminative reflections. This reading is a long-way distant from the left-Hegelian readings, which instead view the constellation as a reworking or sublation of the Hegelian "system" into an "open" structure. I hope, however, to have shown that there are serious problems with the left-Hegelian approach, and to have made the case for the viability of a new reading that limits the specter of Hegel and gives renewed emphasis to Benjamin's legacy.

NOTES

1. This reading is so prevailing that it is difficult to compile a limited list of commentators that adhere to it. A representative sample would include Brian O'Connor, Iain MacDonald, Lauren Coyle, Axel Honneth, Seyla Benhabib, and Michael Rosen. The first three authors celebrate Adorno's alleged emendation of Hegel, while Honneth, Benhabib, and Rosen argue that it ultimately leads to an inconsistent philosophical position. See Michael Rosen, *Hegel's Dialectic and its Criticism* (Cambridge: Cambridge University Press, 1982), esp. 153–80. Axel Honneth identifies not only Adorno but the whole Frankfurt tradition of critical theory with the left-Hegelian legacy, but he finds Adorno's theory particularly problematic as a result of his denial of any rational, normative elements immanent to the world. This type of criticism goes back to Jürgen Habermas, *The Philosophical Discourse of Modernity* (Cambridge, MA: The MIT Press, 1990), 126–30, and is reiterated by Seyla Benhabib, *Critique, Norm, and Utopia: A Study of the Foundations of Critical Theory* (New York: Columbia University Press, 1986),166–89. For the other authors cited above, see Brian O'Connor, "Adorno and the Problem of Givenness," *Revue Internationale de Pilosophie*, Vol. 58, no. 227 (2004/1): 85–99; Ian MacDonald, "The Wounder Will Heal: Cognition and Reconciliation in Hegel and Adorno," *Philosophy Today*, 44 (2000): 132–39; Lauren Coyle, "The Spiritless Rose in the cross of the Present: Retracing Hegel in Adorno's *Negative Dialectics* and Related Lectures," *Telos*, 155 (Summer 2011): 39–60.
2. The fact that Adorno takes the *relations of* exchange (not the forces of production) to hold primacy over social life highlights his rejection of the Marxian idea that when social relations of production begin to hinder rather than foster the forces of production, there inevitably occurs a revolution that installs new and more rational social relations. See Theodor Adorno, "Spätkapitalismus oder Industriegesellschaft?" *Gesammelte Schriften*, vol. 8, pt. 1 (Frankfurt am Main: Suhrkamp Verlag, 2003), 354–73.
3. Ibid.
4. *Minima Moralia* offers countless concrete examples in support of Adorno's claim that market relations have colonized even the most private recesses of life, such as the experience of love (§10–11), gift-giving (§21), family life (§2), and the very possibility of non-instrumental

relations (§3, 97). Adorno finds the logic of exchange at the heart of even the most banal matters of life, such as the structure of doorknobs (§19) and the discovery of dinosaur remains in Utah (§74). See Theodor Adorno, *Minima Moralia*, in *Gesammelte Schriften*, vol. 4 (Frankfurt am Main: Suhrkamp Verlag, 2003).

5. Adorno, like Hegel, holds that the content of any particular concept depends on its relation to other concepts, and that the whole network of concepts has determinate content *because* it reproduces or expresses the relations that obtain in the world of concrete experience. For Adorno, these relations are ordered by exchange; hence, conceptual relations in general reproduce or express the logic of exchange.

6. See Adorno, "Soziologie und empirische Forschung," in *Gesammelte Schriften*, vol. 8, pt. 1 (Frankfurt am Main: Suhrkamp Verlag, 2003), 205.

7. The distinction between appearance and essence should be understood along Hegelian lines: appearance is the appearance *of* essence; it results from and embodies the dynamics of essence (i.e., of exchange), and essence *is* essence only through the facts, experiences, and processes—the appearances—to which it gives rise ("Zur Logik der Sozialwissenschaften," in *Gesammelte Schriften*, vol. 8, pt. 1 (Frankfurt am Main: Suhrkamp Verlag, 2003), 549.

8. Adorno, *Negative Dialektik*, in *Gesammelte Schriften*, Vol. 6 (Frankfurt: Suhrkamp Verlag, 1970), 25.

9. "Das Ganze ist das Unwahre" (*Minima Moralia*, 55).

10. See John Pizer, "Jameson's Adorno, or, the Persistence of the Utopian," in *New German Critique*, no. 58 (Winter 1993),130–31.

11. On the notion of reification see Georg Lukács, "Reification and the Consciousness of the Proletariat," in *History and Class Consciousness* (Cambridge: MIT Press, 1971), 83–222.

12. I am using the term *Merkmale* in the sense used in classical German philosophy, in particular in Kant and Hegel, so that a conceptual mark y of a concept x is a concept partially constitutive of the semantic content of x.

13. I am using the word "riddle" to refer to Adorno's view in "Die Aktualität der Philosophie" (in *Gesammelte Shcriften*, vol. 1 (Frankfurt am Main: Surkhamp, 2003), 325–44.

14. The point is not that the Absolute is non-contradictory, but that the notions of contradiction or non-contradiction do not apply to the Absolute but only to the "finite" viewpoints contained within the Absolute. On this point, see Michael Forster, *Hegel and Skepticism* (Cambridge: Harvard University Press, 1989), 97–116.

15. Hegel distinguishes between correctness and truth. There can be a set of propositions that correctly capture the reality they describe, while that reality is nonetheless ontologically false. See Hegel, *The Encyclopaedia Logic* (Indianapolis: Hackett, 1991), §213. For Adorno's own explanation (and praise) of Hegel's concept of truth, see the first of Adorno's three studies on Hegel in "Drei Studien zu Hegel," in *Gesammelte Scriften*, vol. 5 (Frankfurt am Main: Suhrkamp, 2003), esp. 281–84.

16. *Drei Studien zu Hegel*, 273/Translation in *Hegel: Three Studies* (Cambridge: The MIT Press, 1994), 27.

17. A version of this view can be gathered from Raymond Geuss' discussion of Adorno and Hegel in "Suffering and Knowledge in Adorno," in *Outside Ethics* (Princeton and Oxford: Princeton University Press, 2005), 111–30.

18. See footnote 16.

19. How strong this difference really is depends on one's interpretation of Hegel. Importantly, for Hegel, once consciousness reaches absolute knowledge, it is able to articulate the basic conceptual relations and processes that define an object as an object and that make the world a world. But this does not mean that the non-conceptual is *eliminated*. The very necessity of non-conceptuality is part of the basic relations and processes that constitute the absolute. It is thus possible to interpret Hegel in a manner consistent with the inexhaustibility of the non-conceptual, where the *Logic* actually shows the necessity of non-conceptuality and inexhaustibility.

20. For example, see Adorno, *Negative Dialektik*, 164–65. Alison Stone quotes this passage and notes that it seems to contradict what she claims is Adorno's view that the non-conceptual is beyond expressibility. See "Adorno and Logic," op. cit., 58–60.

21. For Benjamin's notion of nature, see"Über Sprache Überhaupt und Über die Sprache des Menschen," in *Gesammelte Werke I* (Frankfurt am Main: Zweitausendeins, 2011), 206–20, and

the introduction to *Ursprung des Deutschen Trauerspiels*, in *Gesammelte Werke I* (Frankfurt am Main: Zweitausendeins, 2011), 763–955.

22. For Benjamin, the expressive capacity of language that is at its origin survives in its material aspects, such as force, tone, rhetorical devices, imagery, etc.—what Julia Kristeva calls the semiotic as opposed to the symbolic or discursive aspects of language. For Benjamin's theory of language, see "Über Sprache Überhaupt und Über die Sprache des Menschen" (op. cit.) and "Über das Mimetische Vermögen," in *Gesammelte Werke I* (Frankfurt am Main: Zweitausendeins, 2001), 445–48. Translations: "On Language as Such and on the Language of Man" (op. cit.) and "On the Mimetic Faculty," in *Walter Benjamin: Selected Writings*, vol. 1, (Cambridge: The Belknap Press, 1996), 720–22.

23. Critics such as Brian O'Connor and Michael Rosen have interpreted the notion of "sedimented history" in a purely Hegelian way, ignoring the notion's indebtedness to Benjamin. See Brian O'Connor, "Adorno and the Problem of Givenness," op. cit., and Michael Rosen, *On Voluntary Servitude: False Consciousness and the Theory of Ideology* (Cambridge: Harvard University Press, 1996) 226–33.

24. Benjamin's term is *"sinnlose Ähnlichkeit."* Susan Buck-Morss translates it as "non-representational similarity" *The Origin of Negative Dialectics* (New York: The Free Press, 1977), while Edmund Jephcott translates it as "nonsensuous similarity" in "On the Mimetic Faculty."

25. Benjamin provides the example of graphology in "Über das Mimetische Vermögen, 447/"On the Mimetic Faculty," 722.

26. See Benjamin's discussion of truth in *Ursprung des Deutschen Trauerspiels*, 766–68/ *The Origin of German Tragic Drama*, 29–31.

27. Hence Adorno's view that such devices are not extraneous to, but pivotal for, thought that aims at emphatic truth. Adorno explicitly claims that all thinking is exaggeration (*Minima Moralia* §29, 50, 82); interpretation is metaphor, and impulses, affects, and instincts are constituent and necessary parts of thought (ibid., §79, 127).

28. Benjamin, "Doctrine of the Similar," in *Selected Writings*, vol. 2 (Cambridge: The Belknap Press, 1996), 696. Original German: "Lehre vom Ähnlichkeit," in *Gesammelte Werke II* (Frankfurt am Main: Zweitausendeins, 2011), 442.

29. For a very interesting psychoanalytic reading of the concepts of mimesis in Benjamin and Adorno through the lens of Julia Kristeva, see Elaine Miller's "Negativity, Iconoclasm, Mimesis: Kristeva and Benjamin on Political Art," *Idealistic Studies*, Vol. 38, No. 1-2 (2008): 55–74.

30. See Adorno, *Negative Dialektik*, 41–42, where Adorno claims that theory requires "a doubled mode of conduct: an inner one, the immanent process, which is the properly dialectical one; and a free, unbound one, like a stepping out of dialectics."

31. Adorno and Horkheimer, *Dialektik der Aufklärung*, in *Max Horkheimer: Gesammelte Schriften*, Vol. 5 (Frankfurt am Main: Fischer Taschenbuch Verlag, 1997), 217.

32. See Adorno, *Negative Dialektik*, 34/translation by E. G. Ashton in *Negative Dialectics* (New York: Continuum, 2005), 23–24. See also *Negative Dialektik*, 36.

33. Ibid., 11.

34. *Negative Dialektik*, 40.

35. Adorno's use of the literary form of the fragment has a long history in German philosophy, especially with the Romantics, but also with thinkers like Nietzsche. See Friedrich Schlegel, "Athenäumsfragmente," in *Friedrich Schlegel: Kritische Schriften und Fragmente*, eds. E. Behler and H. Eichner (Paderborn: Schöningh, 1988). In Adorno, the use of the fragment is also strongly influenced by Walter Benjamin's idea that the interpretation of the particular makes it expressive of the totality like a monad. See especially the introduction to Benjamin, *Ursprung des Deutschen Trauerspiels*, op. cit.

Chapter Four

The Jargon of Ontology and the Critique of Language: Benjamin, Adorno, and Philosophy's Motherless Tongue

Eduardo Mendieta

There is no philosophy without the history of philosophy, even as some may want to argue that they only philosophize about that which is timeless without the aid of those who came before them. *Philosophia perennis* is itself a historical construct. Philosophy, interestingly, also has a history because individual philosophers have biographies and their thinking itself has a history. When we think about all the major philosophers in the history of philosophy, we are confronted with the philosophical problem that these philosophers underwent a process of maturation. Thus, when we discuss Plato's dialogues, we talk about the early, middle, and late dialogues, by which we mean that we stipulate that they belong to different periods in Plato's philosophical development. We also do something similar when discussing the difference between Aristotle's writings on nature and animals, and his more so-called philosophical texts. We can also talk about the earlier and later writings of Kant, which reflect not only shifts in philosophical preoccupation but also shifts in his own thinking. The same can be done and has been done with respect to Hegel, Marx, Sartre, Heidegger, and more recently Habermas. Of course, there are philosophers who, notwithstanding their *Lebenslauf* and their intellectual itinerary, have remained relentlessly faithful to some key philosophemes, to the point that we can call them philosophical obsessions. Heidegger's *Leitfrage*, for instance, was the question of Being; Habermas' has been that of discourse; Irigaray's sexual difference; Butler's injurability; Nussbaum's gender justice. All of these philosophers have doggedly pursued their key questions or philosophemes, even when they have shifted perspective. Adorno belongs to this latter type of philosopher, namely to the kind to which it is extremely difficult to assign periods, ruptures, turns, disavowals, corrections, and dramatic shifts. While there is an early Adorno, the adjective here refers to a moment in his biography, as in the young Adorno, rather than a period in his thinking. Even a cursory reading of Adorno's corpus reveals a consistency of themes, an unwavering faithfulness to a series of themes; even his writing and speaking style seemed to have emerged already formed and scripted, as if from Zeus' head. One could take pages from volume one of his *Gesammelte Schriften*, and put them in a lottery tumbler with pages from volume six and volume seven, spin and then pull out a page. One would not be able to figure out to which volume, or to which period in his philosophical itinerary, it belongs. This would also happen if one were to throw in the tumbler pages from his lecture courses from the late 1950s and 1960s. Note for instance that in the lecture courses from 1961 through 1969, Adorno inserted, literally, texts he had written in the 1930s, as if three decades, World War II, and his exile in the England and the United States had not taken place in between. In contrast to thinkers who blossom late, such as Plato, Aristotle, Kant, Gadamer, and Rorty, Adorno seems to have been a child genius already preternaturally matured at the early age of twenty-seven, when a lot of his "early" texts were written.

In this chapter, I will focus on a cluster of texts written by Adorno in the early 1930s, shortly after he had met Walter Benjamin and began an intense philosophical friendship that left Benjamin's indelible imprint on everything Adorno would produce from that moment on. These early texts are now gathered in volumes one and two of his *Collected Works*, while another text belonging to this period has appeared in translation in *Notes to Literature*, volume two. The texts in question are: "The Actuality of Philosophy" (1931),[1] "The Idea of Natural History" (1932),[2] "Theses on the Language of the Philosopher" (a manuscript that is not dated but which the editors identified as belonging to the same period),[3] "On the Use of Foreign Words" (also identified by his editor Rolf Tiedemann as belonging to this period),[4] and *Kierkegaard: Construction of the Aesthetic* (1933).[5] These texts need to be considered jointly, as forming part of a constellations of formulations and lines of thinking, because they all gravitate around a series of themes, concepts, and configurations that are decisive and determining for Adorno's thinking in general. As I will argue, these texts need to be read jointly because in them we can read in eloquently articulated, and almost finished, fashion Adorno's philosophy of language as a philosophy of philosophy—where *Sprachkitik* is metaphilosophy—his coupling suffering, truth, and language—where epistemology is transformed into the Golgotha of language—and the entwinement of history and nature that give rise to what he calls "second nature"—where natural history is best thought of in terms of the allegory of *facie hippocrita*, the physiognomy of nature suffering. Before, however, I consider Adorno's text, it is indispensable that I briefly discuss Walter Benjamin's thinking during the late teens and twenties of the twentieth century, as this is the subsoil, the very germinal center of Adorno's own emergent philosophy during the late twenties and early thirties.

THE PURGATORY OF LANGUAGE OR THE THEOLOGY OF LANGUAGE

It is difficult to understand Adorno's philosophy of language without some general understanding of Benjamin's own philosophy of language, or what should more appropriately be called his theology of language.[6] As has been noted by intellectual biographers such as Richard Wolin, Benjamin's thinking about language underwent a transformation in the 1920s, from a Jewish mystical approximation to language towards a Brechtian inflected form of historical materialist critique of language.[7] By the middle of the 1920s, Benjamin had begun to develop a historical materialist theological philosophy of language that explicitly rejected both what he called a "bourgeois" conception of language and a mystical conception of language. In an unpublished manuscript from 1916, evidently working notes towards *The Origin of German Tragic Drama*,[8] for instance, Benjamin identifies tragedy with language, or more precisely, that all human language is at its core, tragic: "Tragedy is not just confided exclusively to the realm of dramatic human speech; it is the only form proper to human dialogue. That is to say, no tragedy exists outside human dialogue, and the only form in which human dialogue can appear is that of tragedy."[9] Proper human dialogue can only appear as tragic because it is caught in what he calls "tragic time" in another manuscript from the same period.[10] Language is tragic because it is caught in the stream of history, or rather because human language is historical, it cannot but be tragic. "Language in the process of change is the linguistic principle of the mourning play."[11] *Trauerspiel* exemplifies the ceaseless decay of language. At the same time, and for the same reason, the mourning play discloses the way in which nature itself is not simply timeless, or the ceaseless cyclicality of winter and spring, but rather that nature itself is caught in the winds of history. "The mourning play is nature that enters the purgatory of language only for the sake of the purity of its feelings; it was already defined in the ancient saying that the whole of nature would begin to lament if it were granted the gift of language."[12] The mourning play, with its allegories in which sunsets intimate the death of a king, and the death of a king a tragedy in nature, becomes a cathedral of murmurs. Language does penance, or it is itself penance. But, language also silences the lament of suffering nature, for its very historicality leads it to become fossilized into slogans and words that

alleged to speak the name of things. This is what Benjamin calls signification, the ruse that language can directly signal that which it names. Signification, however, is the sedimentation of history into language. And thus, nature
"finds itself betrayed by language."[13] This is why human language is tragic.

In yet another text from the same year, 1916, "On Language as Such and
on the Language of Man,"[14] we find a more explicit and expanded fashion
Benjamin's theology of language. There is nothing that is either an expression or trace of human mental life that is not language. The mental life of
humanity does not express itself *through* language, but communicates "*itself*" in it. There is no mind that preexists language, and language that cannot
be dissociated from mental life. As Benjamin puts it: "The linguistic being of
things is their language; this proposition, applied to man, means: the linguistic being of man is his language. However, the language of man speaks in
words."[15] This is not a form of linguistic idealism, as we will see, but at the
very least it announces that there is nothing outside language. Even ideas
must find a linguistic embodiment for them to bear fruit. Without language,
then, all mental, that is *geistige*, life is sterile: "Language communicates the
linguistic being of things."[16] This is not far off from Hans-Georg Gadamer's
formulation that "*Being that can be understood is language*."[17] Beings,
things, here for Benjamin are that which is properly communicative *in* language, and not simply *through* it. The thing does not preexist language, and
language is not some arbitrary system of signification that willy-nilly can be
use to signify the thing. We could say that Benjamin's view of language here
is apophantic and not communicative. Language that names things reveals
them in their linguistic being, and does not simply communicate them. This
power of language, however, is derivate from God's language. Divine language is the incantation of things into being, and it is for this reason that they
always already are in language, and not merely through it. God's word is the
fiat of creation. "In the word, creation took place, and God's linguistic being
is the word. All human language is only the reflection of the word in
name."[18] Human language is an approximation to divine language. More
emphatically, human language is the ruination of divine language, inasmuch
as in the name that humans grant to things, there are traces of the divine
creative power of language. Before the fall, before humans sinned, there was
an Adamic language, a language that participated in God's creation. This
"paradisiacal language," which dwelled in eternal divine temporality, must
have been one of perfect knowledge, in which word, name, and thing were
translucent and congruent. After the fall, however, human language lives off
divine language. And nature itself has become mute, which is why: "It is a
metaphysical truth that all nature begin to lament if it were endowed with
language. . . . This proposition has a double meaning. It means, first, that she
would lament language itself. Speechlessness: that is the great sorrow of
nature (and for the sake of her redemption the life and language of *man*—not

only, as is supposed, of the poet—are in nature)."[19] Even in human sinful-ness, we are the vehicle of redemption in language. Redemption is a linguis-tic event that takes place in human language, and not merely through it. That nature laments, yearns for language, has a second meaning, namely that nature sorrows and suffers in her speechlessness. Lament, however, "is the most undifferentiated, impotent expression of language. It contains scarcely more than the sensuous breath; and even where there is only a rustling of plants, there is always a lament."[20] Nature's language is that of a murmuring suffering that finds echoes in the most powerless form of human language. It could be extrapolated then that human language not only lives off divine language, but is itself the expression of nature's own lament, for we are also nature. Our language is itself the lament of nature.

For Benjamin, furthermore, what the word is to divine language, the name is to human language: in one case created creation and creating creation, in the other an approximation to the lament, "mute magic of nature," in which "God shines forth."[21] The book of nature is written in a divine language for which all human language is an attempt at its translation. Language itself is translation and transposition. Language is a purgatory precisely because it is this process of translation. To summarize thus far: there is no mental being that is not *in* language, all human language is the epiphany of beings, which takes place in the name. For humans, name turns out to be "the language of language."[22] The name lives off of the divine word. Divine word is creation; human name is the rustle or lament of created creation in human language. The name is a translation of the divine word. Human language as such is translation; language is translatability, of suffering into name.

Benjamin's linguistic theology and theological linguistics establishes not only that we cannot separate the mental being of things from their linguistic incantation; it also establishes that all human language, since the expulsion from paradise, is translation.

> It is necessary to found the concept of translation at the deepest level of linguistic theory, for it is much too far-reaching and powerful to be treated in any way as an afterthought, as has happened. Translation attains its full mean-ing in the realization that every evolved language (with the exception of the world of God) can be considered a translation of all others. . . . Translation is removal from one language into another through a continuum of transforma-tions. Translation passes through continua of transformations, not abstract ar-eas of identity and similarity.[23]

I would like to suggest that divine creation is continued in the translatability that is the essence of language itself, for in translation something new is brought forth, and the rustle of mourning nature becomes audible as a new word.

In the extant correspondence between Benjamin and Adorno, there is no evidence that the latter either read these texts or even knew of their existence at the time. There is, however, evidence that both spent days talking about these ideas.[24] We also have evidence that Adorno read very closely Benjamin's *Trauerspiel* book, and in fact dedicated one of his very first seminars to a close study of the text.[25] Many of the ideas touched on above show up in Benjamin's book, but the part that is most decisive for Adorno is the "Epistemo-Critical Prologue." Here, I want to only foreground what Benjamin has to say about philosophy, which defines Adorno's own metaphilosophy, or philosophy of philosophy.

The *Trauerspiel* opens with the affirmation that "philosophy must continually confront the question of representation."[26] The question of representation turns out to be the question of how philosophy communicates its content, which is, however, beyond the power of thought itself to determine in advance. "Historical doctrine is based on historical codification."[27] That is, philosophy's forms of representation, or presentation of its contents, are products of historical sedimentation, the formalization of style into a *Lehre*, a teaching. To echo the opening lines of this chapter, philosophy is historical through and through, because it is the "historical codification" of its styles, the many genres of its articulation. It is for this reason that philosophical thought cannot be "evoke *more geometico*."[28] Philosophy can no more simply be derived from a set of naked and evident axioms than language can simply signify as if word and thing did not have some intimate relationship. For this reason, the task of the philosopher cannot be assimilated to the scientist, for whom it is unessential and unimportant how her discoveries are presented. Scientific presentation is external to its content. For the philosopher, like in language, style is indispensable. Every philosophy worth that name is a sui generis style of presentation. This leads Benjamin to claim that the centrality of style to philosophy has some "postulates." They merit ample quotation as they will find resounding echoes in Adorno: "the art of interruption in contrast to the chain of deduction; the tenacity of the essay in contrast to the single gesture of the fragment; the repetition of themes in contrast to shallow universalism; the fullness of concentrated positivity in contrast to the negation of polemic."[29] This, in short, describes Adornian paratactic writing style and anti-system philosophical prismatics.

The other key themes that are taken up by Adorno from this generative "prologue" are that of "truth as the death of intention,"[30] and the recurring image of "ideas are to objects as constellations are to stars."[31] The former theme announces that truth is predicated on the dispossession of the subject, or rather on the estrangement of the subject from its own plenipotentiary intentionality so that truth can be approximated. The latter transforms linguistic criticism into epistemological critique, hence the title of the prologue. Ideas do not have direct correlations to entities or things. The *Sache*, the matter or content, of thinking, is not to be disclosed by symmetrical and translucent equivalences. Thinking that is true to its vocation must relate to knowledge the way astronomers relate to the constellations they view through telescopes: as meta-cosmic entities that themselves gravitate, gyrating around other invisible constellations, and which are the fading light of dead stars.

In her contribution to this anthology, Marcia Morgan unfolds an eloquent argument for what she calls, following Seyla Benhabib, the "Benjaminian moment" in Adorno's work. Her argument is parsed out into different sections that move smoothly, creating a map of the different ways in which creative subjectivity enters into relation through a series of historically constituted topoi: subjectivity as interiority and turning towards one's inner self (what Ortega y Gasset called in Spanish *ensimismamiento*, that is, the turning oneself into a subject by turning inwards), aesthetic experience as exposure to a space of subdued and quiet reflexivity, of distraction and reverie; and agency as what is enabled by private bourgeois space. Morgan shows powerfully why Adorno, following Benjamin, is so intent on thinking the materiality of the topoi of bourgeois interiority, precisely as they are also the locus of commodification and alienation, which nonetheless are the very site for the subjective refuge from the assault of commodities and the prattle of vacuous communication in the boisterous market-public sphere. In what follows, I want to show how language, and in particular philosophical language, is another privileged topoi in the Benjamin-Adorno thinking constellation, one in which both damage life and the *promesse de Bonheur*, melancholy and redemption, converge.

THE LIQUIDATION OF PHILOSOPHY, OR PHILOSOPHY'S NON-CONTEMPORANEOUS CONTEMPORANEITY

In January 1931, Max Horkheimer, in his capacity as the recently appointed director of the Institute for Social Research delivered his inaugural lecture, "The Present Situation of Social Philosophy and the Tasks of an Institute for Social Research."[32] The lecture begins with a whirlwind overview of the evolution of social philosophy from Kant through Hegel, bringing us to the present state of "social philosophy" in the early part of the twentieth century. The lecture then turns away from historical reconstruction towards the immediate challenges facing European society. Horkheimer then identifies three processes around which the most enduring and important set of philosophical problems cluster: "namely, the question of the connection between the economic life of society, the psychical development of individuals, and the changes in the realm of culture in the narrower sense (to which belong not only the so-called intellectual elements, such as science, art, and religion, but also law, customs, fashion, public opinion, sports, leisure activities, lifestyle, etc.)."[33] According to Horkheimer, investigating these processes is nothing but the reformulation of the perennial philosophical questions concerning the "connection of particular existence and universal Reason, of reality and Idea, of life and Spirit."[34] The spirit of philosophy, so seems to be arguing Horkheimer, now dwells in the workshop of social science. The concepts of philosophy have now migrated into social theory.

In May of the same year, T. W. Adorno delivered his own inaugural lecture, as a recently qualified *Privatdozent*: "The Actuality of Philosophy." While at first blush the two lectures seem to begin with similar *Zeitdiagnosen* of the state of philosophy, Adorno quickly turns away from social philosophy and social theory towards the question of philosophy itself, and more emphatically the question of to what extent philosophy is up to the tasks laid before it by the times. After a synoptic overview of the early twentieth century, Adorno claims that philosophy's claim to grasp the totality has failed. This failure is evident in the crisis of idealism, as well as in the crisis of the two main currents in which philosophy has bifurcated: positivism and ontological phenomenology. The crisis has two sources: one, that philosophy's pretention to provide access to the whole in a conceptual totality is no longer tenable; second, is philosophy's own disintegration via specialization. The crisis of philosophy is Janus faced: one face looks to the promise of a reason that grasps the social whole; the other, in defeat, reconciles itself with piecemeal, fragmentary, glimpses at the shards of a shattered totality. Specialization is the scar of philosophy's collapse and abdication before a reified social existence. But this crisis of philosophy is not evident to these very currents, which are its expression. Instead, they plunge critical thought deeper into obsolescence. Thus, Adorno's dire diagnosis: "Every philosophy which today does not depend on the security of current intellectual and social conditions, but instead upon truth, sees itself facing the problem of a liquidation of philosophy."[35] Only philosophy that does not abdicate its claim to truth, social truth, can recognize that its present crisis is leading to its liquidation. This means that in the face of migration of philosophy's task into the edifice of social science and scientific specialization, philosophy faces its abolition.

It is against the "liquidation of philosophy" that Adorno raises the question of philosophy's actuality: "whether philosophy is itself at all actual. By 'actuality' is understood not its vague 'maturity' or immaturity on the basis of non-binding conceptions regarding the general intellectual situation, but much more: whether, after the failure of the last great efforts, there exists an adequacy between the philosophic questions and the possibility of their being answered at all."[36] The question of philosophy's actuality arises out of its "historical entanglements."[37] In other words, whether philosophical questions can be at all answered or translated into research agendas is both a reflection of a historical situation and itself the result of a historical process, what he later calls the decay of its very symbols. The very currency of philosophical thinking has been effaced by the sands of time. Reading this lecture closely, one can almost hear Adorno protesting that philosophy that is too in tune with the times, that is too contemporary, *Zeitgemäss*, renders itself useless. Against a philosophy that liquidates itself because of its fashionableness, Adorno juxtaposes a philosophy that saves its claim to truth by turning itself non-contemporaneous, which also abjures the claim on the whole (*Das Ganze*) in the name of the microscopic, minute details of fragments, juxtaposed, precariously and provisionally suspended in a constellation of "unintentional elements."[38]

Taking up the difference between philosophy and positive science, Adorno affirms that their central difference resides in the way that the positive and differentiated sciences "accept their findings, at least their final and deepest findings, as indestructible and static, whereas philosophy perceives the first findings which it lights upon as a sign that needs unriddling."[39] To philosophy that is to the height of its calling, no sure or appropriate interpretative key is given, "nothing more is given to it than fleeting, disappearing traces within the riddle figures of that which exists and their astonishing entwinings."[40] But, philosophy, which is itself caught in those historical entwinings, can also approach these fading, vanishing, fleeting evanescent traces if it takes distance, estranges itself, from its time. Philosophy that faces its potential liquidation must render itself *Unzeitgemäss* (unfashionable) and *Ungleichzeitleich* (non-contemporaneous).[41] This is how philosophical interpretation renders itself dialectical. How is that dialectical type of philosophical interpretation to be enacted? Adorno's answer should make us recall Benjamin's postulates about philosophy's umbilical dependence to style: "I bestow upon historical facticity, or its arrangement, the power which actually belongs to the invariant, ontological first principles, practice idolatry with historically produced being, destroyed in philosophy every permanent standard, sublimated it into an aesthetic picture game (*Bilderspiel*), and transformed the *prima philosophia* [philosophy of first principles] into essayism."[42] In short, this philosophy that is both unfashionable and non-contemporaneous makes its claim upon reason by way of the art of invention, but the organon of invention is fantasy.[43] Dialectically practiced philosophy is philosophy that abides by an exact imagination that is attentive to both temporal and spatial estrangements: the microscopic and fragmentary are concretions of history in nature. Here, Adorno's philosophy of language is in accord with Jorge Luis Borges' view on language: "Language is nourished not by original intuitions—there are few—but by variations, happenstance, mischief. Language: to humbly speak thought."[44]

FACIA HIPPOCRATICA, OR THE SUFFERING OF NATURE

In 1932, a year after his inaugural lecture, Adorno presented a paper before the Kant Society in Frankfurt. This is the now famous and extremely important essay "The Idea of Natural History." The essay takes up and expands on many themes already introduced in his "The Actuality of Philosophy." But new themes and, above all, new terms are also introduced. One that is new and key is that of "philosophical terminology." Here, Adorno is developing his own lexicon, his own way of referring to certain problems. Here, also, we see Adorno intensify his critique of Heidegger. In many ways, this text ought to be read as precursor both to *The Jargon of Authenticity*[45] and evidently to *Negative Dialectics*,[46] and arguably to *The Dialectics of Enlightenment*. Adorno clearly positions himself over and against the "ontological" currents of the day, and it is clear he means Heidegger's version of phenomenological ontology, which in his assessment has dissolved the terms of both nature and history into a historicism that does justice to neither concept. But, for Adorno, the question of both nature and history, which tend to be thought in philosophy in opposition to each other, is a matter of how these concepts are either rendered accessible or betrayed by philosophical terminology. "Nature" and "history" are concepts that are rendered intelligible by a constellation of philosophical terms. These constellations are entangled in the history of philosophy but also in the decay, transformation, renewal, and abandonment of key philosophical terms. The issue then calls for a critique of philosophy's terminology.

Adorno's argumentative strategy against phenomenological neo-ontology is to demonstrate that its putative celebration of history, qua elevation of historicity to a key philosophical category, is actually betrayed and rendered vacuous. Historicity cannot "master" the problem of historical contingency, on the one hand. The facticity of Dasein, on the other hand, compels us to think that historicity is the fiat of a will, and in this way history is dissolved in the existential project of individual unmoored from history. Neither history's tychism nor synechism, that is, its ruptures and continuities, can be appropriately accounted for by an existentialist conception of historicity. At the same time, nature disappears from philosophical consideration, or is thrown into the timeless abyss of eternity—the time of nature, and natural time are thus also not properly accounted. The challenge, then, is:

> If the question of the relation of nature and history is to be seriously posed, then it only offers any chance of solution if it is possible *to comprehend historical being in its most extreme historical determinancy, where it is most historical, as natural being, or if it were possible to comprehend nature as an historical being where it seems most deeply in itself as nature.* It is no longer simply a matter of conceptualizing the fact of history as a natural fact *toto*

caelo (inclusively) under the category of historicity, but rather to retransform the structure of inner historical events into a structure of natural events. [47]

Instead, Adorno invites us to think through and with a new concept that he alleges will do justice to both history and nature, in their respective philosophical terminological senses: that is, in that former refers to the horizon of eventuality and that the former refers to the horizon of recurrence. This is the concept is that of natural history. But, against neo-ontology's penchant for creating philosophical terminology ad novo and by fiat, Adorno argues that this concept has emerged from the history of philosophy itself. The concept gathers the historical experience of philosophy itself: "it has its binding identity in the context of historical-philosophical work on particular material, til now above all on aesthetic material."[48] This last remark is particularly telling. It announces that while the term "natural history" has emerged from the historical-philosophical work on the themes of nature and history, its efficacy has been restricted to aesthetics. It is now part of Adorno's agenda to make this concept effective for philosophy in general. This is a transposition of a concept from one sphere to another so as to have it refract throwing a different light.

Adorno traces the origins of this concept to George Lukács' and Walter Benjamin's work. In Lukács, Adorno focuses on the concept of "second nature."[49] By "second nature," Lukács referred to alienated social reality that takes on an ineluctable, intractable, fateful character, but at the same time, it is implicit that "first nature" is also experienced in a reified and alienated way. The scientist approaches nature as a corpse, as a thing to be dissected, analyzed, used, and then thrown away once exhausted or rendered useless. For Lukács, however, "second nature" points to how history is turned into an allegedly obdurate and imperturbable nature. "Second nature" makes us approach history like a charnel house in which the accumulated remnants of past historical moments are calcified into the dance macabre of fate. "Lukács envisioned the metamorphis of the historical qua past into nature; petrified history is nature, or the petrified life of nature is a mere product of historical development,"[50] but, to which should be added, no longer is meaningful, or to be thought as the result of human design. The accumulated bones of humans turn into ciphers of nature. But, while the archeology of the concept of "natural history" may reside in Lukács' *oeuvre*, according to Adorno, it is Benjamin who "marks the decisive turning point in the formulation of the problem of natural-history in that he brought the resurrection of second nature out of infinite distance into infinite closeness and made it an object of philosophical interpretation."[51] Adorno identified two passages in Benjamin's *The Origin of German Tragic Drama* as marking this transition. In one, Benjamin refers to how the "allegorical poets" saw in natural "eternal transience," and, conversely, how "history" is written in "the countenance of nature in the sign language of transience."[52] At the crossroads of this double inversion is the allegory, which is expression. "Allegory is usually taken to mean the presentation of a concept as an image and therefore it is labeled abstract and accidental. . . . What is expressed in the allegorical sphere is nothing but a historical relationship."[53] What "second nature" is for Lukács, the "allegorical" is for Benjamin, namely the process by means of which the natural is to be deciphered as the most historical, and the historical to be read as what has turned into nature.

"Second nature," however, appears most strikingly in Benjamin's work in the allegory of *facie hippocratica*, the suffering and mourning face of nature. Robert Hullott-Kentor, in a translator's note to this term, quotes for us the classical definition of this countenance: "a sharp nose, hollow eyes, collapsed temples, the ears cold, contracted, and their lobs turned out: the skin about the forehead being rough, distended, and parched; the color of the whole face being green, black, livid, or lead colored."[54] Two images, two allegories: charnel house and *facie hippocratica*; two forms to approximate the concept of natural history. Both, however, have at their core the process by means of which history is rendered natural (i.e., timeless and mystical), and nature is rendered speechless but mourning and murmuring: if it could speak, it would speak its torment, which is the torment we inflict on it, the accumulated suffering of history. Adorno has excavated in Lukács and Benjamin two terms that help to draw out a constellation of concepts that through "exact imagination" and dialectical interpretation allow us to mediate nature and history.

> The differential procedure required to arrive at natural-history without antici-
> pating it as a unity consists in firstly accepting these two problematical and
> indeterminate structures in their contradictoriness, as they occur in the *lan-
> guage of philosophy*. This is legitimate in that it appears that the philosophy of
> history increasingly comes to just this sort of intertwining of the originally
> existing and the newly becoming in the findings presented by research.[55]

I would claim, in order to introduce the next section, that in this essay Adorno is not simply critiquing Heidegger, and not simply offering a genera-tive reading of Lukács and Benjamin that offers conceptual tools to deal with the impasse of "contemporary" philosophy, rather, he is also laying out a distinct metaphilosophy, one that says that we should approach concepts by way of a dialectical critique of philosophy's language. Philosophysical termi-nology becomes the site of the accumulation of historical processes. Lan-guage is the ruin of thought, but thought can only dwell in language. Philoso-phy's terminology is the urn of natural and historical suffering, therein are buried semantic contents that may help us exorcise the spell of second nature.

LANGUAGE AS RUINATION, OR *LOS FÍLOSOFOS DESLENGUADOS*

Adorno's philosophy is ineluctably linked with an immanent critique of historical materialism, and most specifically with its inversion of one of Marx's most famous pronouncements, namely the eleventh thesis on Feuerbach: "The philosophers have only *interpreted* the world in various ways; the point is, to *change* it."[56] For Adorno, instead, "Philosophy, which once seemed obsolete, lives on because the moment to realize it was missed."[57] As Adorno argued in his 1931 and 1932 texts, philosophy that is too contemporary is condemned to self-abolition. Its being out of tune with the times is part of its critical task. But, its *Ungleichzeittigkeit* is above all a function of philosophy's dependence on language. There is no philosophizing without language, and language itself is the site of the encounter between truth and history. This is what is at the heart of this beautiful and programmatic text: "Theses on the Language of the Philosopher." Adorno, once again, takes up Benjamin's critique of the bourgeois conception of language, which renders the relationship between "word" and "thing" as contingent, arbitrary, and non-essential. Now, however, this view, which is also associated with linguistic idealism, is articulated in terms of the "distinction between form and content in philosophical language."[58] Here, Adorno also takes aim at the promise of the communicability of philosophical language that alleges to make all truth and philosophical content transparent in the language that is denuded of its historicity. This promise is either "banal" or "untrue." It is banal because it postulates the pregivenness and validity of words. This is banal because it is not the case that we know beforehand which words correspond to which thing or context of enunciation. The historicality of the given demands that what it names or the words by which it is given to us in language also grow out of that historical context. "Through language history wins a share of truth. Words are never merely signs of what is thought under them, but rather history erupts into words, establishing their truth-character. The share of history in the word unfailingly determines the choice of every word because history and truth meet in the world."[59]

The pretention to undistorted communicability, furthermore, is untrue because it projects a positive utopia of transparent communicability that covers over the very problem of what either conditions or disables communicability: historical suffering.[60] In this context, Adorno also brings to bear his critique of neo-ontological language: "All deceiving ontology is especially to be exposed by means of a critique of language."[61] This, in a nutshell, is the thesis that is developed expansively in *The Jargon of Authenticity* and most of *Notes to Literature*, as well as his winter 1951/1952 *Der Begriff der Philosophie* lecture course,[62] and 1962–1967 lecture course, now published as *Philosophische Terminologie*,[63] namely: "All philosophical critique is today possible as the critique of language. This critique of language does not merely have to concern itself with the 'adequation' of words to things, but just as equally with the state of words on their own terms."[64] This requires that we approach philosophical language neither through mere exposition (what words may mean according to philology), nor through mere derivation (by arbitrarily choosing words so as to concatenate axioms into proofs), but rather through what Adorno calls "configurative language": "configurative language represents a third way as a dialectically intertwined and explicatively indissoluble unity of concept and thing. The explicative indissolubility of such unity, which eludes comprehensive logical categories, today compellingly requires the radical difficulty of all serious philosophical language."[65] This configurative language that problematizes the "disintegrated language" of philosophy[66] is one that, more precisely, aims to avoid the "unbroken dignity of words" and the "speechless" intentionality of the subject.[67] Philosophical language has to dwell in the ruins of language that is not simply the instrument of a preexisting intentional subject and one that instead recognizes the broken dignity of words by recognizing the "aesthetic dignity of words."[68] Here, we also find the seeds of Adorno's reflections on what he calls the "Art's linguistic quality,"[69] or its "speech-like character" [*Sprachähnlichkeit*].[70] Works of art, like words, and language in general share something in common precisely because both are the work of history: their content is sedimented history, but also the ruin of history. Language, like works of arts, is also the site of the ruination of history, from which only a negative utopia can be projected. "The growing significance of the philosophical critique of language can be formulated as the onset of a convergence between art and knowledge. While philosophy has to turn itself towards the unmediated unity of language and truth—though up to now only aesthetically—and must measure its truth dialectically against language, art wins the character of knowledge: its language is aesthetic, and only then harmonious, if it is 'true': when words are in accordance with the objective historical condition."[71] But, as Adorno argued insistently and relentlessly, the objective historical condition is one of fragmentation, reification, and commodification. If the work of art is the trace of this ruination, the sentence within language becomes the locus of both a remembrance and hope, the archive of a paradisiacal promises, as William Gass put it: "In the aesthetically interesting sentence, in any case, every materiality of language is employed to build a body for the meaning that will the realize the union of thought and thing that paradise apparently forgot to promise us, and give consciousness the solid presence it constantly yearns for and will never quite realize. Over and over, we think that in the world we shall find the place where mind and matter meet."[72]

The recognition of the ruination of language, however, is not simply a negative diagnosis; it also traces a positive agenda: how is language as the site of history to be also the site of redemption? Insofar as philosophy approaches its terminology in terms of a critique of language that can redeem the "aesthetic dignity of words." In the following formulation, we find Adorno's thinking of the dialectic as a critique of reified, decayed, ruined language: "Today the philosopher confronts disintegrated language. The ruins of words are his material, to which history bind him; his freedom is solely the possibility of their configuration according to the force of truth in them. He is as little permitted to think the word as pregiven as to invent a word."[73] But how is the philosopher to confront its "disintegrated" language so as to lead it to disclose its truth content, without doing violence to its historical content and without re-asserting violent and dispossessing subjective sovereignty? Part of the answer is provided in a text that belongs to the period in which he wrote the "Theses on the Language of the Philosopher." I am referring to "On the Use of Foreign Words," which as the title already intimates is a defense of the use of foreign words against the purism of linguistic nativists. "One must defend them [foreign words] where they are at their worst from the point of view of purism: where they are foreign bodies assailing the body of language."[74] This incursion, however, is for the sake of the health of a language that its detractors would defend on the grounds of its autonomy, purity, of its belonging to a people or an unequivocal historical project (as Heidegger would want us to believe). "[H]istorically, foreign words are the points at which a knowing consciousness and an illuminated truth break into the undifferentiated growth of the aspect of language that is mere nature: the incursion of freedom."[75] Through surgeon-like precision, the dialectical philosopher assails the body of moribund language so as to heal it by inserting in it the "silver rib of a foreign word."[76] The "silver rib" is an expression that Adorno appropriates from Walter Benjamin's *One Way Street*. This very expression is cited in a text from 1959, "Words from Abroad,"[77] but it is one that is also echo in his *Kierkegaard* book, when he writes with respect to Kierkegaard's philosophy of language: "Precisely here Kierkegaard show reverence for the historical scars on the creaturely body of language, the foreign words, for the sake of their function in history."[78]

The "silver rib," the foreign words, "helps the patient, the idea, to survive, while it is sickened from the organic rib. The dialectic of the foreign word is of this nature. It moves away from the organic nature of language when the latter is no longer adequate to grasp ideas. . . . In the foreign word as ray of light from *ratio* strikes the stream of language, which gleams painfully in it."[79] The use of foreign words is the analogue of the dispossession of the subject by way of the constellations of words that approximate the concept through the organon of exact imagination. Foreign words unmask the "second nature" of nativist language. As Adorno will make amply clear through his early 1960s' course on *Philosophical Terminology*, the philosopher has to resist the reification of language by effecting a *Verfremdungseffekt* (distantiation or alienation effect). The dialectical philosopher renders herself *deslenguada*, to use that most propitious expression of Gloria Anzaldúa, when she writes: "*Deslenguadas. Somos los del español deficiente.* We are your linguistic nightmare, your linguistic aberration, your linguistic *mestizaje*, the subject of your *burla.* Because we speak with tongues of fire we are culturally crucified. Racially, culturally and linguistically *we are huérfanos*—we speak an orphan tongue."[80] If for Adorno, "the dialectic is language, the organon of thought,"[81] language can best service thought when it has de-alienated itself, or rather, think through its having become "second nature" by means of unmasking its quasi-biological and quasi-natural character. Philosophy that is truly dialectical and historical, that aims to approximate the "cognitive utopia" by "uncealing" the "nonconceptual" in concepts by way of concepts (i.e., words). But this turns out to be nothing else that to "lend voice to suffering."[82] Language that does not give voice to suffering is mere jargon; suffering that is without language remains mute and unredeemed historical torment. Philosophy can only mediate this historical dialectic when it recognizes that it has no mother tongue, that is always speaks in an orphan language. Its language has to be oppositional in order to be faithful to the truth that language is the "index of the false."[83] As he put it in his essay "Skoteinos: How to Read Hegel": "all philosophical language is language in opposition to language, marked with the stigmata of its own impossibility."[84] If for Heidegger "Language is the house of Being. In its home man dwells,"[85] for Adorno's thinking that is to the task of the reification and commodification of social existence is one that finds itself without a mother tongue, always having to disavow a paternal language, always speaking in accents and borrowed words. Philosophy has no native tongue, it lacks a home, and it is without a native soil. Against Heidegger, Adorno would claim that language is the charnel house of thought, not the house of being, and thus the locus of both mourning and redemption. Philosophy that is still possible must be homeless, and dialectical thinking that is proper to deciphering historical suffering is deliberate exile from any alleged original or perfect philosophical language.

Philosophy has a history also because philosophers in history have only spoken in the adopted languages of their homes. The language of philosophy is always the language of a philosopher, for there is no transhistorical, universal, univocal philosophical language. In *Minima Moralia*, Adorno quotes Nietzsche from the *Gay Science*, "It is even part of my good fortune not to be a house-owner." Then Adorno adds: "Today we should have to add: it is part of morality not to be at home in one's home."[86] In another entry in the same book, Adorno notes: "For a man who no longer has a homeland, writing becomes a place to live. In it he inevitably produces, as his family once did, refuse and lumber." He ends this section laconically: "In the end, the writer is not even allowed to live in his writing."[87] Today we should have to add: the dialectical-redemptive philosopher is not allowed to be at home in his mother tongue, which is why philosophy must be ceaselessly rendered estranged from any linguistic purism.

NOTES

1. Theodor W. Adorno, "The Actuality of Philosophy," *Telos*, No. 31 (March, 1977), 120 33.

2. Theodor W. Adorno, "The Idea of Natural History," transl. by Bob Hullot-Kentor, *Telos*, No. 60 (Summer 1984), 111–24.

3. Theodor W. Adorno, "Theses on the Language of the Philosopher," transl. by Samir Gandensha and Michael K. Palamarek, in *Adorno and the Need in Thinking: New Critical Essays*, eds. Donald A. Burke, Colin J. Campbell, Kathy Kiloh, Michael K. Palamarek, and Jonathan Short (Toronto: University of Toronto Press, 2007), 35–40.

4. Theodor W. Adorno, "On the Use of Foreign Words," in *Notes to Literature*, volume 2, transl. Shierry Weber Nicholsen (New York: Columbia University Press, 1992), 286–91. On the dating of this text, see Tiedemann's "Editorial Remarks from the German Edition," xvii.

5. Theodor W. Adorno, *Kierkegaard: Construction of the Aesthetic*, transl. Robert Hullot-Kentor (Minneapolis: University of Minnesota Press, 1989).

6. See Jacques Derrida, "Des Tours de Babel," transl. by Joseph F. Graham, in *Difference in Translation*, ed. Joseph F. Graham (Ithaca: Cornell University Press, 1985), 165–207; and "Transfer ex Cathedra: Language and Institutions of Philosophy," in *Eyes of the University. Right to Philosophy 2*, transl. by Jan Plug and others, ed. Jacques Derrida (Stanford: Stanford University Press, 2004), 1–82, especially the section titled "Theology of Translation," 64–82.

7. Richard Wolin, *Walter Benjamin: An Aesthetic of Redemption* (New York: Columbia University Press, 1982), especially chapter two: "The Path to Trauerspiel," 29–78.

8. Walter Benjamin, *The Origin of German Tragic Drama*, transl. John Osborne (London: New Left Books, 1977).

9. Walter Benjamin, "The Role of Language in *Trauerspiel* and Tragedy," in *Selected Writings*, volume 1 1913–1926, ed. Marcus Bullock and Michael W. Jennings (Cambridge, MA: The Belknap Press of Harvard University Press, 1996), 59.

10. Walter Benjamin, "*Trauerspiel* and Tragedy," in *Selected Writings*, 55–57.

11. Walter Benjamin, "The Role of Language in *Trauerspiel* and Tragedy," 60.

12. Ibid., 60.

13. Ibid., 60.

14. Walter Benjamin, "On Language as Such and on the Language of Man," in *Selected Writings*, volume 1 1913–1926, ed. Marcus Bullock and Michael W. Jennings (Cambridge, MA: The Belknap Press of Harvard University Press, 1996), 62–74.

15. Ibid., 64.

16. Ibid., 63.

17. Hans-Georg Gadamer, *Truth and Method*, second revised edition, transl. Joel Weinsheimer and Donald G. Marshall (London and New York: Continuum, 2004), 470.

18. Walter Benjamin, "On Language as Such and on the Language of Man," 68.

19. Ibid., 72.

20. Ibid., 73.

21. Ibid., 69.

22. Ibid., 65.

23. Ibid., 70.

24. In the late 1920s, Adorno would retreat to Königstein im Taunus, near Kronberg, to work without distractions. Benjamin visited him there between 1928 and 1930. See Theodor W. Adorno and Walter Benjamin, *The Complete Correspondence 1928-1940*, ed. Henri Lonitz, transl. Nicholas Walker (Cambridge, MA: Harvard University Press, 1999), see especially letters 7 and 110, and editorial note 2 on page 15.

25. See "Adorno Seminar vom Sommersemester 1932," in *Frankfurter Adorno Blätter IV* (München: edition text + kritik, 1995), 52–78. See also Müller-Doohm, *Adorno: A Biography*, 145.

26. Walter Benjamin, *The Origins of German Tragic Drama*, 27.

27. Ibid., 27.

28. Ibid., 27.

29. Ibid., 32.

30. Ibid., 36.

31. Ibid., 34.

32. See Max Horkheimer, *Between Philosophy and Social Science: Selected Early Writings*, transl. G. Frederick Hunter, Matthew S. Kramer, and John Torpey (Cambridge, MA: The MIT Press, 1993), 1–14. For a discussion of this lecture, see Stefan Müller-Doohm, *Adorno: A Biography*, transl. Rodney Livingstone (Cambridge, UK: Polity, 2005), 134–44.

33. Ibid., 11.

34. Ibid., 12.

35. Adorno, "The Actuality of Philosophy," 124.

36. Ibid., 124.

37. Ibid., 124.

38. Ibid., 128.

39. Ibid., 126.

40. Ibid., 126.

41. Here, I am evidently appropriating Ernst Bloch's terminology, see Ernst Bloch, *Erbschaf dieser Zeit*, Erweiterte Ausgabe (Frankfurt am Main: Suhrkamp, 1985), 111–26.

42. Adorno, "The Actuality of Philosophy," 132.

43. Ibid., 131.

44. Jorge Luis Borges, *Selected Non-Fictions*, ed. Eliot Weinberger (New York: Viking, 1999), 39.

45. Theodor W. Adorno, *The Jargon of Authenticity*, transl. Knut Tarnowski and Frederic Will (London: Routledge & Kegan Paul Ltd., 1973).

46. Theodor W. Adorno, *Negative Dialectics*, transl. E. B. Ashton (London: Routledge, 2000).

47. Adorno, "The Idea of Natural History," 117. Italics in original.

48. Ibid., 117.

49. Ibid., 118.

50. Ibid., 118.

51. Ibid., 119.

52. Ibid., 119.

53. Ibid., 119.

54. Ibid., 120, see footnote ten.

55. Ibid., 122. Italics added for emphasis.

56. Karl Marx, *Selected Writings*, ed. Lawrence H. Simon (Indianapolis: Hackett Publishing Company, Inc., 1994), 101.

57. Theodor W. Adorno, *Negative Dialectics*, 3.

58. Adorno, "Theses on the Language of the Philosopher," 35.

59. Ibid., 35–36.

60. Ibid., 36.

61. Ibid., 39.

62. Theodor W. Adorno, "Der Begriff der Philosophie. Vorlesungen Wintersemester 1951/ 52," in *Frankfurter Adorno Blätter II* (München: edition text + kritik, 1993), 9–91.

63. Theodor W. Adorno, *Philosophische Terminologie. Zur Einleitung*, two volumes (Frankfurt am Main: Suhrkamp Verlag, 1973). See Shierry Weber Nicholsen, "Language: Its Murmurings, Its Darkness, and Its Silver Rib," in *Exact Imagination, Late Work: On Adorno's Aesthetics*, ed. Shierry Weber Nicholsen (Cambridge, MA: The MIT Press, 1997), 59–102. See also Peter Uwe Hohendahl, "Adorno: The Discourse of Philosophy and the Problem of Language," in *The Actuality of Adorno: Critical Essays on Adorno and the Postmodern*, ed. Max Pensky (Albany, NY: SUNY Press, 1997), 62–82; Eric L. Krakauer, *Disposition of the Subject:*

Reading Adorno's Dialectic of Technology (Evanston, IL: Northwestern University Press, 1998), especially the "Epilogue: Adorno's Grammar: The Self-Disruption of Language," 139–79; Michael K. Palamarek, "Adorno's Dialectics of Language" in *Adorno and the Need in Thinking: New Critical Essays*, eds. Donald A. Burke, Colin J. Campbell, Kathy Kiloh, Michael K. Palamarek, and Jonathan Short (Toronto: University of Toronto Press, 2007), 41–77; and Samir Gandesha, "The 'Aesthetic Dignity of Words': Adorno's Philosophy of Language" in *Adorno and the Need in Thinking: New Critical Essays*, eds. Donald A. Burke, Colin J. Campbell, Kathy Kiloh, Michael K. Palamarek, and Jonathan Short, 79–102. As well as the essays collected in Gerhard Richter, ed. *Language without Soil: Adorno and Late Philosophical Modernity* (New York: Fordham University Press, 2010).

64. Adorno, "Theses on the Language of the Philosopher," 38.

65. Ibid., 38.

66. Ibid., 37.

67. Ibid., 38.

68. Ibid., 38.

69. Theodor W. Adorno, *Aesthetic Theory*, 166.

70. See Fredric James, *Late Marxism: Adorno, or, The Persistence of the Dialectic* (London: Verso, 1996 [1990]), 207.

71. Ibid., 38–39.

72. William H. Gass, *Life Sentences: Literary Judgments and Accounts* (New York: Alfred A. Knopf, 2012), 341.

73. Ibid., 37.

74. Adorno, "On the Use of Foreign Words," 288.

75. Ibid., 289.

76. Ibid., 290.

77. Theodor W. Adorno, *Notes to Literature*, volume one, transl. Shierry Weber Nicholsen (New York: Columbia University Press, 1991), 197.

78. Adorno, *Kierkegaard: Construction of the Aesthetic*, 35.

79. Adorno, "On the Use of Foreign Words," 290.

80. Gloria Anzaldúa, *Borderlands/La Frontera: The New Mestiza*, twenty-fifth anniversary edition, fourth edition (San Francisco: Aunt Laute Books, 2012), 80.

81. Adorno, *Negative Dialectics*, 56.

82. Ibid., 17.

83. Theodor W. Adorno, *Hegel: Three Studies*, trans. Shierry Weber Nicholsen (Cambridge, MA: The MIT Press, 1993), 105.

84. Ibid., 100.

85. Martin Heidegger, "Letter on Humanism," in *Basic Writings. From Being and Time (1927) to The Task of Thinking (1964)*, revised and expanded edition, ed. Martin Heidegger (New York: HarperPerennial, 2008), 217–65, quote at 217.

86. Theodor W. Adorno, *Minima Moralia: Reflections from Damaged Life*, transl. E. F. N. Jephcott (London: Verso, 1974), 39.

87. Ibid., 87. See also Stefana Sabin, "'For a man who longer has a homeland, writing becomes a place to live' Literary Criticism and Aesthetic Theory," in *Theodor W. Adorno: Philosoph des beschädigten Lebens*, ed. Moshe Zuckermann (Göttingen: Wallstein Verlag, 2004), 83–95.

Chapter Five

"The Polarity Informing Mimesis"

The Social Import of Mimesis in Benjamin and Adorno

Nathan Ross

The concept of mimesis stands at a central crossroads for understanding the philosophical relationship between Adorno and Benjamin, as well as the philosophical import that they give art. Mimesis describes both the relationship between the artwork and society, as well as the relation of the subject to the artwork in a properly aesthetic experience. The artwork is mimetic of social reality not in that it presents a series of theses or judgments about reality, but expresses a "feeling of the world" (*Gefühl der Welt*).[1] The mode of experience proper to the artwork is mimetic in that it involves the subject reenacting the artwork by participating in its enigmatic and processual character.

Most approaches to the concept of mimesis in the secondary literature focus on the way in which mimesis represents a special form of experience.[2] How is mimesis different than conceptual knowledge? How is it different than other modes of experience that characterize modern life?[3] Less attention has been paid, however, to defining the various specific forms of mimesis that Benjamin and Adorno discerningly critique, and about which they develop substantial disagreements. *What* does art mime, and why does it matter what it takes up? How do different forms of mimesis result out of the context in which it is deployed? What special, unique forms of mimesis emerge in the modern arts, and why are they valuable for a critical theory of modern society? The omission of these questions gives us an only partial vision of the role that the concept of mimesis plays in their works, as it ignores the *critical direction* that they give to mimesis. Their aesthetic philosophies are not merely focused on defining art, in relation to other spheres of experience, but even more with *discerning which kinds of art* actually harbor a progressive, transformative truth content. Indeed, this latter question serves as the main point of dispute between Benjamin and Adorno in their correspondences throughout the 1930s.[4] I argue that this second problem, that of a critique of modern art in relation to the ends of critical theory, cannot gain a clear form without considering the specific *direction of mimesis* in Benjamin and Adorno, that is: What kinds of structures and experiences do the arts take as their raw material?

Since Plato, we have often thought of mimesis as a kind of relation to nature: "art imitates nature." Not surprisingly, this view has played a strong role in interpretations of critical theory.[5] It is undoubtedly true that Benjamin and Adorno think of mimesis, its repression or recovery, as an index of humanity's relation to nature. It is my argument, however, that for Adorno and Benjamin, great works of art have to be understood far more as a *mimesis of social practices*, or more precisely, as a mimesis of patterns of consciousness involved in modern society. To be more specific to each thinker: Benjamin, in his late aesthetics, thinks that new artistic media unlock an aesthetic experience that mimes the way that we work and use technology in modern industry and that this mimesis of industry gives art the power to promote a redefinition of how we use technology. Adorno, on the other hand, thinks that great works of modern art mime *false consciousness* in ways that allow us to transform our consciousness, and thus achieve a fleeting, ephemeral experience of aesthetic truth.

"THE POLARITY INFORMING MIMESIS" IN BENJAMIN'S "ARTWORK" ESSAY

Most readers will first encounter Walter Benjamin's seminal essay "On the Artwork in the Age of its Technological Reproducibility" from its final (third) version as a text that examines the transformation that the arts undergo when they are no longer tied to their unique individuality and become inherently reproductions. The essay famously argues that what characterizes this transformation is a loss of aura in the artwork, and it has been interpreted as describing a series of phenomenal transformations in the arts, without giving any deeper theoretical grasp of the meaning of these phenomena.[6] It establishes a variety of dialectical oppositions in the historical form of aesthetic experience: the distinction between auratic and non-auratic art, the ritual value as opposed to the exhibition value of art, the two forms of mimesis (semblance and play), the contrast between fascism as aestheticized politics and communism as politicized aesthetics, and the critique of capitalism in relation to newer aesthetic possibilities. Understanding the political and philosophical intentions of this key text in Benjamin's oeuvre seems to depend on placing all of these dialectical opposites into a kind of narrative about the future direction and political meaning of art.

However, as we read the somewhat more speculative second version of the essay,[7] we see that all of these phenomenal distinctions that Benjamin makes only gain their *world historical* stakes for him in that they allow us to diagnose the potential transition between two distinctive relations to nature: what he calls the first and the second technology.[8] The first technology rests upon *using* nature, while the second technology rests upon *interacting* with nature.[9] For Benjamin, the first, exploitive technology only continues to have a hold on human life because it is supported by a mode of aesthetic experience that is not yet fully adequate to the potential generated by the disappearance of aura. As I will argue, this distinction between two technological regimes is based for Benjamin in a distinction between two modes of mimesis, or two kinds of aesthetic experience. We have to change our perceptual practices to change our political attitudes and our way of laboring, and art plays a key role in this transformation.[10] Ultimately, I will argue that this crucial transformation rests on the way in which Benjamin distinguishes two modes of mimesis, semblance and play, which each support a distinctive relation to technology.

We shall begin with the phenomenon at the heart of Benjamin's aesthetic diagnosis: the loss of aura in contemporary art. He writes: "What then is the aura? A strange tissue of space and time: the unique apparition of distance, however near it might be. To follow with the eye—while resting on a summer afternoon—a mountain range on the horizon or a branch that casts its shadow on the beholder is to breathe the aura of those mountains, of that branch."[11] Benjamin uses a metaphor from the perception of nature to indicate something crucial to art for most of its history: that it rests on the technique of making distance and vertical distinction of rank into something that can be seen and felt as the *nearness* of distance. For Benjamin, this is perhaps most apparent in the role of art within religious rituals, where it is not even meant to be enjoyed or even seen, in some cases, but meant to reinforce the feeling of distinction between sacred and profane. The prevalence of the phenomenon of aura within aesthetic creation and experience reveals the existential structure of a society that is organized around rituals that reinforce the feeling of hierarchy.

Benjamin's thesis on the decline of aura relates to a broader theme in his work: the mimetic nature of art. Throughout his earlier aesthetic thinking, Benjamin views the function of art as essentially *mimetic*. This is apparent as early as his essays "On Language as Such and the Language of Man" and "On the Task of the Translator." As Beatrice Hansen demonstrates, there is already something like a "good" and a "bad" mimesis in Benjamin's writings on language.[12] However, in a challenge to the Platonic conception of mimesis, Benjamin is concerned with the capacity of mimesis to produce truth in a unique, aesthetic manner. Much like Adorno after him, Benjamin criticizes contemporary, rationalized culture with losing the distinctively mimetic mode of comportment that would allow us to gain some "experience" from our engagement with the world.[13] Benjamin's philosophy of mimesis rests on a critical distinction between different forms of mimesis: it is possible for art to imitate nature in a way that renders nature unknowable and inaccessible to experience, but it is also possible for it to produce truth. Art is not merely the imitation of natural objects, but the rehearsal of a way of interacting with the natural. Yet this raises a difficult question that would later become the most significant philosophical question occupying Adorno's *Aesthetic Theory*: how is it possible for art to be *true* as a mode of mimesis? For Benjamin, and Adorno as well, it is not a matter of realism, but of distinguishing the ways in which mimesis can transform consciousness and make it capable of negating an untrue relation to nature. And this concern over the potential veridity of mimesis reaches its point of greatest dialectical sharpness in the second version of Benjamin's "Artwork" essay. Here he argues in a long footnote (that does not make its way into the third and final version of the text) for a distinction between two modes of mimesis: semblance and play, *Schein* and *Spiel*.[14] While he equates semblance with the auratic mode of aesthetic experience, which is coming to an end, he argues that this end frees the way for a new mode of mimesis, namely play.

Here is the key passage from the essay in which Benjamin articulates this mimesis as an oppositional structure:

> Thus we encounter the polarity informing mimesis. In mimesis, tightly inter-folded like cotyledons, slumber the two aspects of art: semblance and play. This polarity can interest the dialectician only if it has a historical role. And that is, in fact, the case. This role is in fact determined by the first and second technologies. Semblance is in fact the most abstract—but therefore the most ubiquitous—schema of all the magic procedures of the first technology, whereas play is the inexhaustible reservoir of all the experimenting procedures of the second. . . . This would then lead to a practical insight—namely that what is lost in the withering of semblance and the decay of aura in works of art is matched by a huge gain in the scope for play (*Spiel-Raum*). . . . In film, the element of semblance has been entirely displaced by the element of play.[15]

Benjamin here interprets the loss of aura as the cutting edge in a critical distinction between two technical ways of relating to the natural. He argues that aura and semblance are the perceptual operations that underlie a way of interacting with nature that he calls "the first technology." For Benjamin, the first technology is characteristic of both the archaic relation to nature as well as capitalism (this is a key theme in early critical theory: that capitalism is actually based on the repetition of an archaic form of society under modern conditions).[16] The first technology is one that organizes nature as a resource to be exploited: It is a material that is outside of us, which we use and use up in a quantitative fashion to preserve ourselves at a distance from it. Of course, the relation of human to nature always also indicates the relation of humans to each other. If we see nature only as a material to be used, then we also see the natural within the human as a force to be exploited for gain. We stand squarely within the first technology when we treat each other as labor power and human relations are organized around the mutual use of each other's labor. One of the key themes from Marx's theory that Benjamin mirrors in his philosophy of technology is the notion that capitalism creates a technology that would reduce the necessary labor time and yet it establishes property relations that do not enable us to reduce the amount of labor to which we are subject. Modern technologies offer possibilities to live together with the earth in non-extractive ways and to make labor into something frictionless and interactive rather than exploitive, and yet these technologies are entrenched in a political property structure that must increase the level of exploitation in order to remain in place. As technology advances, Benjamin notes that war becomes a means by which the ruling class preserves the prevalence of the exploitive first technology even when the second technology comes into view as a political possibility.[17]

The challenge in integrating this discussion of the first and second technology with Benjamin's larger analysis of aesthetic experience is to understand how this first technology is supported by the experience of aura and semblance.[18] He writes: "Semblance is in fact the most abstract—but therefore the most ubiquitous—schema of all the magic procedures of the first technology, whereas play is the inexhaustible reservoir of all the experimenting procedures of the second."[19] Benjamin's argument rests on the link between the first technology, which organizes the human relation to nature around objectifying extraction, and the aesthetic procedure of sacrifice and magic. We have to believe, in a pre-reflective way, in a need for distance between ourselves and nature, and in the need for nature (even in ourselves) to be sacrificed, in order for this first technology to remain compelling even when other ways of existing with nature would be technically possible. Art can reinforce this belief in sacrifice to the extent that it organizes our perception of nature around semblance. The first technology rests on a mode of organizing perception that Benjamin equates to magic: it is a trick played on the percipient to establish a passive and distant relation to the underlying technical procedure. The opposite of such a procedure is not merely the disillusioning of perception, but a mode of perception that allows the percipient to intervene in a non-established way in the material process of nature, in a manner involving both reciprocity and unpredictability. The contrast at work in the essay is not one between art as illusion and art as realistic depiction, a distinction that would point towards the realist aesthetics of thinkers such as Lukács and Siegfried Kracauer. Rather, it is a matter of understanding how the contrast between semblance and play maps on to the distinction between the first and second technology:

> The first technology really sought to master nature, whereas the second aims rather at an interplay between nature and humanity. The primary social function of art today is to rehearse that interplay. This applies especially to the function of film. The function of film is to train the human being in the apperceptions and reactions needed to deal with an apparatus whose role in their lives is expanding almost daily. [20]

This leads Benjamin to a striking metaphor for this shift within the task of artist: while the artist of the first mimesis is like a magician, the artist of the second mimesis is like a surgeon. [21] Like the magician, the painter of natural semblance presents a view of nature that maintains the distance between the viewer and object, but like the surgeon, the filmmaker dissects reality and enters into a natural process in such a way as to reveal its unfinished, provisional space of contingency. The painting's semblance offers a view of nature that is rounded out to completion, while the film offers a series of provisional, experimental views of nature. Just as the surgeon breaks the body's natural surface and enters into it in order to achieve a practical intervention in its functioning, the film breaks apart our view of a common set of social actions in order to insert play in the place of drudgery. It mimes the way in which technology dominates the labor process, the way in which the tool becomes not a means for labor, but an apparatus that controls labor. In so doing, this new art form lays bare the poverty of experience at the root of modern life. [22]

Benjamin thus establishes the opposed notions of the *finished product* and the *provisional* as the key experiential feature in distinguishing the two modes of mimesis and relating them to their embeddedness in the first or second technology: "The results of the first technology are valid once and for all (it deals with irreparable lapse of sacrificial death, which holds good for eternity). The results of the second are wholly provisional (it operates by means of experiments and endlessly varied test procedures)." [23] The first technology operates on the model of extracting from nature and creating a product, while the second operates on that of an interactive, frictionless, reciprocal metabolism with nature. For Benjamin, this distinction is reflected also in two different modes of artistic creation, one in which the goal is a finished product, and the other in which the creative process involves constitutive provisionality. "The state of their technology compelled the Greeks to produce eternal values in their art. . . . Film (on the other hand) is the artwork most capable of improvement. And this capability is linked to its radical renunciation of eternal value." [24] He illustrates this with the way in which Charlie Chaplin would make a film by shooting thousands of minutes of experimental performances only in order to weave them into a film through editing. This closely echoes what Benjamin wrote in his dissertation on German Romanticism on the notion of the fragment: While the fragment of an ancient statue is fragmentary in the sense that it is a broken part of what was meant to be taken as a finished product, the Romantic fragment is *inherently* fragmentary in that it aims to present an incomplete unit of thought that offers space for further development.[25] It would just have to be added that film is now provisional not merely in a conceptual sense, but in its very way of organizing the relation of perception to nature. Beatrice Hansen argues that this relation to completion within time is what distinguishes mimetic play: "It harbors an open-ended, dynamic temporality, an interval for chance, imagination and agency."[26]

Benjamin gives two concrete phenomena from film-making as illustrations of this provisional, playful relation to nature: the altered role of the actor in film, as opposed to theater, and the way that film reveals the physical environment of the city. Whereas in the theater, an actor creates a semblance, that is, evokes a unified character through the projective use of voice and gesture, the actor in film is simply responding to a series of promptings from the director or even from machines. The film director, for example, might get the actor to seem afraid by making a loud noise. Or the director might use a crowd of ordinary people from the street to create a mob scene. Benjamin writes of the role of the actor in modern film: "For the first time—and this is the effect of film—the human being is place in a position where he has to operate with his whole living person, while foregoing its aura."[27] And: "Film makes test performances capable of being exhibited, by turning that ability itself into a test. . . . To accomplish it is to preserve ones humanity in the face of the apparatus."[28] The actor in a film is, at least potentially, more like the athlete of modern sports or the worker in a modern factory, in responding to the demands of a "test," but with the crucial difference that the film *offers us this test procedure as an experience*, and thus gives us the chance to enter into this technical relation to nature in a playful way. Benjamin also captures this point through the way in which film depicts its physical environment:

> The most important social function of film is to establish equilibrium between human beings and the apparatus. Film achieves this goal not only in terms of man's presentation to himself, but also in terms of his representation of his environment by means of the apparatus. . . . It manages to reassure us of a vast and unsuspected field of play (*Spielraum*).[29]

Here we see the second form of mimesis, play, opened up through film's capacity to reveal daily surroundings in a way that is not merely more realistic, but also surrealistic: "It is through the camera that we first discover the optical unconscious."[30] For the realist, film is politically enlightening because it depicts the hidden laws of our daily environment, the factory, schools, etc., while for Benjamin, it is politically useful because it depicts this same world *as if in a dream*. Benjamin's favoring of the play element of mimesis over semblance demonstrates his continued commitment to elements of surrealistic aesthetics, a field of aesthetic experience on which he and Adorno disagreed.[31] As I have argued, to think of aesthetic experience as play involves understanding the dialectical transformation of art into a form of mimesis that inserts provisionality, reciprocity, and unpredictability into our perception of nature and everyday life. The late aesthetics of Benjamin thus calls us to think of art as true not in the sense of a correspondence theory of truth, but in terms of its ability to challenge what is distant and fixed within our relation to nature.

ART'S MIMESIS OF SOCIAL RATIONALITY IN ADORNO'S *AESTHETIC THEORY*

Benjamin is not merely focused on giving a general account of how aesthetic experience is different than other modes of experience, as he also aims to give an account of *what kinds of mimesis*, which specific forms of aesthetic experience, are true; he does so in a manner that refers to the political significance latent in new forms of art. In other words, he develops a discerning account of how art can become *critical* mimesis. Adorno inherits not only the concept of mimesis from Benjamin, but also the problem of distinguishing which forms of mimesis produce truth.[32] We saw in the prior section that Benjamin's late aesthetics seeks to differentiate between an antiquated form of aesthetic mimesis that reinforces the politics of illusion and a redemptive form of mimesis that enables critical experience because it is based on interplay.

As we saw in the prior section, Benjamin tended to see aesthetic forms as progressive that could imitate the staggering impact of technology on the modern subject, and he thus defends modes of art that speak to the subject through a tactile and "distracted" mode of apprehension. Adorno, by contrast, regretted this tendency in Benjamin's thinking and attributed radical truth content to those artworks that continue to demand concentration from the subject in new and dissonant ways. I argue that these disagreements over aesthetic forms represent not so much a matter of differing taste or class pretension between Benjamin and Adorno, but are symptomatic of fundamentally divergent views of how mimesis creates truth.

In *Aesthetic Theory*, Adorno seizes on Benjamin's definition of aura as an aesthetic phenomenon, but draws a radically divergent lesson from it. He cites Benjamin's definition of aura as the "unique appearance of a distance, no matter how near it may be" and argues that "[t]o perceive the aura of nature in the manner that Benjamin demands as an illustration of his concept means to become aware of the aspect of nature that makes an artwork essentially what it is."[33] The ability to relate to the phenomenon of aura is an essential feature of an aesthetic experience for Adorno, as "distance is the first condition for the proximity to the content (*Gehalt*) of works."[34] While the experience of aura has regressive and authoritarian connotations in Benjamin's work, especially in an age when works are democratized and brought closer to us by their technical reproducibility, Adorno argues that there is a critical value to the phenomenon of which Benjamin is critical: "The distance of the aesthetic domain from practical aims appears inner-aesthetically as the distance of the aesthetic object from the contemplating subject."[35] In other words, it is precisely the sensation that the work is withdrawing from us as we contemplate it that reveals the work's ability to distance us from our accustomed, practical consciousness. Art without aura would be art without negativity. Aesthetic experience without contemplation would merge fully with practical consciousness,[36] and would risk becoming a mere mechanism in replicating the social order. While Benjamin dreams of a form of aesthetic mimesis in which our world does not appear to us as an illusion that stands over and against us, Adorno seeks to defend this space of illusion as the only mirror in which we can take a distancing perspective on what we are.

As we saw in the prior section, the phenomenon of aura is rooted for Benjamin in a dialectical distinction between two forms of mimesis, between semblance and play. With the liquidation of semblance comes the possibility to generate a kind of mimesis that enables an interplay with nature. This new, revolutionary mode of mimesis would entail an aesthetic experience that is distracted, tactile, and suggestive of a new form of labor. Adorno suggests that Benjamin's distinction between semblance and play does not truly liberate aesthetic experience: "On a whole, the crisis of semblance might absorb play: what is proper to the harmony established by means of semblance will also prove acceptable to the harmlessness of play. Art that seeks its redemption from semblance in play ends up becoming sport."[37] Writing three decades after Benjamin, Adorno notes ongoing evidence of a "crisis of semblance" in the arts (such as theater performances without costumes or sets), and yet he argues that this crisis does not liberate a dialectically opposed form of mimesis, but threatens the very experience at the heart of art. The concept of play becomes "harmless,"[38] in Adorno's view, if robbed of the element of semblance, because it offers a purely frictionless mode of enjoyment that fits seamlessly with the culture around it. If mimesis became pure interaction without any space for illusion, it would lose the space in which a critical relation to praxis happens. For Adorno, this means that the concept of semblance that had been so vital to the aesthetic thought of Goethe, Schiller, and Hegel has to be rescued. The concept of aesthetic truth is deeply bound up with the possibility to create the experience of illusion, while simultaneously preserving distance from this illusion. As Lambert Zuidervaart has compellingly demonstrated, Adorno's argument that art represents a special kind of truth content rests on its ability to construct a "double illusion" that thereby negates socially held illusions.[39]

Adorno's philosophy of mimesis departs from a distinction between representational knowledge and mimesis. While representation describes a relationship between a subject and an object (I represent the world in my consciousness), mimesis involves a relationship between subject and another subject. I cannot mimic any being, even a natural or inanimate being, without treating the being as something that has its own way of moving and relating to the world. To follow a suggestion of Josef Früchtl, mimesis deals with *natura naturans*, rather than *natura naturata*.[40] In relating this to artistic practice, this distinction means that art represents a mimesis of its subject matter not by taking up some of its objective features and describing them, but by mimicking the way in which they become meaningful for a subject or the way in which they become subject. The painter does not depict the natural, but imitates consciousness in the act of seeing the natural: she does not imitate nature as something fixed and given, but engages with nature as something that is of interest to the subject and organized by a social way of seeing. Artworks imitate a form of consciousness, and in imitating it they transform the consciousness that does the imitating. In imitating another form of consciousness, I do not simply become this other mode of consciousness, but gain an awareness of this other mode of consciousness that sets me at a distance from it. In fact, the artwork may perform its most insightful act of mimesis by imitating latent features of my own mode of consciousness, and thus setting me at a distance from aspects of my own consciousness that are normally too close to reflect upon.

However, like Benjamin, Adorno defines an ambivalence informing the concept of mimesis. In *The Dialectic of Enlightenment*, he articulates, along with Horkheimer, the urge to imitate as one of the basic and most archaic urges of the subject, which does not disappear, but is repressed by rationalized forms of modern culture.[41] The impulse to imitate reaches far into the past: it is tied to magic, ritual, and the archaic relation between human and animal. There is in mimesis something of the desire to control, to manipulate, to command: one might imitate prey in order to catch, imitate hostile natural forces to tame them, or invoke evil spirits in order to neutralize them. There is a mimetic impulse: a "non-conceptual affinity" for nature, an urge to treat everything as a subject and to make oneself aware of its subjectivity. However, in the magical ritual, one merely imitates a foreign mode of subjectivity in order to trick and capture, or in order to gain control of it for one's own purposes.[42] In its archaic form, mimesis also derives from the immense terror that the subject feels at the overwhelming power of nature, which has not yet been brought under the control of the subject. In situations of extreme danger, the archaic human engages in a "mimesis of the dead"; one submits completely to the will of the hostile force, becomes like a stone, because any other subjective movement would further provoke the danger.[43]

This mimetic impulse arises from an urge first to adapt to nature, and then to control it. Yet as the *Dialectic of Enlightenment* argues, mimesis is increasingly repressed in the modern, scientific comportment to nature. Nature cannot be represented with adequate clarity if it is entered into as a subject and imitated, and so the mimetic impulse is treated as antithetical to the project of knowing and mastering nature. He alludes to this thesis on the repression of mimesis in *Aesthetic Theory*, where he describes art as just a remainder of mimesis:

> The survival of mimesis, the non-conceptual affinity of the subjectively produced with its unposited other defines art as a form of knowledge and to that extent as "rational." For that to which mimetic comportment responds is the *telos* of knowledge, which art simultaneously blocks with its own categories. Art completes knowledge with what is excluded from knowledge and thereby once again impairs its character as knowledge, its univocity.[44]

There is a non-conceptual affinity to objects in the subject, which Adorno characterizes here as the *telos* of all knowledge. As Früchtl demonstrates in a persuasive reading of this passage, the true *telos* of knowledge is to give expression to the teleology inherent to the object in coming to know it, a possibility that Kant definitively blocks in barring knowledge from entering into the inside of things.[45] Mirroring Kant's critique of objective teleology, it is precisely this non-conceptual affinity between subject and object that eludes modern scientific knowledge, thus blocking the fulfillment of its *telos*.[46] This affinity is non-conceptual in Adorno's terms precisely because the very nature of the concept is "identifying," making the object similar to the subject's aim, and thus the concept is outside of nature even when it makes correct determinations of natural objects. For Adorno, this mimetic comportment "survives" in art, because art is the inheritor of modes of behavior that were strictly repressed during the process of progressive enlightenment: magic, myth, and ritual. However, art is not *merely* regression, because it elevates the principle of mimesis to its pure character as a form of knowledge, by separating out all those elements of mimesis that were bound up with fear, deception, and domination in the magical ritual. Thus art paradoxically becomes *more true* as its form of mimesis becomes more a reflection of the rational practice that suppresses mimesis. *Critical mimesis* means not a return to the archaic form of mimesis, but a rescuing of its "affinity to the object" under conditions of modern rationality.

In Adorno's account, there is increasingly one subject matter of mimesis that gives modern art its special status as a mode of aesthetic truth: if mimesis is always the imitation of a form of consciousness, then modern art is more specifically the imitation of the social form of rationality. "The logic of

art . . . draws consequences from phenomena that have already been spiritually mediated and to this extent made logical."[47] Art's mimesis is the remainder in consciousness of what is destroyed by the development of rationality;
thus art is increasingly *the imitation of rationality*. However, since the form
that rationality takes in modern society is delusional and dishonest, art has to
take up this rationality in a way that exposes its crevices and shortcomings.
Art imitates the social and historical form that rationality takes; in so doing, it
makes us aware of what is irrational in the rational. In imitating, it transforms.

Adorno uses the writings of Kafka as an illustration of the difference
between a mimetic response to modern society and a realistic or representational one. Rather than the novel that paints a picture of the economic relations of monopoly capitalism, Adorno sees a deeper social truth content in
the prose of Kafka's novels, which describe an exaggerated, imaginary world
in a tone of understated factual objectivity.[48] The sparse, understated irony
and simple orderliness of Kafka's prose serve to mime the blind form that
rationality takes in the administered world. It is because the quality of the
narrative imitates the quality of the world that the works succeed in having
an experiential truth content that goes beyond mere description. They depict
an imaginary world, but in a way that imitates certain basic experiences of
modern subjects in relation to modern institutions.[49]

Mimesis not only describes in Adorno's thought the way in which knowledge sediments itself in the being of the artwork, but also the way in which
the experience of the artwork has an effect on the subject. In aesthetic experience, the subject processually deciphers and relives the form of the artwork.
Thus, just as the artwork does not represent, but imitates reality, the audience
should not be conceived of as passively absorbing or representing the artwork, but rather as *reenacting* the work in experience. Consciousness becomes like the work in its form, and thus consciousness undergoes a subtle
transformation. He writes: "Artworks exercise a practical effect, if they do so
at all, through a scarcely apprehensible transformation of consciousness."[50]
Consciousness undergoes a transformation in that it imitates the form of the
work; this transformation is a practical effect in that it changes the relation of
consciousness to the world.

This dispute between Benjamin and Adorno over the form of mimesis casts a
new light on what is at issue in their philosophies. It is not so much that
Benjamin has a view of art that is "too affirmative"[51]; rather, he seeks to
understand which forms of art could transform our perceptual practices in
ways that would lead to a "second technology," that is, a social and material
experience based on interplay. Benjamin diagnoses two diametrically opposed forms of mimesis as the key to an aesthetic critique of modern society.
Adorno agrees with the crucial, systematic role that Benjamin gives the

concept of mimesis and seeks to define a distinctly modern mode of mimesis as a mode of social critique. His disagreement is with the emphasis that Benjamin places on eliminating the aspect of mimesis that both thinkers call "semblance." In rescuing the view of art as self-distancing illusion, Adorno works towards an account of art as a space in which ideology appears transfigured as an illusion of itself. As Tom Huhn demonstrates in the final chapter of this book, Adorno understands *semblance* as the power to present our own human development to us as something from which we can free ourselves, at least in a provisional manner.

If we focus on the way that Adorno defines aesthetic truth in dialogue with Benjamin, we see that Adorno's emphasis on semblance points to a distinctive model of art as social critique. Art is not merely the negation of rationality or ordinary understanding,[52] but a mimetic process of experiencing the social and historical form that rationality takes as something that can be reformed. It is precisely to the extent that art mimes social rationality that it can free us from what is oppressive and opaque in this rationality. The creation of hypothetical, imitative forms of rationality would heighten our capacity to see through the pretensions of the predominant rationality of society.

NOTES

1. Theodor W. Adorno, *Ästhetik (1958/59)* (Frankfurt: Suhrkamp, 2006).

2. There are many discussions of the theory of mimesis in Adorno's thought and his debt to Benjamin: A classic account of the genesis of this theme in Adorno is Josef Früchtl, *Mimesis: Konstellation eines Zentralbgeriffs* (Würzburg: Königshausen und Neumann, 1986). See also Martin Jay, "Mimesis and Mimetology," in *Semblance of Subjectivity: Essays on Adorno's Aesthetic Theory*, eds. Tom Huhn and Lambert Zuidervaart (Cambridge: MIT University Press, 1997), 29–53. Also Shierry Weber Nicolsen, "Aesthetic Theory's Mimesis of Walter Benjamin," in *Semblance of Subjectivity: Essays on Adorno's Aesthetic Theory*, eds. Tom Huhn and Lambert Zuidervaart (Cambridge: MIT University Press, 1997), 56–91.

3. This general approach of distinguishing aesthetic experience from ordinary experience is reflected in Christoph Menke, *The Sovereignty of Art: Aesthetic Negativity in Adorno and Derrida* (Stanford: Stanford University Press, 1999).

4. See editor's introduction. This debate over the direction of modern art is covered extensively in Susan Buck-Morss, *The Origin of Negative Dialectics* (New York: The Free Press, 1977).

5. See for example Josef Früchtl, *Mimesis*. One of his central theses is that mimesis represents an expression of *natura naturans* rather than *natura naturata*.

6. "Benjamin merely proclaims a fact and abstains from argument." Kai Hammermeister, *The German Aesthetic Tradition* (Cambridge: Cambridge University Press, 2001), 199.

7. Beatrice Hansen calls this the *Urtext* of the essay. It contains a far deeper speculative and theoretical context for the thesis about technological art forms. Interestingly, Benjamin may have eliminated many of these more speculative claims about the history of art at the request of Horkheimer and Adorno. See Howard Eiland and Michael Jennings, *Walter Benjamin: A Critical Life* (Cambridge: Harvard University Press), 512.

8. I cite the second version of the essay throughout. Walter Benjamin, *Selected Writings*, volume 3, eds. Howard Eiland and Michael Jennings (Cambridge: Harvard University Press, 2002), 127.

9. As Uwe Steiner demonstrates, Benjamin's distinction between first and second technology plays a key role in his political thinking and derives from his reading of science fiction author Paul Scheerbart. Uwe Steiner, *Walter Benjamin: An Introduction to his Work and Thought* (Chicago: University of Chicago Press, 2010), 72–79.

10. See Bertram in chapter 1 of this book.

11. Benjamin, *Selected Writings*, volume 3, 105.

12. See Beatrice Hansen, "Language and Mimesis in Benjamin's Work," in *The Cambridge Companion to Walter Benjamin*, ed. David Ferris (Cambridge: Cambridge University Press, 2004), 54–72.

13. Benjamin writes of the "frailty" of mimesis in "On the Mimetic Faculty," *Selected Writings*, volume 2, 721. His famous thoughts on the loss of experience come in "The Storyteller." Benjamin, *Selected Writings*, volume 3, 133

14. Benjamin, *Selected Writings*, volume 3, 127.

15. Benjamin, *Selected Writings*, volume 3, 127.

16. See "Capitalism as Religion" in Benjamin, *Selected Writings*, volume 1, 288–92; this thesis also recurs in his discussion of Blanqui in the *Arcades Project*, and it clearly figures strongly in *The Dialectic of Enlightenment*.

17. Benjamin, *Selected Writings*, volume 3, 121–22.

18. For a very insightful examination of Benjamin's critique of semblance, see Stéphane Symons, "The Ability to Not-Shine. The Word 'Unscheinbar' in the Writings of Walter Benjamin," *Angelaki: Journal of the Theoretical Humanities*, Vol. 18, no. 4 (2013): 101–123.

19. Ibid., 127.

20. Ibid., 108.

21. Ibid., 115.

22. See Symons' exploration of this phenomenon in chapter 7.

23. Ibid., 107.

24. Ibid., 109.

25. Benjamin, *Selected Writings*, volume 1, 154.

26. Miriam Bratu Hansen, "Room for Play: Benjamin's Gamble with the Cinema," *October*, no. 109 (Summer 2004): 3–45.

27. Benjamin, *Selected Writings*, volume 3, 112.

28. Ibid.

29. Ibid., 117.

30. Ibid.

31. Richard Wollin, "Benjamin, Adorno, Surrealism," in *Semblance of Subjectivity: Essays on Adorno's Aesthetic Theory*, eds. Tom Huhn and Lambert Zuidervaart (Cambridge: MIT University Press, 1997), 93–122.

32. Shierry Weber Nicholsen provides a strong account of the way that Adorno inherits the concept of mimesis from Benjamin in "*Aesthetic Theory's* Mimesis of Walter Benjamin," in *Semblance of Subjectivity: Essays on Adorno's Aesthetic Theory*, eds. Tom Huhn and Lambert Zuidervaart (Cambridge: MIT University Press, 1997), 56–91.

33. Theodor W. Adorno, *Ästhetische Theorie* (Frankfurt: Suhrkamp, 2003), 409.

34. Ibid., 460.

35. Ibid.

36. See Martin Seel, *Adornos Philosophie der Kontemplation* (Frankfurt: Suhrkamp, 2004), 20–28.

37. Adorno, *Theorie*, 154.

38. Ibid.

39. Lambert Zuidervaart, *Adorno's Aesthetic Theory: The Redemption of Illusion* (Cambridge: MIT Press, 1993), 178–213.

40. See Josef Früchtl, *Mimesis: Konstelation eines Zentralbegriffs bei Adorno* (Würzburg: Königshausen und Neumann, 1986), especially 84–89. I would take Früchtl's thesis one step further and argue that to the extent that art imitates nature, it imitates either a real or potential way in which society organizes the natural.

41. In the first essay of *The Dialectic of Enlightenment*, Adorno argues that while the magic of the shaman involves a "specific representation" of the imitated object, modern technology

involves a generalized representation of objectivity. See Theodor W. Adorno and Max Hork-heimer, *The Dialectic of Enlightenment*, transl. Edmund Jephcott (Stanford: Stanford University Press, 2007), 11.

42. "The magician imitates demons; in order to frighten them or appease them, he behaves frighteningly or makes gestures of appeasement." Adorno, *Dialectic of Enlightenment*, 9.

43. Früchtl establishes a fruitful comparison between this "mimesis of the dead" in archaic humanity and Hegel's account of the slave's terror in clinging to life in the master slave dialectic from the *Phenomenology*. See Früchtl, *Mimesis*, 43.

44. Adorno, *Theorie*, 58/*Theory*, 54.

45. Früchtl, *Mimesis*, 65. According to his reading, mimesis involves giving the object back the teleology that mechanistic knowing robs from it.

46. Buck-Morss gives a brilliant formulation of the socially critical function of mimesis: "The thinker, like the artist, proceeded mimetically, and in the process of imitating matter, transformed it so that it could be read as monadological expression of social truth." Buck-Morss, *The Origin of Negative Dialectics*, 132.

47. *Theorie*, 205/*Theory*, 136.

48. "Kafka, in whose works monopoly capitalism appears only distantly, codifies in the dregs of the administered world what becomes of people under the total social spell more faithfully and powerfully than do any novels about corrupt industrial trusts. The thesis that form is the locus of social content can be concretely shown in Kafka's language. Its objectivity, its Kleistian quality has often been remarked upon, and readers remark upon the contradiction between that objectivity and events that become remote through the imaginary character of so sober a representation" (*Theorie*, 342/*Theory*, 230).

49. In his lectures on aesthetics from 1958/1959, Adorno uses Kafka's means of writing as a way to illustrate his thesis that artworks offer a "feeling of the world" through their mimesis of the world, and he contrasts Kafka to the realist theory of literature. "The synthesis of these (societal) elements in Kafka's writing is not a definitive 'This is so': there is no conclusion drawn, a statement or judgment derived, but instead precisely the non-judging inherence of all of these social elements is what allows the artwork to take up the fullness of being that is excluded from the logic of judgment." Adorno, *Ästhetik 1958/59*, 328.

50. *Theorie*, 359/*Theory*, 243.

51. See Bertram's treatment of this in chapter 1.

52. Christoph Menke develops this conception of aesthetic negativity out of Adorno. Christoph Menke, *The Sovereignty of Art: Aesthetic Negativity in Adorno and Derrida* (Stanford: Stanford University Press, 1999).

Chapter Six

Walter Benjamin's Critique of the Category of Aesthetic Form

"The Work of Art in the Age of its Technological Reproducibility" from the Perspective of Benjamin's Early Writing

Alison Ross

The singularity of Walter Benjamin's writings poses problems of theoretical classification. The reception of one of his most cited and admired essays— "The Artwork in the Age of its Technological Reproducibility" ["*Das Kunstwerk im Zeitalter seiner technischen Reproduzierbarkeit*"]—is an exemplary case. There are three main versions of the essay. The first version was written in Paris in the autumn of 1935. The second version of the essay, which substantially expanded on and revised the first, was the version that Benjamin originally wanted published.[1] This second version was the source used in the first publication of the essay, which appeared in French and in shortened form in May 1936 in the *Zeitschrift für Sozialforschung*. While the French edition of the essay was in preparation in early 1936, Benjamin worked on the third version, intending it for publication in a German periodical. He modified it several times over 1937 and 1938 before allowing Gretel Adorno to copy it. Benjamin regarded this late version "as a work in progress, rather than a completed essay." Nonetheless, this version was the "source" for the essay's first publication in German in 1955 in Benjamin's *Schriften*[2] as well as its first English language publication in 1968 in Hannah Arendt's edited collection of Benjamin's writings. Unless otherwise noted, I will refer to this third version of the essay.

The essay is comprised of an introduction, fifteen short sections, and an epilogue. The introduction and the epilogue contain pointed comments about the political significance of Benjamin's analysis of the "work of art." In the introduction, Benjamin refers to Marx's analysis of the capitalist mode of production and argues that "[s]ince the transformation of the superstructure proceeds far more slowly than that of the base, it has taken more than half a century for the change in the conditions of production to be manifested in all areas of culture."[3] The changes in culture do not require a grandiose theory of the "art of the classless society," but "theses defining the tendencies of the development of art under the present conditions of production."[4] The superstructure, "no less than . . . the economy" manifests the "dialectic of these conditions of production." As such, the articulation of the "developmental tendencies of art can therefore contribute to the political struggle in ways that it would be a mistake to underestimate."[5]

In both the introduction and the epilogue, this "contribution" is specifically tailored to the struggle against fascism. According to Benjamin, the "tendencies" his essay identifies in the "superstructure" count against the continued pertinence of traditional concepts, including "creativity and genius, eternal value and mystery." In neutralizing these concepts, his essay is meant to place a block on the manipulation of "factual material . . . in the interests of fascism."[6] Benjamin's formulation of the concepts relevant for art under conditions of capitalist production will prove "*useful for the formulation of revolutionary demands in the politics of art [Kunstpolitik].*"[7] The components of this position are reiterated in Benjamin's claim in his epilogue that Marinetti's expectation that war will provide aesthetic gratification "is evidently the consummation of *l'art pour l'art.*" The claim provides further rhetorical ballast for Benjamin's contention that his polemic against traditional aesthetics has political significance.[8]

However, the coordination of the essay's political tasks with the study of the conceptual implications of technological reproducibility for art is largely unmanageable. Benjamin concedes this point in his introduction. He identifies the problem posed by the manipulation of factual material through the use of traditional concepts 'in an uncontrolled way', and acknowledges, in parentheses, that "controlling [these concepts] is difficult today."[9] The conceptual clarification of the "tendencies" of the superstructure under conditions of capitalist production can hardly stay the fascist tide. On the other hand, Benjamin's attempt to harness these tendencies for potential revolutionary political significance is also unconvincing, largely for the same reasons: The approach requires him to force the tendencies he uncovers into the dialectical setting and vocabulary of Marxist theory, whether they fit there or not.[10]

The problems of the essay are particularly pronounced when viewed through the lens of Benjamin's other writing. For instance, it is not clear that

Benjamin's use in this essay of the Marxist concepts of "dialectic," "super-structure," and "base" can be squared with his eccentric deployment of this vocabulary in other works from the same period.[11] Further, if we view the main themes of this essay in relation to the significant works in Benjamin's corpus, there is the crucial question of whether the features this essay iden-tifies as the "optical unconscious" of film images and describes positively as evidence of the "revolutionary" shift in art[12] are not the target of critical analysis in other important works.

Within the essay, the explicitly political framing of the piece is often in conflict with the passages on the changes wrought by technological reprodu-cibility on the experience of art. One of the central problems with Benjamin's position in the essay is that although it is the technical apparatus of film that he credits with revolutionary significance,[13] this political virtue seems to go beyond the mechanisms of production or the topic of medium specificity, and hence his point loses some of its force. The features of "the masses . . . progressive reaction" to film, which are supposedly aligned to the impact on art of its "technological reproducibility" are in fact largely conceptually interchangeable with the collective experience afforded by buildings. Despite the title of the essay, it is less the technical modality of works of "art" in the age of art's reproducibility than the relation of different types of technical production for "experience" that is at stake.

Benjamin seeks an effective opposition to the "fascist aestheticisation of politics" in film: The latter promises a new mass art able to inculcate a distracted, collective relation to non-auratic form. In its analysis of techno-logical reproducibility, the essay cites as exemplary the tactile and optical relations that determine our relation to architectural forms, and the distracted, rather than contemplative, state that structures our use of buildings through these sensory and habitual modes of engagement. Benjamin sees in these relations to architectural form evidence of the type of destruction of the auratic atmosphere of authority in art that he wants to find in the technologi-cally reproducible art form of film. In this regard, he specifically highlights the type of work of evaluation a film requires of its audience as well as its episodic mode of construction, which does not record its scenes in narrative sequence and accordingly deconstructs the mechanisms that build up the aura around the presence of the actor in theater: "for the first time—and this is the effect of film—the human being is placed in a position where he must oper-ate with his whole living person, while forgoing its aura. For the aura is bound to his presence in the here and now. There is no facsimile of the aura. The aura surrounding Macbeth on the stage cannot be divorced from the aura which, for the living spectators, surrounds the actor who plays him."[14] In this respect, the inauthenticity involved in the mechanisms of representation is less significant in the case of film than it is in theater. In film, "the fact that the actor represents someone else before the audience matters much less than the fact that he represents himself before the apparatus." "What distinguishes the shot in the film studio, however, is that the camera is substituted for the audience. As a result, the aura surrounding the actor is dispelled—and, with it, the aura of the figure he portrays."[15] The treatment of the topic of aura, which stands for the false authority accrued to aesthetic form, links the "Artwork" to Benjamin's polemics against the dominating effects of totalizing aesthetic form on human agency in his early essay on Goethe's *Elective Affinities*, as well as to the later version of this position in his treatment of the effects of the phantasmagoria of commodity capital in the *Arcades*.

In this chapter, I would like to reconsider Walter Benjamin's essay on the artwork in relation to the treatment of the category of aesthetic form across his corpus. My aim is to show that Benjamin's early work articulates a critique of aesthetic form that aligns aesthetic institutions and practices with myth understood pejoratively. I will argue that his "Artwork" needs to be evaluated in the light of that earlier position.

My discussion has two parts. First, I look at the points of continuity and discontinuity between the "Artwork" and Benjamin's earlier polemic against aesthetic form. Second, I consider whether and how this polemic fits with his approach to the question of collective experience. The "Artwork" approaches this question in largely positive terms in the way it attaches progressive political significance to the distracted type of reception operative in film. Other essays of Benjamin's, however, offer a different perspective on this question. In conclusion, I consider some of the implications for the politically inflected account of film in the "Artwork" of the different ways that Benjamin treats the questions of collective experience and aesthetic form across his oeuvre.

THE CONCEPT OF AESTHETIC FORM IN EARLY AND LATE BENJAMIN

Benjamin's work contains a number of distinct perspectives, which can sometimes undermine the coherent treatment of topics. For instance, there is some tension between the respective frameworks of the polemic against the totalizing effects of sensuous form and the analysis of modern experience [*Erlebnis*], both of which Benjamin uses to treat the topic of the artwork. In his critical analysis of sensuous form, the artwork falls on the side of semblance and phantasmagoria when deployed as a schema of existential orientation. Viewed in the context of his important 1924/1925 "Goethe's Elective Affinities" essay, such a pejorative classification is the result of the exclusion of sensuous form from truth. Benjamin's essay argues that the characters of Goethe's novel are prey to an anxious, guilt-ridden existence. They live in fear of transgressing unstated rules, a consequence of their submission to the reign of myth. These characters look to the aesthetic arrangements of the landscape and the interior of the house as if these could provide existential orientation for their lives. They show a culpable disregard for tradition when they tear up the tombstones of the ancestors to "beautify" the church grounds in a clover-covered path. Their boundary-less activities of beautification are the key to the reign of fate in their lives: When human beings empower natural forces with disposition over their lives, they become trapped in the snare of fate. For Benjamin, the vital meaning sensuous forms are presumed to bear is silent, and therefore irremediably ambiguous. The fixation on the meaning such forms are presumed to communicate inevitably leads to anxiety and guilt; the ambiguity of their edicts entails that any act may be a "transgression."[16] The more fate unfolds in their lives, the more human beings look to ritual for atonement and security. "Nothing but strict attachment to ritual can promise these human beings a stay against the nature in which they live. Charged, as only mythic nature is, with superhuman powers, it comes menacingly into play."[17] The receding hold of tradition in modernity does not empower human life with new found "freedoms," rather the replacement of tradition with aesthetic "choice" traps human beings in empty ritual propitiations. Against the pernicious hold of sensuous forms over human life, Benjamin places the articulate clarity of the word, which mortifies the mythic nature. In his view, "what is proper to the truly divine is the logos. The divine does not ground life without truth, nor does it ground the rite without theology."[18] The word embodies truth, whereas the mute sensuous form of the image, on account of its unclear communication of meaning, is excluded from it. This early critical perspective on the totalizing sensuous form that prevails over the bourgeois, aesthetic life is modified in Benjamin's *Arcades* when the vantage point of historical emancipation leads to the idea that sensuous form contains redemptive potentials. One of the consequences of this later position is that "truth" is no longer, as it had been in the early writings, entirely external to the perspective of "myth," nor to sensuous form.

In the "Artwork," the traces of Benjamin's early polemic in the essay on Goethe's novel against sensuous form can be seen in the terms he uses to describe the role of aura and ritual in traditional art forms. On the question of the aura, Benjamin aims to cut down the power of authority, which is sustained and cultivated through the imposition of distance. There is a notable difference between these essays on the topic of tradition. In the early essay, the replacement of tradition with aesthetic value is criticized; in the latter, the destruction of tradition is seen as integral to the evisceration of auratic value. The discrepancy is only apparent, however, since the latter position does not reinstate the features of aesthetic life that the early essay targets for criticism. It is clear that Benjamin's "Artwork" maintains a critical perspective on the tendency to empower aesthetic form. On this point, the connection between the essay on Goethe's novel and on the "Artwork" can be seen in the insistent critical references each makes to ritual. The essay on Goethe's novel identifies ritual propitiation as the attempt to manage the dark forces unleashed by the ascendency of form. The "Artwork" connects aura to ritual. Benjamin holds that "it is highly significant that the artwork's auratic mode of existence is never entirely severed from its ritual function. *The unique value of the 'authentic' work of art always has its basis in ritual.*"[19]

On the other hand, the position Benjamin takes in the "Artwork" also seems to pick up on an insistent thematic of his work that only becomes an explicit object of attention after 1927: namely, the concern about the modern dissipation of experience [*Erfahrung*]. The sense in which these frameworks are at odds with one another can be elucidated in relation to the different tactics Benjamin deploys to manage the difficulties each perspective reveals: the focus on detail and the putatively "insignificant," which is supposed to "mortify" sensuous totality, and the use of the sensory experience of distraction in order to undermine the aura of the artwork, respectively.

One of the consistent themes across the entirety of Benjamin's writing is his claim that the "insignificant" has epistemological significance. Hence, even though the stringent opposition in his early work between truth (the word) and myth (the sensuous form) has eroded by the time of the *Arcades Project*, the *Arcades* is arguably the most ambitious version of the claim on behalf of the marginal or exceptional. In the *Arcades*, it is the refuse of the nineteenth century that is the platform for disclosing the truth of human history per se. The detritus collected in the *Arcades* shows not just the vitiated wishes of the nineteenth century, but it gives these wishes contour and definition. Human beings have a creative vocation; their revolutionary energies are dedicated to achieving the non-alienated existence in which neither things nor others are opaque or alien to them. This wish takes recognizable form in the nineteenth century because this century is the first time that the human desire for emancipation becomes definable in real features. Hence the "insignificant" refuse of the century bears the truth of human history and it allows for knowledge of this truth.

One of the earliest versions of Benjamin's claim that the insignificant is the vehicle of genuine knowledge is in the preface to his *Trauerspiel* book. In this work, he argues that it is the knowledge of the extreme case alone that provides knowledge of the ordinary.[20] Another version still can be found in the position defended in his essay on Goethe's novel: It is the slender novella contained in *Elective Affinities* that contains the truth of the work. In this essay, Benjamin advocates a mortification of the ambiguously expressive form of the symbol, and he claims that the articulate clarity of the word opposes the ambiguous expressivity of nature's silent forms in myth. Benjamin seeks in the mortification of the symbol an effective destruction of the false totality of sensuous form. Aspects of the variants of this general position regarding the significance of the insignificant are used in the "Artwork."

For instance, this position underpins the schema of evaluation that distinguishes the different modalities of the arts of the image: painting is criticized as a mode of the total image, and film praised as a fragmentation of the components of the "total" image. To be sure, one of the anchor points here is the idea that the aura and the semblance are qualities of painting rather than film. However, the key assumption behind this classification of different media is that in film the fragmentation of the whole fractures a false totality. The aura and the semblance qualities belong to the image of totality; when this false image is fractured they also dissipate.[21] In the "instructive" comparison he outlines between the camera operator and the painter, Benjamin uses the analogous comparison of the surgeon and the magician. The references to authority inducing distance are intended to recall the earlier discussion of the aura, which counts for the magician-painter, but not for the surgeon–camera operator. It is significant that the surgeon's activity is based in knowledge of the body, unlike the magician's, which is a model of baseless authority. The terms of this contrast echo the stakes of Benjamin's early opposition between the truth of the Revelation and the anxiety-inducing, futile search for vital meaning in myth.

> The attitude of the magician, who heals a sick person by a laying-on of hands, differs from that of the surgeon, who makes an intervention in the patient. The magician maintains the natural distance between himself and the person treated; more precisely, he reduces it slightly by laying on his hands, but increases it greatly by his authority. The surgeon does exactly the reverse; he greatly diminishes the distance from the patient by penetrating the patient's body, and increases it only slightly by the caution with which his hand moves among the organs. In short: unlike the magician (traces of whom are still found in the medical practitioner), the surgeon abstains at the decisive moment from confronting his patient person to person; instead, he penetrates the patient by operating.[22]

The key to the analogy is the status of the image in each practice. For Benjamin, the painter "maintains . . . a natural distance from reality, whereas the cinematographer penetrates deeply into its tissue." Just as distance contrasts with immersion, so, too, the images that each practice obtains "differ enormously. The painter's is a total image, whereas that of the cinematographer is piecemeal, its manifold parts being assembled according to a new law."[23] The piecemeal quality of the cinematographer's work by definition elevates it above the semblance characteristics that Benjamin's writing consistently aligns to the "total image." The cinematographer does not just satisfy the contemporary expectation of the "equipment-free aspect of reality" that is won "on the basis of the most intensive interpenetration of reality with equipment,"[24] but in so doing the cinematographer provides "an object of simultaneous collective reception."[25] The introduction of this factor of the quality of collective reception into the evaluation of film seems to introduce a perspective at odds with Benjamin's paradigm of the critique of totalizing sensuous form. In particular, the perspective of collective experience that Benjamin appeals to attaches a positive value to the immediacy of the experience of images that his earlier critique of totalizing sensuous form seems to align to the disempowering reign of aesthetic form. Can this contradiction be resolved?

DISTRACTION AND COLLECTIVE EXPERIENCE

Benjamin maintains that the reception of works of art accentuates either their cult value or their exhibition value. This thesis provides a schema of ready identification for the different historical functions of what he refers to as the "construct [*Gebilde*]" of the work of art.[26] The contemporary situation is one in which the variety of methods for technologically reproducing art dramatically increase the "scope" for its exhibition. Further, the new functions that art attains in these conditions, such as "the artistic function . . . may subsequently be seen as incidental."[27] The contemporary exhibition value of art contrasts with the magical and religious service of art in ritual practice: "[t]he elk depicted by Stone Age man on the walls of his cave is an instrument of magic. He exhibits it to his fellow men, to be sure, but in the main it is meant for the spirits."[28] The ritual functions of art are preserved in the aura attached to the artwork in its secular age. Accordingly, Benjamin thinks that the "*whole social function of art is revolutionized*" when it is no longer "*founded on ritual*" but on "*politics*" (i.e., the politicization of art that his essay advocates).[29] This political aspiration requires a form of "exhibition" that does not embellish the "artistic function" but rather provides a pathway for simultaneous collective reception that unsettles the conceptual network attached to the artistic function (such as the figure of the contemplative spectator, etc.). The "Artwork" sees in the cinema a mass art able to reintroduce the prized value of distraction as the context for the assimilation of perceptual experience [*Erfahrung*]. More specifically, film is able to "provide an object of simultaneous collective reception, as architecture has always been able to do, as the epic poem could do at one time."[30] In the essay, the model of such reception is provided by the description of architecture. The tactile and optical mode of our habitual mode of engagement with architectural forms is described as that of a distracted rather than contemplative state. The use-based relation to buildings is evidence of the type of destruction of the auratic atmosphere of authority in art that Benjamin also asserts for the technologically reproducible art form of film. The claim about distraction is also made in the discussion of *mémoire involontaire* in his writing on Proust. Proustian *mémoire involontaire* is the pathway to collective experience that conscious recollection can no longer find. These themes undergo a particular inflection in his 1936 essay on the storyteller. In this essay, Benjamin complains about the way the novel, as a work produced (by the writer) and devoured (by the reader) in isolation, has replaced the social fabric that surrounded the story-teller. The hive of activities like weaving and spinning meant that the knowl-edge imparted in the storyteller's tale was absorbed in a distracted mode.[31] However, the storyteller owed his or her experiential impact on the commu-nity of listeners in part because of the "halo," or aura, that he or she bore.[32] The comment reflects the status of the storyteller's authority as a total "per-son" with his or her "audience." The storyteller's authority contrasts with the way the camera operator deals with the actor: not in the framework of a total person but in a "piecemeal" fashion. The remaining dissonant note in the essay on the storyteller is due to the deeply nostalgic tone of Benjamin's treatment of this auratic figure, which contrasts with the effort to take a positive stance towards the destruction of tradition in the "Artwork" essay's embrace of film's shock effects.

Benjamin maintains that like the modes of existence of human collectives the mode of human perception "changes over long historical periods."[33] In film, the "shifts that in literature took place over centuries have occurred in a decade."[34] Cinema is a mass art that provides the possibility of "simultane-ous collective reception."[35] What is crucial is that film enriches "our field of perception"[36] ; it does so in the case of the "progressive reaction" to film "by an *immediate* intimate fusion of pleasure—pleasure in seeing and experienc-ing—with an attitude of expert appraisal."[37]

The key points regarding the repudiation of auratic distance and its re-placement with "an immediate intimate" experience can be unpacked not just in relation to Benjamin's analogical comparison between painting and cine-matography with the magician and the surgeon, which I mentioned above, but in relation to the question of the epistemological stakes of this analogy. How should we understand the relation between Benjamin's call for an im-mediate intimate experience of cinematic images, as if it were politically meritorious, and his earlier call for the mortification of the totalizing sweep of aesthetic form? Do the technical modalities of film and the new perspec-tives it uncovers possess the epistemological significance that, like the "in-significant detail" of the *Trauerspiel* book and the detritus collected in the *Arcades*, would warrant Benjamin's position?

It seems to me that there is a parallel between what Benjamin's early writing describes as the intention-less status of truth and which he locates in language, and the claim about distracted reception of images as key to the progressive claims of film. As we saw, the "Artwork" prizes the immediacy attained by the surgeon, who is likened to the cinematographer, over the surface engagement of the magician, likened to the painter's interest in the confection of a "total image."[38] It is worth comparing the terminology at stake here with Benjamin's formulation of language in his 1916 "Language" essay as "the 'medium' of the communication." Benjamin's formulation makes language as "medium" contiguous with "immediacy." He writes: "Mediation, which is the immediacy of all mental communication, is the fundamental problem of linguistic theory, and if one chooses to call this immediacy magic, then the primary problem of language is its magic."[39]

In the "Epistemo-Critical Prologue" to his *Trauerspiel*, Benjamin comments on the distinction between "truth" and "knowledge": "[u]nlike the methodology of knowledge" truth "does not derive from a coherence established in the consciousness, but from an essence."[40] "For the thing [that is] possessed" in knowledge, its "representation is secondary; it does not have prior existence as something representing itself. But the opposite holds good of truth."[41] In the case of truth, the essence "is self-representation, and is therefore immanent in it as form."[42] This position regarding the independence of the essence clarifies to some extent his view that unlike knowledge, "truth does not enter into relationships, particularly intentional ones."[43] "Truth is an intentionless state of being, made up of ideas. The proper approach to it is not therefore one of intention and knowledge, but rather a total immersion and absorption in it. Truth is the death of intention."[44] He goes on to define these "ideas" as "linguistic"[45] and to claim that they "are displayed, without intention, in the act of naming."[46] These comments need to be seen in the prism of his conception of the paradisiacal state in which "there is as yet no need to struggle with the communicative significance of words."[47] This position on truth echoes the reference in the "Language" essay to the "immanent magic" of language[48] and the general importance of naming language in his thinking as a release from the capture of human life by sensuous form. In the paradisiacal state of Adamic naming, words are "removed from play and caprice."[49] When Benjamin claims that in "philosophical contemplation" the ideas are renewed and that "in this renewal the primordial mode of apprehending words is restored,"[50] he refers to the truth that words bear on account of their intimate relation with the creative intention of divine revelation. The truth that is secured in this manner is replaced in later work with the truth of the human creative vocation. In the *Arcades Project*, the significance of the industrial innovations of the nineteenth century is that they show the human dexterity to mold steel and glass and the realizable wish for a life emancipated from need, "legible" in technological feats. Specifically, the truth of human history per se is recognizable in the industrial innovations of the nineteenth century.

Film offers a version of the same kind of thesis. Here, too, there is a technological innovation that promises a qualitative shift. Film alters and "enriches" our perception. It adds an optical and auditory precision to apperception: "In contrast to what obtains in painting, filmed action lends itself more readily to analysis because it delineates situations far more precisely. In contrast to what obtains on the stage, filmed action lends itself more readily to analysis because it can be isolated more easily."[51] It is this "piecemeal" quality of filmed action that makes it difficult to separate its artistic and scientific value. Like the arcades, technical ingenuity is a testament to the human vocation, which destroys the carapace of "pastness" that obscures the potentially motivating force of the wishes and dreams of past generations in the present.

In the way that it accentuates the "hidden details in familiar objects, and by its exploration of commonplace milieu through the ingenious guidance of the camera," the technical innovation of film "explodes" the "prison-world" of familiarity "so that now we can set off calmly on journeys of adventure among its far-flung debris. With the close-up, space expands; with slow motion, movement is extended."[52] The seemingly insignificant detail and debris play the main role in puncturing an otherwise closed totality. Once again, this refuse is charged with epistemological significance. And yet the problem of film is that the "attitude of expert appraisal" somehow coexists with the immediacy of the image. Like the idea that cinema heralds a techno-logical innovation that is politically progressive, but that requires critical elucidation to be what it is, so, too, this "attitude" of analytic "appraisal" undercuts the "immediacy" of the image and the values it represents such as "distraction" and "heightened attention." These difficulties are all related to the uneven status of the conceptualization of the image across Benjamin's corpus.

In the early work, the perception of meaning in an image was tied to deleterious existential effects, since such meaning was irreducibly ambigu-ous. The situation of ambiguity fostered guilt and anxiety. This early position seems to be at odds with the orientation of the later theory of film since the epistemological clarity secured in the word is absent from the medium. The comparison between painting and film can be cited in support of this point: "The painting invites the viewer to contemplation; before it, he can give himself up to his train of associations. Before a film image, he cannot do so. No sooner has he seen it than it has already changed. It cannot be fixed on." Benjamin goes on to cite Duhamel's description of the structure of film[53] : "I can no longer think what I want to think. My thoughts have been replaced by moving images. Indeed," Benjamin comments, "the train of associations in the person contemplating these images is immediately interrupted by new images. This constitutes the shock effect of film, which, like all shock ef-fects, seeks to induce heightened attention."[54]

The idea that thoughts are replaced by images seems similar to what Benjamin's early work objected to in myth. After all, the absorption in aes-thetic form in that early writing is the object of his critical attention: such attention is disempowering in its inducement of incapacity. The attention it attracts is also problematic, since the object that commands attention does not warrant it. The *immediacy* of the images in film, however, might also be understood as akin to the intention-less state of truth celebrated in Benjamin's prologue to his *Trauerspiel* book. Film provides a medium that cuts away at what the "Language" essay had denigrated as the "play and caprice" of mere communication. The heightened attention caught by the flow of images in film is antithetical to passive absorption in one's own thoughts. And on this perspective, the contrast between the limited position of transitory intention and intention-less truth appears to be sustained across the corpus. The heightened attention won in the shock effect of film directs us to what is pertinent and stokes the motivation to act. On both counts, the shock effect in film is the counter to the depleting feeling of anxiety that takes hold in the face of forms that are marked for our attention, but whose claim on us is ambiguous and de-motivating.

CONCLUSION

Still, odd notes between the "Artwork" and Benjamin's other significant writings persist. In the works after 1929, Benjamin refers critically to modern "lived" experience [*Erlebnis*] and postulates that the collective experience once provided by tradition was characterized by distracted activities (the "Storyteller" essay) and might be glimpsed again through the state of distraction (*mémoire involontaire* in "The Image of Proust" or the discussion of experience in "On Some Motifs in Baudelaire"). And yet the experience of distraction involved in the reception of film in the "Artwork" seems quite different from any of these examples. I have argued here that it has some of the epistemological features that align it with Benjamin's treatment of the refuse and the marginal as bearers of truth and/or knowledge across the corpus. It is noticeable that in Benjamin's major works this epistemological dimension carries an existential significance regarding the difference between a life lived under the pallid light of myth or one that is illuminated by the moral decision. There is a consistent polemic against sensuous form in Benjamin's writing. In his early writing, the pejorative status of sensuous form is connected to Benjamin's conception of myth as external to truth. Later, the polemic is tied to the features of commodity capitalism that produce phantasmagoric effects. In each case, the captivating effects of sensuous forms are seen to induce anxiety, guilt, and helplessness in their victim. The breadth of these themes is truncated in the slogans of political engagement that frame the "Artwork."

Human life ends in a fateful impotence when it is under the sway of aesthetic practices and institutions. This position is fleshed out in other early works from a slightly different angle. In Benjamin's *The Origin of German Tragic Drama*, the theory of allegory mortifies the meaning communicated in sensuous form because it looks beyond form to knowledge. These positions are all quite distinct from the later thesis in the *Arcades* that truth is "more the ruffle on a dress than some idea," which implies that truth is somehow lodged in sensuous forms. [55] However, in each case Benjamin uses the concept of the insignificant or the "detail" to defend the "knowledge" and/or "truth" that he sees defeating the semblance of false mythic totalization in sensuous form.

Are these features sufficient to provide the connection to the idea of the intention-less status of truth given that in the case of film the mode of this immediacy is that of the "image" rather than the "word"? How serious is the clash between the framework of "experience" and that of the "image," or "form" in Benjamin's "Artwork"? To my mind, the key factor in resolving this clash is the existential significance that Benjamin accords to the shock effect of film. The gripping force of the image in the case of film helps to clarify how the politicization of art can be reconciled both with the tenor of Benjamin's early critical position on sensuous form, and with the theme of distracted experience.

In the *Arcades*, Benjamin treats the problem of how to transform the dreamlike experience of the commodity form into the motivating experience of the lost wishes and dreams of past generations. It is the immediacy of this experience of knowledge of the past that is crucial for its motivating effect. The *Arcades* deals with detritus from the past that stimulates revolutionary motivation in the present. The historical index of the nineteenth century points forward to its redemption in the twentieth. The detritus of the nineteenth century embodies the collective past. Viewed from the perspective of the *Arcades*, the reason that the political theses of the "Artwork" seem unwieldy is that the technical apparatus of film stands in for the frustrated wishes of a century, and the distracted state in which vital meaning is experienced is tied to the process of "criticism." In the *Arcades*, revolutionary experience is direct and immediate, and the context of its formation is the exposure to detritus. As in Benjamin's early writing, so, too, in the later work, aesthetic institutions and practices are excoriated for their pacifying effects.

I have argued here that understanding Benjamin's position across his corpus on the topics of sensuous form and distracted (collective) experience can help to qualify the seemingly discrepant propositions about the politicization of art in his "Artwork" essay. This essay presents a twofold discrepancy: first, between the idea that the technological reproducibility of art has political significance and the tenor of Benjamin's early critical position on sensuous form; second, between the endorsement of collective experience in film and the position developed in the *Arcades*, which deals with the substantive issue of how the pacifying experience of commodity forms can be transformed into the motivating, collective experience of the lost wishes and dreams of past generations. The "Artwork," in contrast, cultivates the expectation that a "progressive" experience can be had in the distracted state of film reception. In its specification of the virtues of the medium of film, the essay is unable either to explain the ways this experience is genuinely a collective experience beyond the aesthetic category of an "audience" (however involved this collective body is in the process of meaning construction), or how the peculiar link between film criticism and progressive experience can move beyond the field of the aesthetic reception of a film to action. This is a problem for the cogency of Benjamin's call for the "politicisation of art" since the shift away from "art" and towards "experience" is not only mandated in the "Artwork," it is also consistent with many of the fundamental themes across Benjamin's heterogeneous corpus.

NOTES

1. Walter Benjamin, "The Artwork in the Age of its Technological Reproducibility" (second version), *Selected Writings: Volume 3*, eds. Howard Eiland and Michael W. Jennings, transl. Edmund Jephcott and Howard Eiland (Cambridge: The Belknap Press of Harvard University Press, 1996), 122, Note.
2. Walter Benjamin, "The Artwork in the Age of its Technological Reproducibility" (third version), *Selected Writings: Volume 4*, eds. Howard Eiland and Michael W. Jennings (Cambridge: The Belknap Press of Harvard University Press, 2003), 270, Note.
3. Benjamin, *Selected Writings: Volume 4*, 251–52.
4. Benjamin, *Selected Writings: Volume 4*, 252.
5. Ibid.
6. Ibid.
7. Ibid, emphasis in original.
8. Benjamin, *Selected Writings: Volume 4*, 270.
9. Benjamin, *Selected Writings: Volume 4*, 252.
10. Miriam Hansen, "Benjamin, Cinema and Experience: the Blue Flower in the Land of Technology," *New German Critique*, No. 40 (1987): 180, argues that the "Artwork" essay evinces the influence of Brecht.
11. Benjamin gives an eccentric formulation of the Marxist base-superstructure relation in terms of the vocabulary of "expression" in his contemporaneous drafting of the *Arcades Project*. "Marx lays bare the causal connection between economy and culture. For us, what matters is the thread of expression. It is not the economic origins of culture that will be presented, but the expression of the economy in its culture. At issue, in other words, is the attempt to grasp an economic process as perceptible Ur- phenomenon, from out of which proceed all manifestations of life in the arcades (and, accordingly, in the nineteenth century)." Walter Benjamin, *Arcades Project* [N1a, 6], 460. And: "This research—which deals fundamentally with the expressive character of the earliest industrial products, the earliest industrial architecture, the earliest machines, but also the earliest department stores, advertisements, and so on—thus becomes important for Marxism in two ways. First, it will demonstrate how the milieu in which Marx's doctrine arose affected that doctrine through its expressive character (which is to say, not only through causal connections); but, second, it will also show in what respects Marxism, too, shares the expressive character of the material products contemporary with it." Walter Benjamin, *Arcades Project* [N1a, 7], 460. Indeed, the Marxist notion of the "revolutionary situation" is itself described in the *Arcades* as "inadequate."
12. Benjamin, *Selected Writings: Volume 4*, 266, 262.
13. Benjamin, *Selected Writings: Volume 4*, 264: "The technological reproducibility of the artwork changes the relation of the masses to art. The extremely backward attitude toward a

Picasso painting changes into a highly progressive reaction to a Chaplin film." Emphasis in original removed.

14. Benjamin, *Selected Writings: Volume 4*, 260.

15. Ibid.

16. Walter Benjamin, "The Artwork in the Age of its Technological Reproducibility" (second version), *Selected Writings: Volume 1*, edd. Marcus Bullock and Michael W. Jennings (Cambridge: The Belknap Press of Harvard University Press, 1996), 343.

17. Benjamin, *Selected Writings: Volume 1*, 303.

18. Benjamin, *Selected Writings: Volume 1*, 326.

19. Benjamin, *Selected Writings: Volume 3*, 105, second version.

20. Walter Benjamin, *The Origin of German Tragic Drama*, transl. John Osborne (London: Verso, 2009), 35.

21. Hence the contrast between the false totality of semblance form and Benjamin's definition of the "origin" in *The Origin of German Tragic Drama* in which the "totality of its history" is the schema of revelation for an idea's truth: "On the one hand [the origin] needs to be recognized as a process of restoration and re-establishment, but, on the other hand, and precisely because of this, as something imperfect and incomplete. There takes place in every original phenomenon a determination of the form in which an idea will constantly confront the historical world, until it is revealed fulfilled, in the totality of its history. Origin is not, therefore, discovered by the examination of actual findings, but it is related to their history and their subsequent development" (*Origin of German Tragic Drama*, 45–46). The totality that reveals truth is one that is keyed to imperfection, not semblance. In the *Arcades*, the problem of "fathoming an origin" is pursued in "the origin of the forms and mutations of the Paris arcades from their beginning to their decline" (462 [N2a, 4]). If Benjamin locates "this origin in the economic facts" (462 [N2a, 4]), these facts are not themselves "primal phenomena; they become such only insofar as in their own individual development—'unfolding' might be a better term—they give rise to the whole series of the arcade's concrete historical forms, just as the leaf unfolds from itself all the riches of the empirical world of plants" (462 [N2a, 4]). The reference to the "primal phenomena," which Benjamin also uses in the same convolute to refer to the primacy of the image in history, indicates that it is the "arcade's concrete historical forms" that are the sites in which an idea is lifted out of the process of becoming to become "in the totality of its history" (i.e., in its full development from beginning to decline, an experience of truth). Here, it is decay that is the key to the positive use of "totality."

22. Benjamin, *Selected Writings: Volume 4*, 263.

23. Benjamin, *Selected Writings: Volume 4*, 263–64.

24. Benjamin, *Selected Writings: Volume 4*, 264.

25. Ibid.

26. Benjamin, *Selected Writings: Volume 4*, 257.

27. Ibid.

28. Ibid.

29. Benjamin, *Selected Writings: Volume 4*, 257, his emphasis.

30. Benjamin, *Selected Writings: Volume 4*, 264.

31. Benjamin, *Selected Writings: Volume 3*, 149.

32. Benjamin, *Selected Writings: Volume 3*, 166, N.28.

33. Benjamin, *Selected Writings: Volume 3*, 104, second version, author's italics removed.

34. Benjamin, *Selected Writings: Volume 4*, 262.

35. Benjamin, *Selected Writings: Volume 4*, 264.

36. Benjamin, *Selected Writings: Volume 4*, 265.

37. Benjamin, *Selected Writings: Volume 4*, 264, emphasis added.

38. Benjamin, *Selected Writings: Volume 4*, 263.

39. Benjamin, *Selected Writings: Volume 1*, 64.

40. Benjamin, *The Origin of German Tragic Drama*, 30.

41. Benjamin, *The Origin of German Tragic Drama*, 29.

42. Benjamin, *The Origin of German Tragic Drama*, 30.

43. Benjamin, *The Origin of German Tragic Drama*, 35.

44. Benjamin, *The Origin of German Tragic Drama*, 36.

45. Ibid.

46. Benjamin, *The Origin of German Tragic Drama*, 37.

47. Ibid.

48. Benjamin, *Selected Writings: Volume 1*, 71.

49. Benjamin, *The Origin of German Tragic Drama*, 37.

50. Ibid.

51. Benjamin, *Selected Writings: Volume 4*, 265.

52. Ibid.

53. Duhamel, writes Benjamin, "detests the cinema and knows nothing about its significance, though he does know something about its structure" (Benjamin, *Selected Writings: Volume 4*, 267).

54. Benjamin, *Selected Writings: Volume 4*, 267.

55. Walter Benjamin, *The Arcades Project*, transl. Howard Eiland and Kevin McLaughlin (Cambridge: Belknap Press, 1999), N 3, 2, 463.

Chapter Seven

Walter Benjamin and the "Highly Productive Use of the Human Being's Self-Alienation"

Stéphane Symons

It seems safe to say that it has by now become an altogether impossible task to add something genuinely new to the enormous mass of secondary literature that has been published about Walter Benjamin's seminal text *The Work of Art in the Age of Its Technological Reproducibility*. It remains quite stunning to see that a single text could spark discussions in, among others, the fields of philosophy, sociology, art history, psychology, literary studies, education, and technology studies alike and that, after all these decades, it is still being read as one of the foundational manifestoes of the one academic discipline that seems to borrow freely from all the other ones just mentioned: cultural studies. It is to a large extent thanks to this mass of literature and by virtue of the many brilliant analyses that it has brought forth that the subtlety of Benjamin's text and the many conceptual layers it contains have for the most part been identified and explored. When some of a single generation's sharpest cultural theorists and philosophers (Miriam Bratu Hansen, Susan Buck Morss, T. J. Clark, Samuel Weber, Beatrice Hanssen, or Eli Friedlander, to name but a few) decide to devote attention to one and the same text (or rather, to one single set of texts, if we take the different versions of the "Artwork" essay into account), the intellectual harvest this yields is as rewarding as could be expected: it seems that, at last, almost all of the most complex and far-reaching issues that run through Benjamin's essay have been accurately described and that there is hardly an argument or idea left that has not yet been adequately mapped. From all this, it has become clear that it is in the first place a set of conceptual dualities that has bestowed Benjamin's essay with the solidity and reliability of strong scaffolding, fit to be deployed in very diverse environments and usable for a large variety of purposes. Most of the interpretations so far, that is to say, zoom in on the difference between, for example, an auratic artwork and a technologically (re)produced one, an experience of absorption and a reception in distraction, cult value and exhibition value, a *Bild* and an *Abbild*, an aestheticized politics and a politicized aesthetics or the multitude as a mass and the multitude as a matrix. In what follows, I will elaborate at length on some of these issues but, rather than focusing in the first place on yet another systematic overview or one more exploration of the conceptual framework that is set up in the body of the "Artwork" essay, I will most often take recourse to mere bits and pieces from it in order to use them, initially, as a clarification of some of the broader, philosophical stakes of Benjamin's theory.

This clarification will start from the place where, in the second version of the "Artwork" essay, Benjamin describes what is ultimately at stake in the issue of technologically (re)produced art: "the representation of human beings by means of an apparatus has made possible a highly productive use [*eine höchst produktive Verwertung*] of the human being's self-alienation [*Selbstentfremdung*]."[1] This phrase will be dropped from the third (and canonical) version of the essay, most likely under pressure from Adorno, but its brief occurrence comes with a familiar ring to it. Remarkably enough, that is to say, the same intuition, albeit described with different words, had already made a first appearance ten years earlier in Benjamin's book on the German baroque. "[D]epersonalization [*Depersonalisation*]," it is stated there, can be "set in an incomparably productive context [*einen unvergleichlich fruchtbaren Zusammenhang*]."[2] There are, of course, obvious differences between both contexts and Benjamin's philosophical interests of the mid-1930s had shifted away, in many and important regards, from those of the mid-1920s. It is, however, worthwhile to explore some of the most interesting similarities.

THE ORIGIN OF GERMAN TRAGIC DRAMA (MOURNFULNESS)

The above quotation from the *Trauerspiel* book is lifted from Benjamin's discussion of the baroque *Grundgefühl* of mournfulness [*Trauerigsein*], which is described as the uncanny experience that a seemingly *in*significant object somehow resonates with a strange layer of meaning. Mournfulness, that is to say, is "the pathological state, in which the most simple object [*jedes unscheinbarste Ding*] appears to be a symbol of some enigmatic wisdom because it lacks any natural, creative relationship to us."[3] For Benjamin, as has been repeated extensively in secondary literature, this state of mournfulness symptomatizes the "unredeemed" universe that is conjured in the literary texts on which his analysis focuses. The inability to discover "any natural, creative relationship to us" in a "most simple object" is thus, first and foremost, a token of a "fragmented" world "that knows no eschatology"[4] and epitomizes "the hopelessness of the earthly condition [*die Trostlosigkeit der irdischen Verfassung*]."[5] Yet, much more intriguing to Benjamin than this confrontation with a "depersonalizing" repetition of the same is the irreducible possibility that it be lifted with a sudden "one about-turn [*mit jenem einem Umschwung*]."[6] For what drives Benjamin's descriptions of the baroque "play of mourning" is less an interest in the phenomenon of "mourning" [*Trauer*] as such, than the feeling that it, under the hands of some of the authors his analysis focuses on, was transformed into a form of "play" [*Spiel*]. It is this process through which *a* play is modified into an instantiation of play which marks the difference between, on the one hand, a "most simple object" with alienating and depersonalizing features and, on the other, "a symbol of some enigmatic wisdom."[7] As is well known, the literary mode that was privileged by the *Trauerspiel* authors, allegory, is an essential element to understand the nature and possibility of this "about-turn." The mode of allegory thrives on a potential for meaning that arises, not *in spite of* but *due to* an object's or story's puzzling and incomplete reference to something altogether different from what could ordinarily be expected. Allegory, in other words, reveals an object to be simultaneously a "fragment" [*Bruchstück*] *and* more than the mere part of a lost whole:

> It will unmistakably be apparent especially to anyone who is familiar with allegorical textual exegesis, that all of the things which are used to signify derive, from the very fact of their pointing to something else, a power which raises them onto a higher plane, and which can, indeed, sanctify them. Considered in allegorical terms, then, the world is both elevated and devalued.[8]

One of the more implicit arguments in Benjamin's book on the *Trauerspiel* is that, on account of its indulgence in the mode of allegory, it is to be considered less as an "artistic genre" than as a "function" or, in Samuel Weber's terms, a "medium" that positively affects our "ability to respond" to the surrounding world: giving up the *telos* of capturing the world as a completed "work" and rejecting the (Aristotelian) aim of purifying the contingencies of history into a coherent "plot" or "story," the *Trauerspiel* is first and foremost to be read as the quest for an "*arcanum*, immune to the assaults of melancholy" and something "housed and roofed"[9] for the spiritually homeless (the historical context of the Reformation is, of course, a crucial element in this regard).[10] With the help of allegory, the *Trauerspiel* can unexpectedly but drastically up the ante of our normal outlook at history and, by way of a "restaging" of the world, restore the belief that it is not utterly depleted of the possibility of change. For Benjamin, the allegorical gaze does not therefore merely shatter the promise of a clear and direct grasp of the whole, opposing itself wholly to the "false semblance of totality" that is rendered by the symbol. It is, rather, in this very moment of fragmentation that it shows itself as capable of charging the remaining parts with a novel dynamic of meaning ("the most simple object appears to be a symbol of some enigmatic wisdom"). When allegorized in this manner, a fragment acquires a significance that is fully its own, that is, it does not any longer merely derive its meaning from the overarching unity it naturally belongs to.

Benjamin emphasizes the unexpected and even alienating nature ("depersonalization") of this renewal of meaning, but he indicates at the same time that it cannot be released from a "will"[11] and an "astounding tenacity of intention."[12] It is therefore vital to note that a given fragment can only yield a form of play by virtue of a specific form of attentiveness or presence of mind on our part. *Spiel* is not at all antithetical to "pensiveness" and "its natural affinity . . . for gravity,"[13] but it denotes a sustained ability to respond actively and creatively to a world that has nevertheless lost its coherence and continuity. In the most exemplary cases (Calderón), "the secular drama must stop short on the borders of transcendence," but it "seeks, nevertheless, to assure itself of this indirectly, in play."[14] In this regard, as was suggested by Martin Jay, the *Trauerspiel* is wholly at odds with *Trauerarbeit* in that it, unlike the latter, explores the immanent capabilities and infinite possibilities of *Trauer* itself, rather than being primarily driven by the aim of working through it in a supposedly "healthy" manner.[15] Driven by a "will to allegory," the *Trauerspiel* carves out the uncertain ground that is needed for play, that is, the unstable place where the mere 'stuff' of ruins and debris can, against all odds, be experienced as "speaking more impressively [*eindrucksvoller*]" and as "preserving the image of beauty to the very last."[16]

THE WORK OF ART IN THE AGE OF ITS TECHNOLOGICAL REPRODUCIBILITY (POSSIBILITY)

Many commentators have noted that Benjamin's interest in the Baroque penchant for the "petrified, primordial landscape" and all things "untimely, sorrowful, unsuccessful"[17] cannot be disentangled from the chaotic times that his generation had lived through no more than a couple of years earlier. Susan Buck-Morss, for instance, even goes as far as to claim that the *Trauerspiel* book needs to be read as a "response to the horrifying destructiveness of World War I." The *Trauerspiel*'s radicalized exploration of an uncertain connection between the hardships suffered in this world and the possibility of redemption in the next must have indeed taken on a shifted urgency for readers who, centuries later, had just come out on the losing end of the first industrialized war in the history of mankind. In many texts that are written around the same time as the "Artwork" essay, Benjamin describes his own generation as having had to undergo "from 1914 to 1918 . . . one of the most monstrous experiences in the history of the world [*eine der ungeheuersten Erfahrungen der Weltgeschichte*]" and the many parallels with the earlier statements from the *Trauerspiel* book are striking:

> [N]ever has experience been contradicted more thoroughly: strategic experi-
> ence has been contravened by positional warfare; economic experience, by the
> inflation; physical experience, by hunger; moral experiences, by the ruling
> powers. A generation that had gone to school in horse-drawn streetcars now
> stood in the open air, amid a landscape in which nothing was the same except
> the clouds and, at its center, in a force field of destructive torrents and explo-
> sions, the tiny, fragile human body. With this tremendous development of
> technology, a completely new poverty of the soul [*ganz neue Armseligkeit*] has
> descended on mankind. [18]

It is quite clearly with this bleak outlook on the world and history in mind that we have to understand Benjamin's above quoted, urgent reminder that "the representation of human beings by means of an apparatus has made possible a highly productive use of the human being's self-alienation." As Peter Osborne puts it, "it is the first world war which provides the traumatic background of Benjamin's culture theory, fascism its ultimate context."[19] Underlying this statement is indeed, first and foremost, the politically charged idea that what Benjamin calls the "apparatus" is structurally ambiva-lent, an ambiguity that is elsewhere reframed as the distinction between the (fascist) "first" and the (utopian and revolutionary) "second" technology.[20]

Taking the title of Benjamin's essay at face value means that this issue of the "productive use of the human being's self-alienation" should not be tack-led directly but through the analysis of the nature of technologically repro-duced artworks. Most relevant to our discussion, namely, is that Benjamin puts into place his famous distinction between the auratic original and its technological reproduction with the purpose of understanding how and why the latter can no longer be reduced to a mere reference to the former. Unlike a reproduction made by hand, that is to say, a technological reproduction dis-lodges the original that it refers to from its natural context of meaning: a technological reproduction "can bring out aspects of the original that are accessible only to the lens [and] . . . [it] can place the copy of the original in situations which the original itself cannot attain."[21] It is for this reason that the project that underlies the "Artwork" essay can be read as an extension of the one that inspired him to write the *Trauerspiel* book: Technological repro-duction ought to be understood as an allegorizing practice in that the result-ing copy acquires, on account of this fragmentation itself, a significance that it does not simply derive from the original. Anticipating the Derridean ac-count of the added, differential meaning that comes out of the dynamic of iterability, Benjamin makes the claim that a technological reproduction re-news the meaning of what is being reproduced in a puzzling and non-anticipatable manner: "By replicating the work many times over, it substitutes a mass existence for a unique existence. And in permitting the reproduction to reach the recipient in his or her own situation, it actualizes that which is reproduced [*aktualisiert sie das Reproduzierte*]."[22] It is, in other words, on account of the *difference* and not on account of the *similarity* between an original artwork on the one hand and its technological reproductions on the other that the latter become significant. Exploiting a form of contingency that lies at the heart of the relationship between an image and its meaning a copy can "actualize" a way of being that was dormant in the original but could not possibly have become present at its initial moment of creation.

On account of this actualization of what one could call an added meaning or "meaning-in-excess" (exhibition value), Benjamin claims that "the work of art becomes a construct [*Gebilde*] with quite new functions."[23] A firmer grasp on these "quite new functions" requires that we understand the nature of an artwork that is not merely technologically *re*produced, but technologically *produced*. This will not only bring us to the heart of Benjamin's views on the artistic use of photography and film, but it will just as well further our insight into the essential connections with the *Trauerspiel* book. In a crucial passage in the "Artwork" essay, Benjamin describes how the artistic use of the technological apparatus genuinely *produces* a *world*, rather than that it would merely *re*produce a *work*. "Our bars and city streets, our offices and furnished rooms, our railroad stations and our factories," writes Benjamin, "seemed to close relentlessly around us. Then came film and exploded this prison world with the dynamite of the split second, so that now we can set off calmly on journeys of adventure among its far-flung debris."[24] Like the *Trauerspiel*, in other words, a technologically produced artwork rids the world it indexes of its ultimate unity and internal coherence and for this reason provokes a sense of "self-alienation." However, with this same *Trauerspiel*, a technologically produced image of the world shares the capacity of somehow *overturning* this dynamics of fragmentation, thus evidencing that "self-alienation" is not a *merely* alienating process ("we can set off calmly on journeys of adventure"). According to Benjamin, that is, on account of this very assault on anything that is supposedly pure, authentic, or internally unified, a technologically produced image of the world presents a viewer with a mode of signification that, even though it had always already been part of the reproduced reality, could only be actualized in and through its image. It is this moment that allows technologically produced images to "recast" the surrounding world as a universe full of hitherto unforeseen possibilities, thus preparing the ground for play.

> On the one hand film furthers insight into the necessities governing our lives [*Zwangsläufigkeiten*] by its use of close-ups, by its accentuation of hidden details in familiar objects, and by its exploration of commonplace milieux

through the ingenious guidance of the camera: on the other hand, it manages to
assure us of a vast (strange) and unexpected room-for-play [*eines ungeheuren
und ungeahnten Spielraums uns zu versichern*].[25]

A technologically produced image of the world thus discovers an unexpected
layer of possibility within the very heart of what can otherwise only appear
as necessary and ineluctable. Its "vast (strange) and unexpected room-for-
play" renews from within our ordinary outlook on the world: It forces our
gaze to take in what is a fact (it furthers "insight into the necessities govern-
ing our lives"), but, more importantly, it re-opens it towards that which is
not. It is with the aim of highlighting the puzzling and disorienting nature of
this experience that Benjamin emphasizes that the newly created "room-for-
play" is *ungeheuer* (a German term that can be likened to the more common
term *unheimlich* ["uncanny"] and associatively connects with *nicht geheuer*
["suspect"]) and that it is "[c]learly *another* nature which speaks to the camera as compared to the eye."[26] From Benjamin's perspective, a technologically produced image of the world genuinely reproduces it, that is, it creates it
anew and thereby reveals its original and supposedly "natural" set-up to be
but one of its many possible instantiations.

As Miriam Bratu Hansen has suggested in her brilliant analysis of Benjamin's concept "room-for-play," it "names an intermediary zone not yet fully
determined in which things oscillate among different meanings, functions,
and possible directions. As such, it harbors an open-ended, dynamic temporality, an interval for chance, imagination and agency."[27] In what follows, we
will come back to the various connections with concepts like "mimetic repetition" and "bodily presence of mind," but what is important at this stage of
the discussion is that the sudden appearance of "room-for-play" does indeed
come together with the discovery of a utopian dimension within a work of
art. In the second version of the "Artwork" essay, Benjamin focuses on the
concept of a "second" technology, that is, an apparatus of which the "origin"
lies in play, and which is directed towards an "interplay [*Zusammenspiel*]
between nature and humanity" and not, as is the "first" technology, towards
the sheer "mastery" of the former by the latter.[28] In a footnote, he adds that
"[j]ust as a child who has learned to grasp stretches out its hand for the moon
as it would for a ball, so humanity . . . sets its sights as much on currently
utopian goals as on goals within reach. . . . Because this [second] technology
aims at liberating human beings from drudgery, the individual suddenly sees
his room-for-play [*Spielraum*] immeasurably expanded. He does not yet
know his way around this space. But already he registers his demands on
it."[29] This utopian dimension of a technologically produced image of the
world needs to be taken seriously (and literally) since Benjamin emphasizes
that the non-place such a technologically produced image constitutes is not at
all to be confused with mere semblance or illusion: "In film," rather, "the

element of semblance [*Schein*] has been entirely *displaced* by the element of play."[30] In an argument that runs parallel to Gilles Deleuze's later analysis of the concept of non-sense [*nonsense*], Benjamin suggests that the non-reality of the technologically produced image (it is, after all, an image) is not at all antithetical to its capacity to indicate a reality. For Benjamin, on the contrary, it is only when the technological apparatus creates "ordinary" reality anew *as an image* that it can reveal what is, in fact, most real to that reality: the presence of the (virtual) possibilities that were not in fact acted upon but that nevertheless subsist in and through the image. Similar to how, according to Deleuze, "what is *saying* its own sense can only be *nonsense*," the very *non*-reality of such images (their being nothing less than *ungeheuer*) can become sign and token of their *reality*: "The equipment-free aspect of reality has here become the height of artifice, and the vision of immediate reality the Blue Flower (Novalis's term to denote the highest object of imagination, ss) in the land of technology."[31] This somewhat puzzling argument can best be illustrated by way of Benjamin's concept of the "optical unconscious." Revealing the presence of elements that belong to the world but can only be grasped in and by its technologically produced image, the camera allows for "a space informed by human consciousness [to] give way to a space informed by the unconscious."[32] Such an unconscious proper to the apparatus itself is in the first place a reservoir of all things seemingly irrelevant and non-noteworthy in daily life, having escaped from our conscious attention and natural perception: "We are familiar with the movement of picking up a cigarette lighter of a spoon, but know almost nothing of what really goes on between hand and metal, and still less how this varies with different moods. This is where the camera comes into play, with all its resources for swooping and rising, disrupting and isolating, stretching or compressing a sequence, enlarging or reducing an object."[33] The argument is the same as the one that underlies Benjamin's essay on Proust: It is on account of the very *non*-reality of an artwork that it can disclose a "Penelope work of forgetting"[34] and "actualize"[35] a past that could not in fact have become fully actual in ordinary life. In this manner, a seemingly most insignificant part of reality (Marcel's "taste of the little madeleine on Sunday mornings in Combray," Benjamin's "what really goes on between hand and metal") comes back as a "dewy fresh 'instant'"[36] in a medium that is, itself, nevertheless experienced as *non*-real (a literary text, an image). A technologically produced image of the world does not bring back a part of reality *because* it is meaningful, any more than the *mémoire involontaire* does, but it is, rather, the other way around: In and through a technologically produced image, bits and pieces of a seemingly trivial reality *become* meaningful because they, against all possible odds, resurface again. In this way, a technologically produced image of the world acquires the same "rejuvenating force" [*verjüngenden Kraft*][37] that marks the *mémoire involontaire*, confronting us with the fact that what is real always and necessarily exceeds what is being actualized. [38]

From the very first pages of the essay onwards, Benjamin is uncharacteristically clear about the political agenda that motivates his theses on technological (re)production: they are "completely useless for the purposes of fascism . . . [but] useful for the formulation of revolutionary demands in the politics of art [*Kunstpolitik*]." [39] To give this statement its proper weight, what has been said about technological (re)production needs to be connected to the issue of a "productive" use of "self-alienation." Throughout his writings of the mid-1930s, Benjamin defines the *Armseligkeit* or *Erfahrungsarmut* ("poverty of experience") of his generation most consistently as the failure to "embed" events into "the great inscrutable course of the world" [40] and align the "individual past" with the "collective" one. [41] "It is as if," writes Benjamin, "a capability [*Vermögen*] that seemed inalienable to us, the securest among our possessions, has been taken from us: the ability to share experiences." [42] Underlying the "Artwork" essay, I would suggest, is the idea that a "productive" use of "self-alienation" entails that what seems to be a mere *in*capability (*Armseligkeit, Erfahrungsarmut*) can be transformed into what we would like to call a "negative" capability. With this, I mean that what appears to be nothing but a privative "*im*potentiality to" can and should in fact be made visible as a "potentiality *to-not*": The *in*ability "to share experience," that is to say, needs in truth to be understood as the very precondition for a sustained ability *to-not* fall victim to the allure of deeply ambivalent ideals like "purity," "unification," or "naturalness." For, it is of course no mere coincidence that the vocabulary that Benjamin takes recourse to for his descriptions of the experience that in his mind "has fallen in value . . . may fall into bottomlessness" [43] was in fact, in the mid-1930s, more enthusiastically deployed than ever before: One by one, values like a feeling for the "great inscrutable course of the world" and an "amalgamation" of the individual and the collective past [44] had ceased to be part and parcel of what Benjamin calls "wisdom" and had been tainted by the reactionary, pseudoromantic rhetoric of fascism. For this reason, Benjamin emphasizes that the claim that his generation is "poor in experience" does not indicate that it would be merely "ignorant or inexperienced" and he describes it as an excess rather than as a lack: the members of his generation have "'devoured' everything, both 'culture and people,' and they have had such a surfeit that it has exhausted them." [45] The most problematic element of the *Armseligkeit* or *Erfahrungsarmut* that Benjamin diagnoses is, as a consequence, that it prepares the ground for an ideologically motivated revitalization of the aura, that is, for an "*aestheticizing of politics*" that appeals to an immediate connection between the individual and the collective and the supposedly fated temporality of an objective spirit. [46] "Tiredness," he writes, "is followed by sleep, and then it is not uncommon for a dream to make up for the sadness and discouragement of the day—a dream that shows us in its realized form the simple but magnificent existence for which the energy is lacking in reality."[47] As Susan Buck-Morss brilliantly puts it, what matters most to the Benjamin of the 1930s is the transformation of this (fascist) *an*aesthetics into a (revolutionary) aesthetics, whereby the former denotes "a viewing of the 'scene' with disinterested pleasure, even when that scene is the preparation through ritual of a whole society for unquestioning sacrifice and ultimately, destruction, murder, and death."[48]

CONCLUSION

The stakes of Benjamin's "Artwork" essay are to describe the technological apparatus as a means to awaken the masses from this most recent instantiation of a "dogmatic slumber" and thereby, as he puts it elsewhere, "to win the energies of intoxication for the revolution."[49] Taking Benjamin's plea for a "new, positive form of barbarism" seriously means therefore, in the first place, to exploit the structural ambivalence of the technological apparatus and to use the very means that have helped put a collective to sleep as the tool to re-awaken it. The technological apparatus can thus, with and through the non-real space that is its own, be discovered as a "training instrument" [*Übungsinstrument*][50] for the ability *to-not* respond to anything that is pregnant with the merely illusionary, dreamlike qualities of the aura ("authenticity," "unification," the "unique apparition of a distance, however near it may be," an "undulating life").[51] It is only when *Armseligkeit* and *Erfahrungsarmut* can become visible as such "potentialities *to-not*" that human beings can learn how to discover meaning *within* the very heart of what is fragmented and incomplete and to construct a sustained responsiveness to what is, despite all, still in change and not-(yet-)actual.

NOTES

1. Walter Benjamin, *Selected Writings, Volume 3*, eds. Michael W. Jennings, Marcus Bullock, Howard Eiland, and Gary Smith (Cambridge: The Belknap Press of Harvard University Press, 1999–2004), 113; in German, Walter Benjamin, *Gesammelte Schriften VII*, eds. Rolf Tiedemann and Hermann Schweppenhäuser (Frankfurt am Main: Suhrkamp Verlag, 1991), 369. O will stand for *The Origin of German Tragic Drama*, transl. John Osborne (London: Verso, 2003). AP will stand for *The Arcades Project*, transl. Howard Eiland and Kevin McLaughlin (Cambridge: The Belknap Press of Harvard University Press, 2004).

2. Walter Benjamin, *The Origin of German Tragic Drama*, transl. John Osborne (London: Verso, 2003), 140; *Gesammelte Schriften*, I-1, 319.

3. Ibid., 140; ibid., I-1, 319.

4. Benjamin, *Origin*, 66.

5. Ibid., 81.

6. Benjamin, *Origin*, 232; *Gesammelte Schriften* I, 406.

7. In an important passage in the *Trauerspiel* book, Benjamin defends the view that the Spanish baroque (and Calderón in specific) was "superior" to the German *Trauerspiel* in this

regard and that it, on account of "[t]he very precision with which the mourning and the play can harmonize with one another" takes on "exemplary validity." "Nowhere but in Calderón," writes Benjamin for this reason, "could the perfect form of the baroque *Trauerspiel* be studied." The explanation for this is that the Spanish "play of mourning" oftentimes resolve "the conflicts of a state of creation without grace . . . by a kind of playful reduction, within the sphere of the court, whose king proves to be a secularized redemptive power," whereas its German counterpart is marked by a "rash flight into a nature deprived of grace." Benjamin, *Origin*, 81. Nevertheless, Benjamin makes quite clear that, though "this element of play is not unfolded with the brilliance of the Spanish drama . . . [i]t does however have the motif." Ibid., 82.

8. Ibid., 175.

9. Ibid., 141; *Gesammelte Schriften* I, 320.

10. The reference to "ability to respond" is borrowed from Samuel Weber, "Introduction," in *Theatricality as Medium* (New York: Fordham University Press, 2004), 29. For a brilliant analysis of the stakes of this discussion, see Samuel Weber, "Storming the Work: Allegory and Theatricality in Benjamin's *Origin of the German Mourning Play*" in *Theatricality as Medium* (New York: Fordham University Press, 2004), 160–80, primarily 168–78, where Weber focuses on the *Trauerspiel*'s "lack of symbolic immanence" which "opens the theatrical site to a potentially endless, if by no means simply arbitrary, series of possible allegorical interpretations, which in turn call into question the stage itself" (176).

11. Benjamin, *Origin*, 92.

12. Ibid., 139.

13. Ibid., 140.

14. Ibid., 81.

15. See Martin Jay, "Against Consolation: Walter Benjamin and the Refusal to Mourn," in *Refractions of Violence* (New York: Routledge, 2003), 11–24, especially 15–16. For the same distinction between *Trauerspiel* and *Trauerarbeit* in the context of a discussion of the work of Friedrich Hölderlin, see Philippe Lacoue-Labarthe, "The Caesura of the Speculative," in *Typography: Mimesis, Philosophy, Politics*, ed. Christopher Fynsk (Stanford: Stanford University Press, 1998), 208–35, especially 234–35. The description of a "disarticulation of the work" and the reference to the transition of a "*melodic* conception of the work to a *rhythmic* one" in which it is prevented "from carrying along its representations exclusively in one sense or another" will have an implicit relevance to our discussion of Benjamin's interpretation of the concept of rhythm in some of the following pages.

16. Benjamin, *Origin*, 235; *Gesammelte Schriften* I, 409.

17. Benjamin, *Origin*, 166.

18. Benjamin, *Selected Writings: Volume 2*, 731–32; *Gesammelte Schriften* II-1, 214 (translation modified).

19. Peter Osborne, quoted in Martin Jay, "Against Consolation: Walter Benjamin and the Refusal to Mourn," 224.

20. Benjamin, *Selected Writings: Volume 3*, 107.

21. Ibid., 103.

22. Ibid., 104; *Gesammelte Schriften* VII, 353.

23. Ibid., 107.

24. Ibid., 117.

25. Ibid., 117; *Gesammelte Schriften* VII, 375–76 (translation modified).

26. Ibid., 117 (my emphasis).

27. Miriam Bratu Hansen, "Room for Play: Benjamin's Gamble with the Cinema," *October*, no. 109 (Summer 2004), 3–45.

28. Benjamin, *Selected Writings: Volume 3*, 107.

29. Ibid., 124 (translation modified).

30. Ibid., 127 (my emphasis).

31. Ibid., 115.

32. Ibid., 117.

33. Ibid., 117.

34. Benjamin, *Selected Writings: Volume 2*, 238.

35. Ibid., 244.

36. Ibid.

37. Ibid.

38. See also Howard Caygill's description of the optical unconscious as a "possibility of creating an openness to the future" in his *Walter Benjamin. The Colour of Experience* (London: Routledge, 1998), 94. See also Miriam Bratu Hansen, *Cinema and Experience* (Berkeley: University of California Press), 155–62. The reference to the word "rejuvenating" when denoting an experience of the reality of what is not(-yet-)actualized is revelatory given Benjamin's earlier analysis of a "metaphysics" that is specific to youth. In both his essay with the same name, written in 1913-1914 and "The Life of Students" (1914-1915), Benjamin connects the unique existential dimension of youth with an "interval" in the flow of time and an accompanying "birth of immortal time" (*Selected Writings: Volume 1*, 12), "transformation" or "unceasing spiritual revolution" (ibid., 43). With words that refer forward to his later philosophy of history and the concepts of "interruption" and "now-time" [*Jetztzeit*], Benjamin understands the "youthful" experience of a given moment as one in which the "present that has been eternally will come again" [*die ewig gewesene Gegenwart wird wieder werden*] (ibid., 8; *Gesammelte Schriften* II, 93): what is youthful is thus both "filled with the being of our fathers and ancestors" (ibid., 6) and "laden with future" (ibid., 10). See also Howard Eiland and Michael W. Jennings, *Walter Benjamin: A Critical Life* (Cambridge: Harvard University Press, 2014), 43–60. And, for a further development of this argument, my own "The Ability to Not-Shine. The Word "Unscheinbar" in the Writings of Walter Benjamin," *Angelaki: Journal of the Theoretical Humanities*, Vol. 18, No. 4 (2013): 101–23.

39. Benjamin, *Selected Writings: Volume 3*, 102; *Gesammelte Schriften* VII, 350.

40. Benjamin, *Selected Writings: Volume 3*, 153.

41. Benjamin, *Selected Writings: Volume 4*, 316.

42. Benjamin, *Selected Writings: Volume 3*, 143; *Gesammelte Schriften* II, 439)

43. Benjamin, *Selected Writings: Volume 3*, 143.

44. Benjamin, *Selected Writings: Volume 4*, 316.

45. Benjamin, *Selected Writings: Volume 2* 734.

46. Benjamin, *Selected Writings: Volume 3*, 122.

47. Benjamin, *Selected Writings: Volume 2*, 734.

48. Susan Buck-Morss, "Aesthetics and Anaesthetics: Walter Benjamin's Artwork Essay Reconsidered," *October*, Vol. 62 (Autumn 1992): 39.

49. Benjamin, *Selected Writings: Volume 2*, 215.

50. Benjamin, *Selected Writings: Volume 3*, 120; *Gesammelte Schriften* VII, 381.

51. Benjamin, *Selected Writings: Volume 2*, 104–05; *Gesammelte Schriften* I, 340.

Chapter Eight

The Composer as Producer

Joseph Weiss

Music says We immediately,
regardless of its intentions.
—Anonymous music critic

By now, it has become second nature to assume that the desire to determine the truth or falsehood of a work of art is a relic from the bygone years of modernism.[1] Who could disagree with Arthur Danto's Hegelian declaration that, in the post-historical world, *theory* (i.e., that which apparently stands above sensuous or material embodiment) is now the primary factor in the production and reception of artworks?[2] Any appeal to the capacity to discriminate between truth and falsehood, the correlate of which finds expression in the antiquated political categories of true and false consciousness, revolutionary versus reactionary *praxis*, becomes downright comical by virtue of seemingly maintaining what Hegel called the "ludicrous contrast between its own opinion of itself and its immediate existence."[3] Perhaps this decline in the politics of art was always latent within the matter itself. Perhaps, in other words, we can in retrospect see that the full development of the historical process, in which there is no longer anything new under the sun, was secretly playing itself out from the start. After Dadaism and, later, Warhol's pop art, the joke that calls out the lack of culture in the elite culture of the art world appears to be a first hint of the fact that subjective intention, the abstract game of mere discourse, was, in reality, the condition for the possibility of baselessly deeming certain art objects praiseworthy or true.[4] If everything is really that arbitrary, then, despite many of the radical claims of twentieth-century experimental and avant-garde artists, the truth of their practice would simply consist in pointing out the burgeoning knowledge that there is no longer any basis for the truth claims of aesthetic judgment.[5] In short, this would mean that Walter Benjamin's claim that *the technically most advanced artwork is also, of necessity, the politically most advanced artwork,*[6] no longer holds for us, or can no longer serve as the basis for determining the truth of artworks. From this perspective, we must count Benjamin's claim among those same naïve artifacts of a bygone era, and declare our unwavering commitment to historicism.[7] Especially after the failures of the anti-capitalist movements of the early and mid-twentieth century, searching for the links between the formal or technical structuring of aesthetic material and the political promise of new modes of human organization seems to be an increasingly untenable or misguided task.

Well before John Cage's famous *4'33"*, which has, of course, often been compared to works like Duchamp's anti-art *Fountain*, Benjamin seems to have, in fact, detected something of this historical trajectory towards the "anything goes" relativism of the post-modern world.[8] In his essay from 1934, entitled "The Author as Producer," he maintains, for example, that the caption alongside the photograph becomes as important, if not more important, than the content presented.[9] Against his own intention of discovering artistic practices that, without descending to propaganda, were dedicated to the socialist revolution, it is as if Benjamin sensed the impending dissolution of so-called tendentious (*Tendenz*) aesthetics before it actually occurred.[10] In place of this aesthetics, which calls into question the producer's role *in* the process, his or her material support or resistance to the reproduction of coercive social relations, an explanatory model built on the groundless play of endlessly fluctuating post-modern subject-positions gradually took precedence. The desire for alternatives, for the qualitatively new, was no longer explained as the collective social labor that is stored up and objectively impinging upon the *sensus communis,*[11] the "We" that waits to be unleashed in the technical struggle against the stultifying forms of atomized, fetishistic (aesthetic) production. Rather, it became a simple manifestation of the abstract attitude or spirit of the idiosyncratic artist,[12] whose separation from the narrow category of class is seen as a strength.

This prioritization of spirit (*Geist*), which, to state it more directly, allegedly bears no essential relation to the real apparatus within which art and politics are produced, at first glance seems to be especially at play in that artistic medium whose social and political significance has always been the most difficult to pin down. Moreover, of the various artistic media, this one in particular appears to exhibit the least egalitarian tendencies, or it appears to require the greatest degree of specialization. I am speaking, of course, of music. If one is not initiated, not schooled in its idiom, history, and technique, it seems that one is almost certain to miss the nuances of its expression. Probably sensing something of a potential elitism, Benjamin went so far as to claim that, in keeping with the need to have photo captions produced from out of the workers' own self-activity, both the listener and performer of revolutionary music now require the power of the word, that is, language or lyrics, in order to truly instigate a politics that might go beyond subservience to the paid experts of the bureaucratic state.[13] We thus see why Benjamin likely focused on the radical character of the musical collaboration between Eisler and Brecht,[14] instead of, for instance, addressing the primarily instrumental innovations already abundantly present in Schoenberg's free atonality and serialism from the same historical period. Although it parallels his famous hope that collective production processes might be opened up with the advent of film,[15] this choice to prioritize the word is especially interesting given that Schoenberg explicitly highlighted an affinity between composing and another practice that Benjamin repeatedly counted amongst the constituents of modern disenchantment, namely gambling.[16]

However we gauge the success or failure of Benjamin's emphasis, the specific form of his challenge was not the only way to question the insulated, self-perpetuating knowledge administered by critics and artists with a vested interest in either restoring or perpetuating the crisis-ridden social relations that constitute the status quo.[17] Notwithstanding his connection with, as I have suggested, the coming historicism of post-modern capitalism, it is arguably John Cage, above all others, who most successfully challenged the conventional forms of musical production in the mid-twentieth century.

Let us, accordingly, play the role of the comic critic, who ludicrously supports the lost cause and attempts to seize the truth, for a moment. If we take Benjamin's claim about the most advanced artistic technique (*Technik*) corresponding to the most advanced politics and apply this criterion for determining the truth content (*Wahrheitsgehalt*)[18] of artworks to some of the more striking technical innovations of experimental music from this same period, then I maintain we will glean the as yet unfulfilled promise at work in the attempts of the mid-twentieth century to radicalize music. As opposed to the narrative of the "hack writer"[19] who all too conveniently pledges allegiance to the de-politicized, bourgeois space from which art of the post-historical world is destined to ineffectually express itself, I aim to prove that this promise set in motion in the 1930s and 1940s continues to encroach upon the activity of those concerned with driving the technical possibilities of musical production to their outermost (political) extreme. To be more specific, I will argue that, from Cage's early theory and practice on both the incorporation of city-scape noise and improvisational techniques to the insights of his contemporary, Pierre Schaeffer, concerning how *musique concrète* or the "sonorous object" is causally dissociated from its sound source, one historically dominant impulse in particular comes to the fore. Instead of the wanton celebration of the supposedly equally valid musical possibilities to which I have alluded, the experimentation of this period was guided by the desire to release music from the false projections, egoism, or abstract impositions of the Western tradition. Just as in the same crisis period

Edmund Husserl was compelled to critique the "natural standpoint" that unwittingly projects a theoretical gaze upon the pure appearing of the appearances,[20] Cage and Schaeffer attempted to get "back to the matter at hand" by, as Schaeffer put it, achieving "direct contact with the sound material."[21] After examining some of the most provocative contributions of these two musicians, we will come to see that the contemporary failure to fully play out the latent implications of their experiments is, in the final analysis, grounded in our inability to recognize that the technical organization of sound becomes stunted, as is it were, when it is not compelled to take up what Benjamin suggested all along. It becomes stunted, that is, when we fail to recognize that the truth of the work is indissolubly bound up with the degree to which the author has become producer, or in case of music, the degree to which the production and organization of sound—in short, its technology—has begun to rupture the fetishized individualism of the current process, the uni-directional causality from which it allegedly springs. The audience must, in a word, become producer.

LOCATING THE TRUTH OF TECHNICALLY REPRODUCED MUSIC

As we unpack what, on the face of it, must appear to be a rather audacious claim about the truth of musical production, it is helpful to note that the old Marxist category of the forces of production retains its critical potency. It is virtually impossible, for example, to contest the fact that the transformations in aural perception parallel the transformations in visual perception, both of which are based, as Benjamin famously argued, on the decline in the "aura."[22] The technical reproduction of the image and the possibility of employing photomontage, slow and fast motion, splicing, etc., cannot be dissociated from the material nexus within which the radio broadcast and the sound studio emerge. Importantly, the "original" or "authentic" version of visual and sound objects are, only at this historical hour, first called into question. It is clear, then, why in his later writings Schaeffer emphasized the Pythagorean endeavor of giving lectures to his students from behind a curtain in order to best enable learning.[23] Just as with his *epoché* Husserl bracketed spatio-temporal or mathematical coordinates when attempting to capture the essential structures of cognition,[24] Schaeffer contended that once the visual drops out of the perception process (i.e., once the performers on stage need not stand over and against the audience, and explicitly unveiling the causal link between each note and its instrument need not dominate the listening process), the "in-itself-ness" or "pure texture" of the sound can be isolated in a new way.[25] Prior to this technical possibility of reproducing found-sounds electronically, we simply fail to realize the extent to which the visual always intrudes upon our musical perception. The child who mistakenly hears three separate instruments in the multi-layered texture of a solo violin cadenza is closer to the "sonorous object" than the specialist who hears the sound by visually connecting it to the fingering. Despite at a later point in his development renouncing the last vestiges of what might be called Schaeffer's transcendental idealism (i.e., renouncing the comportment that scientistically seeks to grasp the "pure," *a priori* sound), Cage continued to be guided by a desire similar to that of Schaeffer's. As Branden Joseph has suggested, there is a clear similarity between Benjamin's conception of "distraction" (*Zerstreuung*) or "absent-minded" viewing and Cage's hope to instill the ability to "hear music," instead of "understand[ing]" it.[26] This similarity follows the same logic as the attempt to dislodge sound from the causal misunderstandings of visual projection. Cage's futurist call to incorporate "oscillators, turntables, generators, [and] means for amplifying small sounds,"[27] already on display in his 1939 work, *Imaginary Landscape No. 1*, is thus part of the attempt to train the ear to listen to the entire field of sound within which we are already experientially immersed.

In a wonderfully ambiguous formulation that echoes with this attempt to call a halt to the abstractions that cloud the concrete experience of sound, Cage asks, "[w]hy is this so necessary that sounds should be *just* sounds?"[28] The justice of the sounds, their political and technical truth, paradoxically relates to how they are just mere sounds, in contrast to being, as Cage continues, "burdened by psychological intentions."[29] Here, while attempting to bridge the gap between life and music, Cage might as well have been Schaeffer. Yet, both "sound engineers"[30] seem to wholly discard Benjamin's politics of production on this occasion. Their task once again appears to be Husserlian in nature. In Schaeffer's terms, they were now guided by the attempt to capture the "reality of the sound as such, as distinguished from the modes of its production."[31] Expressed differently, "deny[ing] cultural conditioning"[32] is allegedly the condition under which the original confines of music are exploded. And this practice, paralleling the consequences of the downfall of the cultic stage of art,[33] first opens up what Schaeffer calls the "direct montage" of experimentation.[34] Because the chiming bells are removed from their identity as bells, the train engine from its identity as a train engine, "imperceptible improvisations of chance,"[35] outside of anticipation or outside of the search for prescribed rhythmic and harmonic patterns, inevitably come to the surface when reproduced, reassembled, and meshed together in the studio. Soon, in a stroke of good fortune, the composer will discover that, like the affinity between a whistling refrigerator and the chirping song of crickets (*Grillen*),[36] the surge of electric static is indistinguishable from the ocean's crashing waves. The line between nature and history, nature and culture, begins to blur.

If, along these lines, resisting subjective intention while also upsetting the boundary between "nature" and the simulacrum becomes all the more pronounced in the age of technical reproduction, then we are but a short step from underscoring the indispensability of the chance operations, aleatory procedures, or indeterminate compositions that historically followed from these initial gestures. Chance—the gamble—is in music presumably the moment of humility, of resigning oneself before the impossibility of completely mastering the material that, from this period onward, includes the noise of the "explosive motor, wind, heartbeat, and landslide."[37] Despite living in the era where all that is solid has melted into air, where, in other words, every sound could now be part of the game (*Spiel*) of real-time improvisation, we continue to neglect the potential musicality of the concrete objects of our everyday environment. Think of the ease with which we frantically plug into the constant beat of an always-at-hand, 4/4 time, the ease with which we accept the pre-digested melodies of the latest icon, however "underground" he or she may appear. Is this not the source of the rigid dichotomy between "music" and "nature," between the sounds of the city-scape and the nature-scape? Pumped into every waiting room and every supermarket, constantly streaming, no matter the occasion, from every set of headphones and every living room stereo, who could deny just how much the neatly packaged hits drown out the noise of experience, the song of nature-history (*Naturges-chichte*), especially when a genuine chance for silence, for a deep pause of breath (*Atem holen*),[38] presents itself? In the era of omnipresent kitsch, the discipline of clock time, posing as music, recapitulates the uniform rhythm of the heartbeat. This doubles the creaturely existence from which humans allegedly escaped.[39] It is as though Schiller's play-drive (*Spieltrieb*) were in truth designed to carry out brutally, in the words of one left-wing author, the "reactive transformation of physical displeasure into secondary pleasure, without [anyone] noticing that the contraband of *praxis* has slipped into it."[40] In passively adapting, then, to the temporality of forced labor while also failing to heed Benjamin's insight that hoping for "new masterpieces" that appeal to the "long-since-counterfeit wealth of the creative personality" is a "privilege of fascism,"[41] we continue to pay tribute to the composer *as artist*, instead of the composer *as producer*. In a world where the tenuous bond between capitalism and democracy is rapidly disintegrating, should we not, accordingly, assume that preserving the long-since-antiquated specialization of the artist marks the ascendance of something even worse than the fascism of the previous century?

Denying these political implications, which are always indexed in music, would be akin to pretending that the ebb and flow of passing trains, the deep bass that rises and subsides, the grinding gears and high-pitched screeching that jar the body and echo through the "landscape of the future"[42] like a distant chainsaw, have not radically altered the attunement of every human being. Should we really pretend that this cacophony of electrically powered embodiment, of being in an urban soundscape whose circuits are jammed and thus cry out for interruption (*Unterbrechung*), is not precisely that which, through our collective disavowal, propels the unspeakable boredom of the present? Should we maintain, in other words, that better or worse confrontations with this state of affairs are impossible to distinguish, that the mimesis of the petroleum that runs through our veins is doomed to join the chorus that diverts attention from the screams accompanying the overflowing currents of misappropriated energy? Should we, moreover, go on declaring confidently that this state of affairs does not present the latent possibility of technically unleashing something far more profound, or better, far more silent, than the monotony perpetually offered up by a society hopelessly devoid of music?

To say nothing, then, of the historically based dissociation between sound and instrument, it is no surprise that, from the start, Cage implicitly connected the chance operations that rupture our pre-digested listening[43] to that which resists the stupidity of still believing in the artist as the fetishized creator whose genius is the sole source of sound. Already in his 1934 essay, "Counterpoint," this illusion was a central object of his attack. The appearance of a univocal causality that would somehow spring from the isolated individual, instead of the nexus of *frustrated* social labor, became all the more preposterous. Cage thus succinctly expressed his desire for the new when he insisted that a "period of Music, not [of] Musicians"[44] was needed. Soon thereafter, resonating once more with Benjamin, Cage asserted that, following medieval practice, we are in need of *anonymous* producers[45] in order to highlight just how much music is, in truth, not in the least based on the cowardly myopic lens of private property.

And yet, even if this theory and its attendant practices are, as should now be evident, inextricably tied to a certain type of politics, the question of how far this politics goes persists for critical consciousness. Do the progressive tendencies outweigh the reactionary elements, or, as we have suggested, is there something at work in these composers that nonetheless points to the coming de-politicization of the post-modern world? As a perceptive critic explained some time ago,

> [t]here is an echo of that ideology [concerning noble sounds] in the credo that the raw material, the note in itself, is more than simply just there and actually enjoys a real existence. If this ideology is eradicated from the whole conception, then nothing remains of the much-vaunted material to which the composer submits, except for natural, physical qualities. As such, however, they are pre-artistic, crudely factual and incapable of guaranteeing anything of aesthetic worth. Whatever one does, one does it falsely [*falsch*]. The first task is to establish consciousness of the *aporia* [*Bewußtsein der Aporie*]. Schoenberg's dictum, "Indeed, and do they actually compose with [the twelve-tone technique]?" opens the door to the abuse of operating with the twelve notes as if

they still belonged within the scheme of tonality. But the hypothesis that the note "exists" rather than 'functions' is either ideological or else misplaced positivism. Cage, for example, perhaps because of his involvement with Zen Buddhism, appears to ascribe metaphysical powers to the note once it has been liberated from all supposed superstructural baggage. This destruction of the superstructure is conceived along natural-scientific lines [*naturwissenschaftlich*], in the sense that either the tone's basic acoustic material is scooped out from it, or else the composer relies on chance, placing his trust in probability theory.[46]

Behind this analysis, we detect the false choice between an antiquated positivism and the pre-artistic primitivism of new age mysticism,[47] both of which are guided by the ideology of false immediacy, the illusion of direct access to the material. Schaeffer and Cage respectively fail to recognize, in other words, that the need propelling the withdrawal from the "bad" superstructure is itself guided, in part, by that very superstructure. Were it otherwise, experimental music would simply flail aimlessly, it would be a blooming buzzing confusion that, speaking to no one, schematizing nothing, can only muster contentless abstractions concerning mere existence. Whether one is compelled to seize that elusive, tension-filled moment of musical expression, or that elusive moment that critiques expression by syncopating or withholding the expectation of it, some conceptual orientation, some technique (*Technik*), must enter into the process at the opportune moment, if the music is to avoid ringing hollow, avoid losing at the odds that are already stacked against it. The difficulty is that, today more than ever, hyper-reproduction seems to indicate that determining the truth-content of these minute moments—intimately related, among other factors, to what Schoenberg called the "right solutions"[48] —is virtually impossible.

With a similar problematic in mind, Schaeffer insisted that the sonorous object is neither "the instrument that was played," nor the magnetic tape.[49] Devoid of a determinate source, the sonorous object appears to exist, on the contrary, in a kind of "no-man's land."[50] At the precise historical moment when it is first possible to transpose one transposition into another transposition *ad infinitum*, the composer is forced to admit that there are diverse sonorous objects within each sonorous object, or that every sonorous object is *"contained entirely in our perceptive consciousness."*[51] Here the implication is that, while the phenomenological turn no doubt increases an appreciation for the perspectivism involved in apprehending the shifting cluster of sound textures (i.e., the indeterminate angle from which one might fixate on the upper or lower pitch of each tone), it simultaneously appears to inaugurate a limitless range of equally valid interpretations. The indetermination of consciousness now apparently mirrors the indetermination of the technically reproduced sound, especially when the once-solid touchstone of a material substrate—the tape, the instrument, or the individual—has ostensibly lapsed into so much fodder for the caprice of the virtual world. Even though these sound objects are, in Schaeffer's estimation, communicable like any other form of knowledge,[52] today's hyperreal world[53] leaves us wondering what might pull this ethereal music back from the abyss of bourgeois relativism, or more accurately, what might drive it through the abyss, so that it can at last shed its semblance of political neutrality.

We can, in my view, begin to resolve this problem of a reproducibility that arguably signals the post-historical idealism of the present by once again asking, in another variation on a Benjaminian theme, how the sound material is, despite Schaeffer's protestation, connected to the process of production.[54] This time, if we take notice of the fact that the mythology of a pure or singular origin has justifiably lost its substantiality, one answer in particular strikes the listener. I am referring to how the clang (*Klang*) of the sound material is, indeed, bound up with the thwarted possibilities of our collective labor; how the unfulfilled lament (*Klage*) of the past echoes in each "object" that has been produced by the ever-swelling aggregation of our combined effort. Despite and because of the technical variations it undergoes, the trace of labor, all of its unfulfilled hope, is detectable in both the sound itself and the means of capturing that sound. Hence, even if it is the case that, as our above critic suggests, Cage and Schaeffer all too quickly spurn the moment of ego strength, of subjective mediation—both of which are also, incidentally, products of millennia of combined energy—Cage seems to have nonetheless chanced upon this essential relation between music and the collective production process. As early as 1937, he maintains that, "[a]s soon as . . . methods are crystallized into one or several widely accepted methods, the means will exist for group improvisations of unwritten but culturally important music."[55] It is, first and foremost, *group* improvisation that speaks to the promise of technology (*Technik*) and politics coalescing in revolutionary practice. For, on the one hand, this potential for a crystallized method is nothing other than the possibility that the congealed apparatus, the technical machinery that is our stored up, dead-labor, might be turned against the momentum of history and thus finally employed in the task of responding to the needs (*Not*) of living-labor. In other words, this method either fulfills or betrays the struggles, the grievance (*Klage*) of our forebears, it either recognizes or disavows that, in truth, *nature appears as history mediated to the extreme*, just as *history appears as nature mediated to the extreme*,[56] and, therefore, *praxis*, understood as a form of technical reproduction, remains as proportionally open today as it is alleged to be closed by the prognosticators of doom, the apologists for the contingent relations of production. On the other hand—and this may be an expression of the same historical need weighing down on both musical and political methodology (i.e., the same historical need working towards the organization of the *right* solutions), giving voice to the expressionless suffering of nature—on the other hand, improvisation continues to preserve the weak (*schwache*) possibility of tearing down the barriers of convention, of hoping amidst hopelessness, resisting the irrational rationality of total calculation, especially when the domination or mastery that it seeks to assuage is challenged through a process of discovering just how much each individual (sound) is inexorably bound to the collective (sound).

Of course, this importance attributed to collective practice also lends support to the fact that a technique of (musical) production divorced from political content is, at bottom, a hypostatization.[57] Such a notion perpetuates the fetish of progress by forgetting that technology is always a means, and only functions well if it functions at a specified task, rather than realizing the empty abstraction of "efficiency," "complexity," or production for the sake of production. In this respect, the stunted form of the current sociopolitical condition is expressed ideologically in a phenomenological and aesthetic discourse that to this day denies the radical anti-capitalist impulses that necessarily return when the crisis conditions that first produce such a restorative, or "back to" alternative are perpetuated. This does not mean, however, that the shortcoming of past and present discourse, past and present art, consists in a lack of commitment to the "revolutionary cause," or a failure to state directly its collectivist political intentions. Benjamin, on the contrary, teaches us that these collective impulses are immanent to the material, or better, immanently waiting to be seized by the real transformation of the technical means of production. The more frantically they are denied or physically blocked from fulfillment, the more they fester, and the more obvious it therefore becomes that radical alterations to the modes of (aesthetic) production are still possible. We might, accordingly, follow Benjamin and say that, "by dint of a secret heliotropism" (i.e., by dint of the "real movement" of communism[58]), each sound is the resonance of a past labor that, regardless of its intention, strives "toward that sun which is rising in the sky of history."[59] The infant's first cry, the squealing that rings out from the productive consumption of animal genocide, the hissing currents flowing through colossal hydroelectric dams and monstrous nuclear power plants, the electric hum of swarming insects that blends with the buzzing of industrial engines—each of these moments help to form the literal and figurative musical spine, the underlying drone of our stored up energy, whose historical tensions have yet to be tapped, yet to be rechanneled in the revolutionary practice of group improvisation.

In this way, we can see that, precisely when we put the emphasis back on the shifting possibilities of the production process, the technically most advanced work *must*, indeed, also be the politically most advanced work. For a technology that is actually capable of keeping open the moment of chance, playing at or tweaking the collective tensions of the sound material, driving them to their logical extreme, to the point at which something genuinely new or unforeseen emerges, is a technology that has, in truth, already pointed to and inaugurated an advanced form of politics. Seizing control of the forces of production, that is, the collective social labor congealed as technology, is, in other words, synonymous with reorganizing technology politically, collectively. [60] The one implies the other, or rather, the one could not occur without the other. The sound would not sound this way if it were not organized this way. Hence, if the most advanced technology and politics did not appear simultaneously, we would, to repeat, have to assume that, indifferent to the relations of production, that is, indifferent to how and what it organizes, technology is merely an abstract force, an ahistorical hypostatization, incapable of ever advancing beyond its current (political) use, or shaping sound, humans, and nature—all of which are intimately bound to one another—in a manner different from that of the present (political or relational) boundaries. In a word, we would have to maintain that it is not the depraved (*verworfen*) reproduction of the status quo that is the problem, not the current flow of technology that, resembling death, "gave shape to the apocalyptic face of nature and reduced nature to silence—even though," as Benjamin's insists, "this technology had the power to give nature its voice."[61]

Even the revolution requires a little bit of luck. Collectively seizing its chance in the "moment of . . . recognizability"[62] has always been rehearsed in the production of advanced music.

CODA: THE PUBLIC STUDIO

In the end, the glaring failure to actualize, let alone initiate, this possibility of group improvisation, brings us back to the beginning of our discussion.[63] *4'33"* is not simply the Dadaist joke that it is regularly taken to be. It is also Cage's attempt to bring to the fore the dynamic contrast of collectively produced sounds. It is an attempt to teach us to hear and produce a music that is already being produced *as our collective music*, but sadly continues the masquerade whereby only the initiated "musicians," the specialists, appear to be doing the improvisations "within" a delimited space. One's breath is potentially music. The same is true of the crescendo of one's laughter. Why should we exclude these phenomena from running through the reproductive circuits as well? Space is, in a certain sense, nothing other than the act of composing music, *together*. What happens, then, when every sound, down to the least audible quiver, is subject to technical transformation? What happens when, beyond even that which Cage and Schaeffer could imagine, every single note that was ever recorded, every single micro-interval of sound, waits to be harnessed by and for everyone, waits to pass through the as yet unutilized circuits of digital mixing consoles and turn-of-dial amplitude modulation, waits, in sum, to be seized by the public, as public property?[64] Do we not already have inklings of this in the latest craze for Spotify and Groove-shark[65]—inklings, that is, which are continually frustrated from their own-most possibility, since the antiquated property relations that form them cannot help but perpetuate the passive reception of the listener? The home studio in the suburban basement will not suffice either. There are lifetimes at play in the space between every interval of time. Why have these "molecular vibrations"[66] yet to be seized, actively, collectively, in the *public studio*? Why shouldn't the indeterminate chance operation that spontaneously turns the nobs of the radios in *Imaginary Landscape No. 4* give way to our attempt to turn the volume switch of the infinite array of sounds that currently clog the cyber passageways? This turn-of-dial access could, as Schaeffer observes, transform quantity into an unforeseen quality,[67] highlighting, like never before, their dialectical entwinement. Slowing each interval down infinitesimally, speeding them up, running them through filtered pattern delays, ring modulators, countless vibrator pedals, expanding them, without fear of defiling their "pure sound," is now more possible than ever *in real time*. "[T]he proliferation of forms," continues Schaeffer, "cancels out form, which turns back into matter."[68] Mimetic immersion now approaches, where sound and source bleed into each other, where cause and effect reverse, where the difference between the outside and the inside falls away, the passing vehicle or distant siren now but improvisational moments in the musical "happening" itself. The least "organic," most mediated sounds now ring truer as the supplement to the fleeting bird song that, long ago, broke through the cacophony of nature's acoustic *tableau*, promising without anticipation that one day peace would become a reality.

Yet unlike Cage—beyond Cage, in fact—all of these technical mechanisms can now line the anti-bourgeois space. The pre-artistic movements of the shuffling audience are only the beginning. In addition to providing these "audience" members with ready-to-hand instruments of an untold variety, every inch of a new productive space could be miked and fed to different electro-acoustic settings, every corner outfitted with internet technology that puts the infinite looping capacity of the public domain's sound at each participant's fingertips.[69] If, during a live performance, an unexpected affinity between the streaming music and a found-sound or orchestral fragment should strike the listener, he or she can incorporate the latter by typing in a search and, within an instant, plugging in the random results. All the while, the feedback and static generated from crossing the miked streams is registered when the movement of amplified and digitized footsteps punctures the entire acoustic field. Incorporating the most advanced technology, *all space becomes a Theremin*, every tablet computer but a chance for music to emerge without specialization. And perhaps most importantly, we at last realize that, as Benjamin puts it, "neither the veil nor the veiled object is the beautiful but the *object in its veil*."[70] Nowhere is this call to grasp the mediation of nature *in its history* truer than in a space that funnels every sound, from raindrops and harmonicas to construction sites, pianos, and gloom (*Grillen*) back into the veil of a multi-effects unit. The familiar becomes strange again: not by unveiling the object, not by the realism of direct sound-recordings, but rather by maintaining the semblance or veil of reproduction, driving mediation to its dialectical extreme, to the point at which the appearance of nature reverses (*umschlagen*), shocks, into culture, and the appearance of culture folds back (*umschlagen*),[71] leaps, into nature. The tone of an industrial generator becomes as eloquent as the texture of the river. Intentionality relents through technology.

Everyone, to be sure, hears from a different angle as the channeled tones ricochet from wall to wall. Yet, each phase interference is subtly united by virtue of sending a ripple through the tightly enmeshed sound-web. The more we compress, short circuit, and intersect the energy-jammed flows of our labor, the more explosive and shocking are the results.[72] The ensuing silence is the voice of our collective labor, the truth, which longs, now as ever, for redemption (*Erlösung*), for an escape from the constraints (*Zwänge*) of the status quo. With practice, participation in the enveloping sound of this shared public studio would almost of necessity trigger the recognition of one's role within the totality of the productive field. We need only commit to teaching ourselves the implicit musicality of our spatial movement.

At the same time, we no longer have to remain faithful to that part of Cage and Schaeffer's innovation that we have seen joins them to the "anything goes" or politically neutral mentality of the present. While loosening up specialization and combating rigidly imposed hierarchy is certainly the goal, composers at the helm of a central operating system could control the initial frivolity, redirect the missteps that would naturally flow from the early stages of habituation. From behind a cylindrical curtain, in the middle of an open hall that is equipped with the latest Dolby 5 technology,[73] these producers could take provisional and restricted leadership over the balance of effects, the shifting levels and emphases, which need to be adjusted on the spot if the organization of sound is to avoid regressing to nonsense. They could, similarly, provide that first push, or capture and amplify the tone of a current flow, a labor flow, which often emerges of its own accord once it is turned on, or once the circuits have been appropriately routed through the endlessly randomized combinations of a universal effects board. The undulating bass line or sinusoidal waves that propel the trajectory of a work that is for the first time grounded in the direct investment of nature's surplus labor, paves the way for a new attunement. Cage's humor and expressionless gesture meets the torture of Merzbow. Stockhausen's computer chip ambiance meets the disjointed kitsch of Nurse With Wound's surrealist show tunes. Yet, like Brecht's tactic, these composers at the operating system are, with humility, compelled to listen to the suggestions of those who are only just learning the power of self-determination. This avoids the above-mentioned problem of false immediacy while also heeding the call to strike the note at the right moment. Like Engel's famous claim that abolishing authority in one stroke is the naïve business of anarchism, the early arrangement of the public studio would merely open up another space for the ongoing struggle between capital and labor, that is, capital and nature. In time, it too would surely overcome its original instantiation.

With this first sketch of a new productive space in mind, we finally grasp why Benjamin's call for a collective "literarization" (*Literarisierung*) of all life[74] must be accompanied, if not preceded, by a collective *Musikalisierung* of all life. The power of the word will certainly be indispensable in the coming class struggle of the twenty-first century. But, undermining its own intention, it will just as certainly remain stifled and caught within the impotent realm of communicative action,[75] if it is not complemented by the improvisational attempt to merge life and music in unforeseen ways.[76] Music, after all, speaks like no other. Music is a greater intensity, as Deleuze says.[77] The technology at our disposal points, as always, in the direction of this embodied, intensified synthesis with life. This is Cage's most lasting lesson. This is his attempt to transform music and life for the sake of a new society. Thus, following the ancient Mondo style of question and answer, Cage's cynical questioner asks, "[b]ut, seriously, if this is what music is, I could write it as well as you." His response: "Have I said anything that would lead you to think I thought you were stupid."[78] Indeed, the audience must become the producer of music, but this is only because it was always the producer of music, always the voice of nature's silent lament.

NOTES

1. It is noteworthy that, even among thinkers who are dedicated to taking up the lineage of the early Frankfurt School, there is widespread agreement about how the rise of the postmodern condition propels the departure from this desire to determine the truth of artworks. See, for example, Aleš Erjavec, "Aesthetics and the Aesthetic Today: After Adorno," in *Art and Aesthetics After Adorno*, eds. J. M. Bernstein, et al. (Berkeley: University of California Press, 2010), 201. See also, Albrecht Wellmer, *Versuch über Musik und Sprache* (München: Verlag, 2009).

2. Arthur C. Danto, "The Artworld," in *Aesthetics and the Philosophy of Art: The Analytic Tradition*, eds. Peter Lamargue, et al. (Malden: Blackwell Publishing, 2004), 32.

3. G. W. F. Hegel, *Hegel's Phenomenology of Spirit*, transl. A. V. Miller (New York: Oxford University Press, 1977), 451.

4. We could add to this prioritization of discourse the parallel argument made by Pierre Bourdieu, which essentially claims that, despite all the appeals to grandeur or "distinction," aesthetic taste remains blinded by its social position and therefore devoid of any "truth-content." See Bourdieu, *Distinction: A Social Critique of the Judgment of Taste*, transl. Richard Nice (Cambridge: Harvard University Press, 1984). For a criticism of this position that resembles my argument, see Jacques Rancière, *Aesthetics and its Discontents*, transl. Steven Corcoran (Malden: Polity Press, 2004), 1–17.

5. Cf. Peter Bürger, *Theory of the Avant-garde*, transl. Michael Shaw (Minneapolis: University of Minnesota Press, 1984).

6. Walter Benjamin, "The Author as Producer," in *Selected Writings*, volume 2.1, ed. Michael W. Jennings (Cambridge: Harvard University Press, 2003), 769; "Der Autor als Produzent," in *Gesammelte Schriften*, volume 2.1, eds. Rolf Tiedemann and Hermann Scheppenhäuser (Frankfurt a.m.: Suhrkamp Verlag, 1974), 684. Hereafter, all works from the *Selected Writings* will be cited as *SW* with the corresponding volume number, and all works from the *Gesammelte Schriften* will be cited as *GS* with the corresponding volume number.

7. Walter Benjamin, "On the Concept of History," in *SW* 4, ed. Michael W. Jennings (Cambridge: Harvard University Press, 2003), 396; "Über den Begriff der Geschichte," in *GS* 1.2, eds. Rolf Tiedemann and Hermann Scheppenhäuser (Frankfurt a.m.: Suhrkamp Verlag, 1974), 702.

8. See Arthur C. Danto, *After the End of Art: Contemporary Art and the Pale of History* (Princeton: Princeton University Press, 1997), 47. For more on Cage's complicated relationship to postmodernism, see Alastair Williams, "Cage and Postmodernism," in *The Cambridge Companion to John Cage*, ed. David Nicholls (New York: Cambridge University Press, 2002) 227–41.

9. Benjamin, *SW* 2.2, 775/*GS* 2.1, 693.

10. For further analysis of the concept of tendentious (*Tendenz*) art, see the texts gathered in Fredric Jameson, et al., *Aesthetics and Politics* (Brooklyn: Verso, 2007).

11. Cf. Immanuel Kant, *Critique of the Power of Judgment*, transl. Paul Guyer and Eric Matthews (New York: Cambridge University Press, 2000), 171–75.

12. Benjamin, *SW* 2.2, 772/*GS* 2.1, 689.

13. Benjamin, *SW* 2.2, 775–76/*GS* 2.1, 694.

14. Ibid.

15. Walter Benjamin, "The Work of Art in the Age of Its Technological Reproducibility: Third Version," in *SW* 4, ed. Michael W. Jennings (Cambridge: Harvard University Press, 2003), 251–83; "Das Kunstwerk im Zeitalter seiner technischen Reproduzierbarkeit: Dritte Fassung," in *GS* 1.2, eds. Rolf Tiedemann and Hermann Scheppenhäuser (Frankfurt a.m.: Suhrkamp Verlag, 1974), 471–508.

16. See Walter Benjamin, *The Arcades Project*, transl. Howard Eiland and Kevin McLaughlin (Cambridge,: Harvard University Press, 1999). *Passagenwerk*, in *GS* 5.1, eds. Rolf Tiedemann and Hermann Scheppenhäuser (Frankfurt a.m.: Suhrkamp Verlag, 1974).

17. Benjamin, *SW* 2.2, 774/*GS* 2.1, 691–92.

18. Benjamin's most explicit formulation of his concept of truth-content (*Wahrheitsgehalt*) is in the early work, *Goethe's Elective Affinities*, in *SW* 1, ed. Michael W. Jennings (Cambridge: Harvard University Press, 2003), 300; *Goethes Wahlverwandtschaften*, in *GS* 1.1, eds. Rolf Tiedemann and Hermann Scheppenhäuser (Frankfurt a.m.: Suhrkamp Verlag, 1974), 128. Understanding this concept requires that we neither reduce it to the historical circumstance from which the work of art was formed, nor reduce it to the direct material-content that is presented or immediately on display in the work. Truth-content is, rather, that part of the work that says something more, that silently promises, or negatively reveals a truth that is perhaps too untimely for its age.

19. Benjamin, *SW* 2.2, 774/*GS* 2.1, 691–92.

20. Edmund Husserl, *The Crisis of European Sciences and Transcendental Phenomenology: An Introduction to Phenomenological Philosophy*, transl. David Carr (Evanston: Northwestern University Press, 1970).

21. Pierre Schaeffer, *In Search of Concrete Music*, transl. Christine North and John Dack (Berkeley: 2012), 7.

22. Benjamin, *SW* 4, 254/*GS* 1.2, 477–78.

23. Pierre Schaeffer, "Acousmatics," in *Audio Culture*, eds. Christoph Cox and Daniel Warner (New York: Continuum, 2010), 76–77.

24. Edmund Husserl, *Ideas: General Introduction to Pure Phenomenology*, transl. W.R. Boyce Gibson (New York: Routledge, 2002).

25. Schaeffer, *Concrete Music*, 13–15.

26. Branden W. Joseph, "'A Therapeutic Value for City Dwellers': The Development of John Cage's Early Avant-Garde Aesthetic Position," in *John Cage: Music, Philosophy, and Intention, 1933-1950*, ed. David W. Patterson (New York: Routledge, 2002), 143.

27. John Cage, "Future of Music: Credo," in *Silence* (Middletown: Wesleyan University Press, 1961), 6.

28. John Cage, "History of Experimental Music," in *Silence*, 70 (my emphasis).

29. Ibid., 71.

30. Schaeffer, *Concrete Music*, 9.

31. Schaeffer, "Acousmatics," 77.

32. Schaeffer, "Acousmatics," 81.

33. Benjamin, *SW* 4, 257/*GS* 1.2, 482–83.

34. Schaeffer, *Concrete Music*, 25.

35. Schaeffer, *Concrete Music*, 12.

36. See Friedrich Nietzsche, *The Gay Science*, transl. Walter Kaufmann (New York: Vintage Books, 1974), 348: "Who will sing a song for us, a morning song so sunny, so light, so fledged that it will *not* chase away the gloom [*Grillen*] but invite the crickets [*Grillen*] instead to join in the singing and dancing?" (translation modified).

37. Cage, "Credo," 3.

38. Walter Benjamin, *The Origin of German Tragic Drama*, transl. John Osborne (New York: Verso, 1998), 44; *Ursprung des deutschen Trauerspiels*, in *GS* 1.1, eds. Rolf Tiedemann and Hermann Scheppenhäuser (Frankfurt a.m.: Suhrkamp Verlag, 1974), 225–26.

39. Ibid., 84–91/*GS* 1.1, 260–70.

40. T. W. Adorno, *Aesthetic Theory*, transl. Robert Hullot-Kentor (Minneapolis: University of Minnesota Press, 1997), 318; *Ästhetische Theorie*, in *GS* 7, ed. Rolf Tiedemann (Frankfurt a.m.: Suhrkamp Verlag, 1972), 471.

41. Benjamin, *SW* 2.2, 777/*GS* 2.1, 695–96.

42. "It's not a physical landscape. It's a term reserved for the new technologies. It's a landscape in the future. It's as though you used technology to take you off the ground and go like Alice through the looking glass." Quoted from Susan Key, "John Cage's Imaginary Landscape No. 1: Through the Looking Glass," in *John Cage: Music, Philosophy, and Intention*, ed. David W. Patterson (New York: Routledge, 2002), 105.

43. For more on this concept of "pre-digested" listening, see T. W. Adorno, "On Popular Music," in *Essays on Music*, ed. Richard Leppert (Los Angeles, CA: University of California Press, 2002), 443.

44. John Cage, "Counterpoint," in *Writings about John Cage*, ed. Richard Kostelanetz (Ann Arbor, MI: University of Michigan Press, 1993), 16.

45. Ibid., 149.

46. T. W. Adorno, "Vers une musique informelle," in *Quasi una Fantasia: Essays on Modern Music*, trans. Rodney Livingstone (New York: Verso, 1998), 286–87 (translation modified); "Vers une musique informelle," in *GS* 16, ed. Rolf Tiedemann (Frankfurt a.m.: Suhrkamp Verlag, 1972), 508–09. For an excellent account of how Adorno's musical criticism is tied to his critique of phenomenology as well as his understanding of Benjamin's conception of temporality, see Stephen Decatur Smith, "Awakening Dead Time: Adorno on Husserl, Benjamin, and the Temporality of Music," *Contemporary Music Review*, Vol. 31 (2012): 389–409.

47. For further analysis of how Cage's use of the chance procedure of the *I Ching* reveals a rebuke of the metaphysics of presence, instead of his tacit support of the above mentioned positivism, see Yasunao Tone, "John Cage and Recording," *Leonardo Music Journal*, Vol. 13 (2013): 11–15.

48. For more on this concept of finding the right solution or the right answer to compositional problems as it relates to both Cage and Schoenberg, see David W. Bernstein, "John Cage, Arnold Schoenberg, and the Musical Idea," in *John Cage: Music, Philosophy, and Intention, 1933-1950*, 37.

49. Schaeffer, "Acousmatics," 79.

50. Schaeffer, *Concrete Music*, 132.

51. Schaeffer, "Acousmatics," 79.

52. Schaeffer, "Acousmatics," 81.

53. Jean Baudrillard, *Simulacra and Simulations*, transl. Sheila Faria Glaser (Ann Arbor, MI: University of Michigan Press, 1995).

54. The intentional ambiguity of the phrase, "process of production," should now be clear. For Benjamin, it, on the one hand, signifies the process of producing particular sound combinations or particular aesthetic configurations, and, on the other hand, signifies the collective social labor that attends or channels those configurations via a particular politics.

55. Cage, "Credo," 5.

56. See Adorno, "The Idea of Natural History," transl. Robert Hullot-Kentor, *Telos*, Vol. 60 (Summer 1984): 117, 119; "Die Idee der Naturgeschichte," *GS* 1, ed. Rolf Tiedemann (Frankfurt a m : Suhrkamp Verlag, 1972), 354–55.

57. For an account that, echoing with this claim, attempts to follow out the imbrications of scientific technique and politics (i.e., that attempts to part ways with the elitism involved in alleging that one has escaped the fabricating or constructive moment operative within both "nature" and "culture," facts and fetishes), see Bruno Latour, *Pandora's Hope: Essays on the Reality of Science Studies* (Cambridge, MA: Harvard University Press, 1999), 266–93.

58. Karl Marx and Friedrich Engels, "Die deutsche Ideologie," in *Werke*, volume 3 (Berlin: Dietz Verlag, 1962), 34; "The German Ideology," in *Collected Works*, volume 5, eds. James S. Allen, et al. (New York: International Publishers, 1975), 49. For discussion of how this notion of communism as the "actual" or "real" (*wirklich*) movement of history might still be at work in the present socio-political circumstance, see Bruno Bosteels, *The Actuality of Communism* (New York: Verso, 2011).

59. Benjamin, *SW* 4, 390/*GS* 1.2, 694–95.

60. Cf. Adorno, *GS* 7, 69/AT, 42: "Social reflection [*Gesellschaftliches Denken*] on aesthetics habitually neglects the concept of productive force [*Produktivkraft*]. Yet deeply embedded in the technological processes this force is the subject, the subject congealed [*geronnen*] as technology."

61. Walter Benjamin, "Theories of German Fascism," in *SW* 2.1, 319; "Theorien des deutschen Faschismus," in *GS* 3, 247.

62. Benjamin, *SW* 4, 390/*GS* 1.2, 695.

63. The public studio that is described below might give the impression of a musical space that copies David Byrne's well-known attempt at the Battery Maritime Building in New York City to spatialize music, or literally turn the building into an instrument.

64. Cf. Benjamin, *SW* 2.2, 772/*GS* 2.1, 688.

65. Spotify and Grooveshark are music streaming services that allow users to store music and access a collectively held database.

66. Gilles Deleuze and Felix Guattari, *A Thousand Plateaus: Capitalism and Schizophrenia*, transl. Brian Massumi (Minneapolis: University of Minnesota Press, 1987), 308. Echoing with both Nietzsche's call to seize the song of nature and Benjamin's call to listen to her mute sorrow (*Trauer*), Deleuze and Guattari attempt to capture the link between the "molecular vibrations" of insects, frustrated labor, and the electronics of a compounded energy that elicits the truth.

67. Schaeffer, *Concrete Music*, 14.

68. Schaeffer, *Concrete Music*, 18.

69. Infinitelooper.com is a website that allows users to loop any interval of time from any YouTube video or audio clip.

70. Benjamin, *SW* 1, 351/*GS* 1, 195 (my emphasis). The careful reader will observe that this claim about the importance of semblance (*Schein*) and the veil is apparently tied to a previous stage of art that has been definitively surpassed with the decline of the aura. I have argued elsewhere, however, that this view on semblance and aura, which fomented an *allegedly* irresolvable debate between Benjamin and Adorno, is only especially operative in Benjamin's "Technology" essay. Close examination of his *corpus* makes clear that, on the whole, Benjamin actually came to side with Adorno. That is to say, he realized just how much, even amidst the radical disenchantment of technical reproduction, semblance and aura are preserved in a transformed manner, instead of being undialectically canceled altogether.

71. For more on the role of the speed and rhythm of the turnover (*Umschlag*) in the production process, see Karl Marx, *Capital: A Critique of Political Economy*, volume 2, transl. David

Fernbach (New York: Penguin Books, 1978); *Das Kapital*, volume 2, in *Werke*, volume 24, ed. Karl Dietz (Berlin: Verlag, 1963).

72. There are several connections between this conception of a public studio that seizes the electric flows of collective social labor and Gilles Deleuze's conception of the flows of capitalist social production. See Deleuze and Félix Guattari, *Anti-Oedipus: Capitalism and Schizophrenia*, transl. Robert Hurley, et al. (New York: Penguin Books, 1977), 222–71. For further discussion of Deleuze's relationship to music theory, see the essays gathered in Ian Buchanan and Marcel Swiboda, *Deleuze and Music* (Edinburgh: Edinburgh University Press, 2004).

73. Although Dolby technology is normally used for the surround sound of home video or theater production, it is likely the best mechanism for capturing the spacialization of time or the *Musikalisierung* of movement involved in the public studio.

74. Benjamin, *SW* 2.2, 776/*GS* 2.1, 688.

75. Jürgen Habermas, *The Theory of Communicative Action: Reason and the Rationalization of Society*, volume 1, transl. Thomas McCarthy (Boston: Beacon Press, 1984).

76. This dialectic of life merging with art and art merging with life echoes with Jacques Rancière's attempt to grasp the politics of aesthetics. See Rancière, "The Aesthetic Revolution and Its Outcomes," in *Dissensus*, transl. Steven Corcoran (New York: Verso, 2010), 115–33.

77. Deleuze and Guattari, *A Thousand Plateaus*, 337. A great deal of work could also be done comparing Deleuze's aporetic claim that "the forces of a *people*, . . . is what is still lacking [in music]" to the politics of production presented by Benjamin.

78. John Cage, "Experimental Music: Doctrine," in *Silence*, 17.

Chapter Nine

The Aesthetic Experience of Shudder

Adorno and the Kantian Sublime

Surti Singh

In *Aesthetic Theory*, the shudder [*Schauder/Schauer*] is one of Adorno's most visceral descriptions of aesthetic experience. It is "a response, colored by fear of the overwhelming"[1] and the "act of being touched by the other."[2] There is an emotional and somatic dimension to this experience: "aesthetic comportment is to be defined as the capacity to shudder, as if goose bumps were the first aesthetic image."[3] On the surface, Adorno's treatment of the shudder appears to be a version of the aesthetics of effect, which focuses on the psychic or bodily effect that the art object produces in the recipient.[4] Yet Adorno explicitly distances the shudder from this kind of aesthetic experience, which he terms lived experience [*Erlebnis*]. This view of aesthetic experience assumes an equivalency between the emotional expression of the artwork and the subjective experience of the recipient; if the artwork expresses something like excitement, the recipient of the artwork will also feel excited.[5] For Adorno, lived aesthetic experience is a partial or reductive view of art, and only one element in the fuller, comprehending experience [*Erfahrung*] associated with the shudder.[6] Not simply an emotional response, the aesthetic experience of shudder involves a cognitive moment that transforms the subject.[7] "Shudder, radically opposed to the conventional idea of experience [*Erlebnis*], provides no particular satisfaction for the I; it bears no similarity to desire. Rather, it is a memento of the liquidation of the I, which, shaken, perceives its own limitedness and finitude."[8] Rather than emotional confirmation of the subject, the aesthetic experience of the shudder is double-edged. It negates the subject and at the same time provokes an awareness of itself.

Adorno explicitly recalls Kant's notion of the sublime in his discussion of the aesthetic shudder. What Kant had reserved exclusively for nature as sublime penetrates art and comes "increasingly into conflict with taste."[9] For Adorno, the invasion of the sublime into art beginning in the late eighteenth century persists into the late, advanced works of the twentieth century. As an instance of the sublime, the aesthetic shudder is analogous to the horror and fear the empirical subject feels in response to the overwhelming power of nature in Kant's *Critique of Judgment*, but it plays a significantly different role in Adorno's aesthetics.[10] On Kant's account, the empirical subject's fear of nature is overcome by the transcendental subject's assertion of its rational superiority. In contrast, the sublime in Adorno's account of modern art reveals an enlightenment subject who shudders at its own limitations without positively overcoming this experience. The relationship between the empirical subject and the transcendental subject in Kant's account of the sublime is transfigured into a tension that the shudder evokes between the enlightenment subject and an anticipatory subjectivity that "stirs without yet being subjectivity."[11] In this chapter, I explore the shudder's relation to these two forms of subjectivity in order to clarify the role of experience in Adorno's aesthetics. Albrecht Wellmer has argued that Adorno can only invoke an anticipatory subjectivity by relying on an illegitimate metaphysical position belonging to the philosophy of reconciliation. According to Wellmer's reading of Adorno, "The word 'I' is the name of a utopian hope: nothing that exists corresponds to this hope; only in the state of redemption would human beings be justified in saying 'I' to themselves."[12] I show, in contrast, that the shudder offers a bridge between these two forms of subjectivity without recourse to an illegitimate metaphysical position. The transcendence that the shudder provokes is not a utopian hope; it opens real, historical possibilities.[13]

THE KANTIAN SUBLIME AND THE EXPERIENCE OF MODERN ART

The transplantation of the sublime into art is coextensive with what Max Weber called the disenchantment of the world and the subsequent loss or explosion of metaphysical meaning.

For Wellmer, modern art is sublime because it *withstands* this loss or crisis of meaning by aesthetically reconstructing it. Wellmer helpfully schematizes three instances in *Aesthetic Theory*—the energetic, the structural, and the dynamic—that reproduce the logic of the Kantian sublime in art. All three characterizations of the sublime violate the standard of taste—the energetic by way of shock, the structural by way of a negation of formal beauty, and the dynamic by way of the progress of consciousness that revolts against

The Aesthetic Experience of Shudder 131

art's traditional limits. Wellmer does not mention the shudder, but it comes closest to his description of the sublime from the energetic point of view:

> The sublime appears as shocking, shattering, moving, overpowering. If one understands the moment of aesthetic experience as one of a condensed presence, through which the temporal continuum of ordinary experience is suspended, the experience of the sublime may be characterized by an additional element of violence, a violence that bursts into the interior space of the aesthetic distance, shaking up, dislodging or disquieting the subject, generating a tremor, a vertigo, loosening the confines of the experiencing ego. To be sure, this happens *under conditions* of aesthetic distance: the shaking up of the subject, its stepping out of itself, is part of an *aesthetic* experience only where the subject at the same time remains within its own boundaries in a state of utmost concentration.[14]

The energetic point of view reveals a sublime experience that shocks and overwhelms the subject. Since the experience of shock is an aesthetic experience, it does not actually dissolve or destroy the subject. On the contrary, this experience is sublime because the subject is able to withstand the shock of art under the conditions of aesthetic distance. The subject, momentarily shaken and disturbed, maintains its integrity. While Wellmer's account of the energetically sublime captures the shocking, overwhelming, and disturbing quality associated with the shudder, it remains short of Adorno's analysis. Importantly, the shudder involves a reflective process that Wellmer's characterization of the energetic does not pursue.[15]

For Adorno, aesthetic comportment is bound up with the process of rationalization but it does not merely replicate the dominant logic of enlightenment thinking. Central to art's autonomy is its disavowal of magical practices, which implies its participation in rationality and the progress of consciousness. Yet, art also preserves the mimetic comportment central to the magical practices it disavows: It contains a "nonconceptual affinity of the subjectively produced with its unposited other."[16] In this respect, art maintains the rationalization process and at the same time contains another form of mimetic knowledge. The dialectic of rationality and *mimesis* is a central tension in modern art: "Art is pulled between regression to literal magic or surrender of the mimetic impulse to thing-like rationality."[17] Since art resists affirming only one pole of this tension, it challenges the separation of feeling (*mimesis*) and understanding (rationality) historically inscribed in subjectivity.[18] From the point of view of their separation, feeling becomes the sphere of sentimentality when it turns away from thought and is closed off from truth; reason becomes tautological when it "shrinks from the sublimation of the mimetic comportment."[19] While the dominant rationality masks their interdependence, the shudder is a corrective to this separation:

> Consciousness without shudder is reified consciousness. That shudder in
> which subjectivity stirs without yet being subjectivity is the act of being
> touched by the other. Aesthetic comportment assimilates itself to that other
> rather than subordinating it. Such constitutive relation of the subject to objec-
> tivity in aesthetic comportment joins eros and knowledge. [20]

The shudder, which Adorno defines as the act of being touched by the other,
is made possible by art's mimetic comportment that fosters a passivity toward the other—assimilating itself to the other instead of subordinating it. [21]
This experience of being touched by the other evokes a subjectivity that is
not yet subjectivity—it is an anticipatory subjectivity that emerges from the
momentary suspension of the dominant rationality. Art temporarily bridges
the separation between reason and *mimesis* by challenging the cognitive
capacities of the subject. The subject, momentarily shocked and shaken in
this experience, does not reassert its rational superiority. Instead, the overwhelming encounter with otherness produces a mimetic response in the subject.

For Kant, when the empirical subject confronts the magnitude of nature—
witnessing the size of massive mountains (mathematically sublime) or the
might of crashing waves (dynamically sublime)—it powerlessly quivers in
the face of overwhelming nature. This experience initially produces a feeling
of displeasure, as the faculty of the imagination strains to account for an
object that exceeds its capacity. At the same time, since the imagination
strains beyond its capacities, it elicits the realm of the supersensible. The
initial displeasure "arouses in us the feeling of our supersensible vocation,
according to which finding that every standard of sensibility is inadequate to
the ideas of reason is purposive and hence pleasurable." [22] In the experience
of the sublime, the subject who feels terrified and overwhelmed by the im-
mensity of nature and experiences a sense of deficiency realizes its own
power of reason far surpasses any power of sensibility and is greater and
superior to nature. By recognizing its own faculty of reason, the subject
establishes its superiority over nature and derives pleasure from this experience. In the experience of modern art, however, the shudder reveals the
subject's *inability* to withstand the other, and it is momentarily assimilated to
it. In this sense, the sublime experience of modern art precipitates a loss of
subjectivity, a loss that reveals the subject's limitations. Kant notes that it is
incorrect to call the object of nature sublime. Rather, it is the subjective
experience of becoming conscious of our own rational superiority: "Hence,
sublimity is contained not in any thing of nature, but only in our mind,
insofar as we can become conscious of our superiority to nature within us,
and thereby also to nature outside us (as far is it influences us)." [23] The
cognitive dimension of the sublime, where it is elicited by the subject's
experience of its own faculties, plays a double role in Adorno's reading of

the shudder in modern art. On the one hand, it is the cognitive experience of the recipient who shudders in response to the artwork. On the other hand, it is constitutive of the artwork itself. This occurs in two ways: Both the movement of consciousness within the artwork—its spiritualization—and the ideal of beauty release the shudder. [24]

The spiritualization of art, as a process of disenchantment, paved the way for the entry of the sublime into art. Spiritualization released art from its old bondage to magic and myth, and its subservience to other activities. In this process, art's origins were negated to the extent that modern artworks no longer need to account for their earlier, dependent manifestations. [25] Artworks "are not to be called to account for the disgrace of their ancient dependency on magic, their servitude to kings and amusement, as if this were art's original sin, for art retroactively annihilated that from which it emerged." [26] The modern artwork embodies a spirit that overcomes its bondage to nature and asserts its autonomy. But this is not a straightforward transplantation of the sublime into art.

> The sublime was supposedly the grandeur of human beings who are spiritual and dominate nature. If, however, the experience of the sublime reveals itself as the self-consciousness of human beings' naturalness, then the composition of the concept changes. Even in Kant's formulation it was tinged with the nothingness of man; in this nothingness, the fragility of the empirical individual, the eternity of his universal destiny—his spirit—was to unfold. If, however, spirit itself is reduced to its natural dimension, then the annihilation of the individual taking place within it is no longer transcended positively.

As the progress of enlightenment consciousness, spiritualization retains the logic of domination. In the artwork, however, spiritualization is both domination *and* its overcoming. By cutting art loose from its dependent manifestations, the spiritualization of art establishes a sphere of immanence. In this respect, the spirit that dwells in the artwork becomes something fundamentally different from the spirit that negates nature. In the artwork, spirit ignites on the materiality of art, which it cannot transcend. In separating itself from nature, the spiritualization of art leads to spirit's recognition of itself as natural, as not only housed or confined by the materiality of art, but inseparable from it.

> Rather than that, as Kant thought, spirit in the face of nature becomes aware of its own superiority, it becomes aware of its own natural essence. This is the moment when the subject, vis-à-vis the sublime, is moved to tears. Recollection of nature breaks the arrogance of his self-positing: "My tears well up; earth I am returning to you." With that, the self exits, spiritually, from its imprisonment in itself. Something of freedom flashes up in that philosophy, culpably mistaken, reserves for its opposite, the glorification of the subject.

> The spell that the subject casts over nature imprisons the subject as well:
> Freedom awakens in the consciousness of its affinity with nature.[27]

Instead of establishing its superiority over nature, spirit recognizes its own natural condition. This is a realization that the recipient of art is unable to transcend positively. Spirit's confrontation with its own natural condition results in the subject's tears rather than its domination. The work of art in which its form is forced to transcend itself under pressure from the truth-content reflects the sublime structure that Kant reserved for nature. This tension in the artwork is created by the conflict between spirit and material—the spirit of the artwork finds itself unable to be represented sensually, and the material that is continuous with what exceeds the artwork finds itself irreconcilable with the unity of the artwork. "Art is redemptive in the act by which the spirit in it throws itself away. Art holds true to the shudder, but not by regression to it. Rather, art is its legacy."[28] The spiritualization of art, while designating a process of formation by which art achieves autonomy from the realm of nature, is also the chief force by which the undesirable, the rejected, and the foreign enter into art.[29] "The more art integrates into itself what is non-identical, what is immediately opposed to spirit, the more it must spiritualize itself. Conversely, spiritualization for its part introduced into art what is sensually displeasing and repugnant, and what had previously been taboo for art."[30] In this respect, spiritualization preserves the shudder in art—it introduces into art the ugly, the aspects of nature that generated terror and fear, in the aesthetic realm. The shudder designates both the tension within the artwork, between spirit and nature, and the experience of the recipient who is shocked and disturbed by its experience of the artwork. Adorno discusses the presence of these elements in art through the concept of the ugly.

It is from the perspective of the domination of nature that the ugly emerges as something to be excluded from art. Participating in the dialectic of enlightenment, artworks historically rejected whatever was threatening, fearful, and traditionally associated with the archaic. It is these elements that return in modern art, appearing as dissonance:

> What appears ugly is in the first place what is historically older, what art
> rejected on its path toward autonomy, and what is therefore mediated in itself.
> The concept of the ugly may well have originated in the separation of art from
> its archaic phase. It marks the permanent return of the archaic, intertwined
> with the dialectic of enlightenment in which art participates.[31]

The ugly is not unique to modern art—archaic and traditional works of art routinely portrayed ugly subjects—but something qualitatively different emerges in modern art. In archaic and traditional art, the ugly was integrated into the ideal of beauty. For example, a subject matter considered ugly could still be part of a beautiful artwork in the way that it was pictorially represented. In modern art, however, the ugly challenges the ideal of beauty. The ugly is more than a formal element that is ultimately harmonized within the artwork: "The anatomical horror in Rimbaud and Benn, the physically revolting and repellent in Beckett, the scatological traits of many contemporary dramas, have nothing in common with the rustic uncouthness of seventeenth-century Dutch paintings."[32] The ugliness of modern art is qualitatively different from previous artworks because it is the appearance of what is historically older, what art rejected in order to establish itself as art. In this respect, the ugly in modern art is a negativity that is not reconciled within the artwork.[33] It produces contradictions that cannot be transcended in the manner of the "positivity of negation that animated the traditional concept of the sublime." Since ugliness is a result of the domination of nature, it is inseparable from the ideal of beauty that originates in the rejection or renunciation of what was feared. It is only because of this renunciation that certain elements become ugly; beauty has its origin in the ugly.

> The image of beauty as that of a single and differentiated something originates with the emancipation from the fear of the overpowering wholeness and undifferentiatedness of nature. The shudder in the face of this is rescued by beauty into itself by making itself impervious to the immediately existent; beauty establishes a sphere of untouchability; works become beautiful by the force of their opposition to what simply exists. Of that on which it was active the aesthetically forming spirit allowed entry only to what resembled it, what it understood, or what it hoped to make like itself. This was a process of formalization; therefore beauty is, in terms of its historical tendency, formal.[34]

Rather than pure, platonic beginnings, the beautiful in art is established through a separation from the fear of overwhelming nature. Through the spiritualization of art, the process of rationalization overcomes the terrifying by reductively assimilating what can be known, what is familiar or non-threatening. In other words, the process of formalization that Adorno associates with beauty rejects the formless—the overwhelming, undifferentiated quality of nature—in order to establish its own self-contained sphere. Through the assertion of its autonomy and rejection of empirical reality, the ideal of beauty establishes a sphere of untouchabilitiy. Artworks become beautiful by their opposition to what exits—they withstand or overcome empirical reality, and in this way, beauty reproduces the dynamic of the sublime. In doing so, it recreates the illusion of its transcendence and purity in the face of ugly, mutilated, empirical existence. In this respect, the formal process of separation, dependent on art's spiritualization retains the dominating logic of enlightenment reason. Yet, through this illusion of autonomy and the formal process of separation, beauty recreates the sphere of untouchability that generated archaic fear. Beauty separates itself from the terrifying but at the same time invites the return of the shudder. Not only does the beautiful take on features of the sublime by its ability to withstand the empirical world, it also negates the sublime by recreating the formlessness that it rejects: By becoming "cryptically shut," art releases the shudder.[35] In this respect, the sublime subverts the ideal of beauty in art; in modern art, the beautiful is contingent on the sublime. At the same time, the sublime is negated—beauty cannot establish its dominance over the ugly,

> for the terrifying digs in on the perimeter like the enemy in front of the walls of the beleaguered city and starves it out. If Beauty is not to fail its own telos, it must work against its enemy even if this struggle is contrary to its own tenden-cy. Terror itself peers out of the eyes of beauty as the coercion that emanates from form.[36]

In this sense, there is a reversal of the beautiful and the ugly in art. As Hohendahl notes, there is a shift from early art that attempts to establish its autonomy from magic to modern artworks that reject classical reconciliation by rejecting the harmony associated with beauty.[37]

ARCHAIC FEAR AND SUBJECTIVITY

With respect to both spiritualization and beauty, the shudder is tied to the archaic fear of the unknown, which in the *Dialectic of Enlightenment*, Hork-heimer and Adorno describe as the experience of *mana*. It is something "primal and undifferentiated, it is everything unknown and alien; it is that which transcends the bounds of experience, the part of things which is more than their immediately perceived existence."[38] In his reconstruction of the prehistory of rationality that Horkheimer and Adorno trace out in the *Dialec-tic of Enlightenment*, Gordon Finlayson notes that the appearance of *mana* belongs to pre-animistic stage and is "born from the shudder (*Schauder*) in the face of the unknown."[39] *Mana* contains the first inkling of the separation between subject and object since it implies a doubling of nature into essence and appearance. A natural object appears as itself, and at the same time as the location of *mana*. Finlayson schematizes four subsequent stages—the ani-mistic, myth, metaphysics, and the enlightenment—that culminate in the dominant instrumental reason that prevails modern society.[40] Each stage re-sponds to the fear of the unknown in a progressively more distanced and conceptual way, to the point where it is historically assuaged through demy-thologization and the advent of enlightenment thinking. If the shudder marked an overwhelming fear of nature, enlightenment thinking reflects the total domination of nature. In this sense, the shudder is the initial impulse that gives rise to the desire to control nature and that culminates in the development of instrumental reason. At the same time, as Finlayson notes, it also reflects an "impulsive, somatic experience that momentarily registers the presence of what occasions it."[41] Art preserves this dual character of the shudder: The shudder is a reaction to the incomprehensibility of art, but it is also a reaction to the memory of what was repressed.[42]

Art's capacity to release the shudder has a profound impact on the recipient. The development of the enlightenment subject rests on the mastery of nature. This frees the subject from its old submission to nature, but this mastery of nature is not a straightforward accomplishment. The technological domination of nature, rather than edifying the subject, impoverishes it. The enlightenment subject's domination of nature produces a reification of the self—a hardening and ossifying of its human traits—and an objectification of the outer world of which the self is a part. In this context, the resurgence of the sublime in modern art has a powerful impact on the reified, empirical subject of instrumental reason. Like the experience of the dynamically sublime, the subject is overcome by fear when it encounters the undifferentiated wholeness of nature in the artwork. However, if the sublime experience of nature according to Kant resulted in an assertion of the rational powers of the phenomenal subject, the sublime experience of modern art results in a temporary disintegration of the reified empirical subject and its instrumental reason. The reversal of the experience of the sublime from Kant to Adorno, where the subject is disturbed rather than fortified, reflects how the initial cognitive failure in the experience of the sublime is resolved. Aesthetic judgments are rooted in "the mental state that we find in relation between the presentational powers [imagination and understanding] insofar as they refer a given presentation to *cognition in general*." In reflective judgments, the imagination and understanding harmonize in a way that is necessary for cognition in general, but a concept is not produced. Our liking is connected to a concept, but the concept is indeterminate. Since there is no concept involved, the cognitive powers brought together by the presentation are in free play; they are not restricted by any particular rule of cognition. Adorno theorizes a similar overwhelming encounter with the artwork. Unable to be subsumed under a concept, the artwork escapes understanding; unlike the resolution in Kant's concept of the sublime, the subject who experiences the incomprehensibility of art has an involuntary, mimetic response.[43]

> The subject, convulsed by art, has real experiences; by the strength of insight into the artwork as artwork, these experiences are those in which the subject's petrification in his own subjectivity dissolves and the narrowness of his self-positedness is revealed. If in artworks the subject finds true happiness in the moment of being convulsed, this is a happiness that is counterposed to the subject and thus its instrument is tears, which also expresses the grief over one's own mortality. Kant sensed something of this in the sublime, which he excluded from art.[44]

The sublime construction of the artwork shakes the subject's rigid categories by making it aware of the suppressed otherness—nature—upon which its autonomy is based. The shudder is a reminder of what is sacrificed in the formation of enlightenment subjectivity. The subject finds true happiness in being convulsed, but this is happiness counterposed to the subject, thus its instrument is tears. There is at once the possibility of reconciliation with nature, and yet, a realization that this is at the expense of the subject, the sacrifice of its present form—an aesthetic annihilation of the self that mimics death. Once the metaphysical framework that allowed for the establishment of a transcendental subject over and above the empirical subject collapses with the advent of enlightenment thinking, spirit is reduced to nature. In Adorno's reading of the sublime, Kant's distinction between the empirical and the transcendental subject is transposed into a duality within the empirical subject, between the subject of instrumental reason and the stirring of subjectivity "without yet being subjectivity."[45] The shudder, in which this not-yet subjectivity stirs, is the act of being touched by the other.[46] Adorno conceives a tension within the empirical subject itself, which, while occupying a world increasingly hollowed of metaphysical meaning, continues to register this emptiness on a real, somatic level—particularly in the aesthetic experience of art—provoking a response to its deadened and reified existence. In this respect, the tension between the empirical subject and the transcendental subject in Kant is reconfigured as that between an empirical subject and a subjectivity to come.

For Wellmer, Adorno's refiguring of Kant's distinction between the empirical and noumenal subject falls prey to what he labels the philosophy of reconciliation. Wellmer asks how we can conceive of the sublime in modern art when the polarity between the empirical and noumenal, which for Kant gave rise to the feeling of the sublime, is no longer valid. According to Wellmer, Adorno's answer can be parsed into two frameworks: the philosophy of reconciliation and post-metaphysical philosophy. The former conceives of the tension between the empirical and the noumenal subject as one between "the reality of the world and a utopia veiled in black, between a condition of complete negativity and a condition of redemption."[47] The latter framework conceives of the tension as one between the "explosion of metaphysical meaning" in modernity and the emancipation of the subject.[48] Wellmer takes issue with Adorno's claim that the two frameworks are internally connected, that the explosion of metaphysical meaning implies a condition of complete negativity. For Wellmer, we can conceive of the tension between the explosion of metaphysical meaning and the emancipation of the subject positively, as implying the freedom of the subject from the past and the possibility of entering into a shared communicative context. Through a more robust philosophy of language and a conception of intersubjectivity, Adorno could have linked the disenchantment of the world, the explosion of metaphysical meaning, to a gain in communicative rationality. The second claim, then, "contains the elements of a post-metaphysical conception of the sublime that makes it possible to interpret Adorno's *Aesthetic Theory* in terms of a theory of communication."[49] According to Wellmer, the fundamental tension that Kant theorized between the empirical subject and the noumenal subject, and that Adorno theorizes between the explosion of metaphysical meaning and the emancipation of the subject, can be reconceived as a tension within the intelligible subject itself. Within the paradigm of linguistically shared meaning, this tension hovers between the negativity of the subject and its transcendence into the communicative world of shared meaning. For Wellmer, this solves the problem of the metaphysical residue in Adorno's work and transitions his insights toward a post-metaphysical aesthetics.[50]

While Wellmer reads the problem of reconciliation as one that can be solved once the notion of transcendence is understood as occurring toward a shared communicative context, I argue that the shudder is an instance in Adorno's work where transcendence is only a momentary overcoming of the limitations of the reified self, and therefore does not imply reconciliation. That is, turning to Horkheimer and Adorno's early critique in the *Dialectic of Enlightenment* and reading its continuity with *Aesthetic Theory* reveals a shaking of the instrumental subject that momentarily becomes open to an alternative relationship to otherness than one that dominates. For Adorno, the experience of the sublime is double-edged, for while it terrifies and overwhelms the subject, it also reveals the subject's limitations that otherwise remain obscure in a world ruled by instrumental reason. In being forced to confront its own limitations, the subject experiences a momentary liquidation or disintegration that temporarily brings into view the possibility of an alternative relationship to the otherness—nature—it suppresses within itself. This is not reconciliation as Wellmer imagines it—as a return to a paradisiacal nature in a utopia to come. Rather, it is the opening of real, historical alternatives to the reified enlightenment subject.

THE SHUDDER AND THE SUBJECT TO COME

The shudder is linked to enlightenment reason not only as the experience that instigates the eventual domination of nature. The disappearance of the shudder in modern society is also an anxiety that enlightenment reason carries within it, since the disappearance of the shudder all together would eradicate enlightenment reason's link to its original aim—the discovery of truth.

> For if at one time human beings in their powerlessness against nature feared the shudder as something real, the fear is no less intense, no less justified, that the shudder will dissipate. All enlightenment is accompanied by the anxiety that what set enlightenment in motion in the first place and what enlighten-

ment ever threatens to consume may disappear: truth. Thrown back on itself,
enlightenment distances itself from that guileless objectivity that it would like
to achieve; that is why, under the compulsion of its own ideal of truth, it is
conjoined with the pressure to hold on to what it has condemned in the name
of truth. Art is this mnemosyne.[51]

The initial impulse to know the unknown arose from the desire to release the
proto-subject from its bondage to nature, yet its development into the instrumentality of enlightenment thinking detaches the enlightenment from its
original goal—to know nature. The disappearance of the shudder is the disappearance of this impulse to know, and it is replaced with an automatic
rationality that no longer needs to know—it controls. If the world has become thoroughly disenchanted, art preserves the shudder. If in the experience
of *mana*, the only recourse was to flee from the mortal danger that nature
presented, through art, the subject can experience the shudder at an aesthetic
distance. It can momentarily be open to the overwhelming otherness of the
object without risking itself in the process. "Artworks remain enlightened
because they would like to make commensurable to human beings the re-
membered shudder, which was incommensurable in the magical world."[52] If
the experience of shudder drove the development of reason to master nature,
now in a dialectical reversal, our reified subjectivity that becomes abstract
and unknowable like inert nature produces the same response of fear, and
thus becomes the means by which this subjectivity is unravelled. The shudder is an *Erinnerung* or remembrance of the archaic shudder in the face of an
overwhelming nature, which the experience of modern works of art awakens
in the subject.

It is art's fundamental challenge to what the subject has become that
allows the subject to forget itself. The experience of shudder dissolves the
primacy of the subject over the object and initiates a process of self-reflec-
tion in the subject that becomes aware of itself as semblance. Adorno notes
that in an administered world—one ruled by instrumental reason—art can
function as the "communication of the uncommunicable, the breaking
through of reified consciousness."[53] Kafka's writings, for example, "violate
the collusion of the novel reader by the explosive empirical impossibility of
what is narrated, it is precisely by virtue of this violation that they become
understandable to all."[54] The incomprehensibility of modern art, similar to
the overwhelming power of nature that the subject cannot cognize, leads to
"interventions in consciousness."[55] The paradoxical status of advanced modern art has the capacity to negate the everyday experience of culture. "Everything depends on this: whether meaning inheres in the negation of meaning
in the artwork or if the negation conforms to the status quo; whether the crisis
of meaning is reflected in the works or whether it remains immediate and
therefore alien to the subject."[56] Whereas the shock of the culture industry

reinforces the subject's instrumental reason, the shock of the artwork challenges it by initiating a cognitive failure in the subject. Although the shudder successfully disturbs the dominating relationship that the subject has with the object, it is momentary and unable to be sustained as a real alternative. Even though in this experience the subject recognizes itself as semblance and for a moment self-preservation falls away, the subject can never fully discard its drive for self-preservation in the conditions of modern society. Similarly, even though the artwork in this experience expands beyond its boundaries, it can never fully transcend them, for then it would no longer be art. Ultimately, the experience of aesthetic shudder would require the counterpart of philosophical analysis in order to make this experience intelligible, an issue that eludes the constraints of this chapter. In the context of art, the experience of shudder fulfills the condition that would give priority to the object but only in the aesthetic realm.

> Stumbling along behind its reification, the subject limits that reification by means of the mimetic vestige, the plenipotentiary of an undamaged life in the midst of mutilated life, which subverts the subject to ideology. The inextricability of reification and mimesis defines the aporia of artistic expression. There is no general test for deciding if an artist who wipes out expression altogether has become the mouthpiece of reified consciousness or of the speechless, expressionless expression that denounces it. Authentic art knows the expression of the expressionless, a kind of weeping without tears.[57]

The distinction between authentic art and the commodity remains unclear, since all authentic works of art share the fetish-character. In establishing their own sphere separate from empirical reality, artworks intensify their reification. Yet, it is because of this intensification of reification within the artwork that its fetish-character becomes mimetic—its fetish character allows it to mimic the non-illusory world through the creation of an autonomous realm. While this *mimesis* is illusory, Adorno believes that the redemption of this mimetic impulse within art is key to the restitution of experience. The shudder is this *mimesis* that artworks rescue.

NOTES

1. Theodor W. Adorno, *Aesthetic Theory*, transl. Robert Hullot-Kentor (Minneapolis: University of Minnesota Press, 1997), 245.

2. Adorno, *Theory*, 331.

3. Adorno, *Theory*, 331.

4. Christoph Menke, *The Sovereignty of Art: Aesthetic Negativity in Adorno and Derrida*, transl. Neil Solomon (Cambridge, MA: MIT Press, 1998), 151.

5. Adorno, *Theory*, 244.

6. Adorno, *Theory*, 244. For further discussion see Martin Jay, *Songs of Experience: Modern American and European Variations on a Universal Theme* (Berkeley: University of Cali-

fornia Press, 2005), 11–12. See also Scott Lash, "Experience," *Theory, Culture & Society*, Vol. 23 (2006): 335–40.

7. Adorno, *Theory*, 245.

8. Adorno, *Theory*, 245.

9. Adorno, *Theory*, 196.

10. Immanuel Kant, *Critique of Judgment*, transl. Werner S. Pluhar (Indianapolis: Hackett, 1987).

11. Adorno, *Theory*, 331.

12. Albrecht Wellmer, "Adorno, Modernity, and the Sublime," in *Endgames: The Irreconcilable Nature of Modernity*, transl. David Midgley (Cambridge, MA: MIT Press, 1998), 171–72.

13. Herbert Marcuse gives a good explanation of the non-metaphysical sense of transcendence central to critical theory: "The terms 'transcend' and 'transcendence' are used throughout in the empirical, critical sense; they designate tendencies in theory and practice which, in a given society, 'overshoot' the established universe of discourse and action toward its historical alternative (real possibilities)" (*One-Dimensional Man* [Boston: Beacon Press, 1964], xliii).

14. Wellmer, "Adorno," 163.

15. Espen Hammer, who also takes up this tripartite schema of the sublime, gives a description of the energetic that includes the shudder and emphasizes the resulting confrontation that the subject experiences with its own limits. "The Touch of Art: Adorno and the Sublime" *SATS*, Vol. 1, no. 2 (2000): 91–105.

16. Adorno, *Theory*, 54.

17. Adorno, *Theory*, 54.

18. Adorno, *Theory*, 331.

19. Adorno, *Theory*, 331.

20. Adorno, *Theory*, 331.

21. Adorno, *Theory*, 331.

22. Kant, *Critique*, 115.

23. Kant, *Critique*, 123.

24. Adorno, *Theory*, 196.

25. Adorno, *Theory*, 3. J. M. Bernstein describes this dual aspect of spiritualization as follows: "Art's participation in spiritualization, which here means first humanization as disenchantment, is its becoming autonomous, making traditional forms into art forms. In art, however, this movement is double: disenchantment entails the continuance of the mimetic taboo; but in this continuance the art work attempts to rid itself of externality, to become purely immanent" (*The Fate of Art: Aesthetic Alienation from Kant to Derrida and Adorno* [Penn State Press, 1992], 203).

26. Adorno, *Theory*, 3.

27. Adorno, *Theory*, 276.

28. Adorno, *Theory*, 118.

29. Adorno, *Theory*, 196.

30. Adorno, *Theory*, 196.

31. Adorno, *Theory*, 47.

32. Adorno, *Theory*, 46.

33. See Peter Uwe Hohendahl, "Aesthetic Violence: The Concept of the Ugly in Adorno's *Aesthetic Theory*," *Cultural Critique*, Vol. 60 (2005): 170–96, for a discussion of the ugly in Adorno's aesthetics. Hohendahl argues that the ugly is not simply the negative of the beautiful, but is compatible with the autonomy of art.

34. Adorno, *Theory*, 51.

35. Wellmer explains the relationship between the beautiful and the sublime in the following way: "Adorno's construction of art is at the same time an aesthetics of the sublime. This also means that the beautiful and the sublime are not opposed to each other in Adorno's aesthetics in the same way as they are in Kant's; they are rather opposed to each other like two poles of aesthetic coherence (*Stimmigkeit*) of which I have spoken, that is, like semblance (illusion) and truth" ("Adorno," 158). For Wellmer, this is something plausible in Adorno's thought, but it has to be extricated from the context of the philosophy of reconciliation.

36. Adorno, *Theory*, 73.

37. Hohendahl, "Aesthetic,"192.

38. Max Horkheimer and Theodor W. Adorno, *Dialectic of Enlightenment*, transl. Edmund Jephcott (Stanford: Stanford University Press, 2002), 10.

39. Gordon Finlayson, "Adorno: Modern art, Metaphysics, and Radical Evil," *Modernism/Modernity*, Vol. 10 (2003): 79.

40. Finlayson, "Adorno," 80.

41. Finlayson, "Adorno," 80.

42. See Bernstein, *Fate* for a discussion of memorial aesthetics.

43. J. M. Bernstein discusses the link between Adorno's notion of *mimesis* and Kant's reflective judgment: "The activities of reflection without determination, of following along afterward and coexecution, are what Adorno means by mimetic conduct. *Mimetic cognition is understanding intransitively;* reflective judgement is the heir of mimetic understanding" (*Adorno: Disenchantment and Ethics* [Cambridge: Cambridge University Press, 2001], 313–14).

44. Adorno, *Theory*, 269.

45. Adorno, *Theory*, 331.

46. Adorno, *Theory*, 331.

47. Wellmer, "Adorno," 161.

48. Wellmer, "Adorno," 161.

49. Wellmer, "Adorno," 162.

50. Hammer's "Touch" has rightly pointed out that Wellmer misunderstands the notion of reconciliation in Adorno's work. In response, Hammer defends Adorno's notion of the sublime and via its manifestation as the shudder, reads it as an opening, which is ultimately a silence.

51. Adorno, *Theory*, 80.

52. Adorno, *Theory*, 80.

53. Adorno, *Theory*, 196.

54. Adorno, *Theory*, 196.

55. Adorno, *Theory*, 196.

56. Adorno, *Theory*, 154.

57. Adorno, *Theory*, 117.

Chapter Ten

Ecological Experience

Aesthetics, Life, and the Shudder in Adorno's Critical Theory

Rick Elmore

There has been a growing interest in the past decade in the connection between Adorno's critical theory and ecology.[1] These works argue, in particular, that Adorno's materialism and critique of capitalism emerge out of his critique of natural history, highlighting the fundamental role the concept of nature plays in these aspects of Adorno's work. While nature is an important and relevant place to begin charting the ecological possibilities of critical theory, it is only one of a number of aspects of Adorno's work that parallel key concerns of ecological thought, the others being his thoroughgoing critique of capitalism, and, perhaps most importantly, his relentless concern for the question of life. It is this final issue that has received the least attention in works such as Cook's, a somewhat odd omission given that, for Adorno, "the question of whether it is still possible to live is the form in which metaphysics impinges on us urgently today."[2] However, the question of "life" is also crucial to Adorno's aesthetics, as he links the redemptive power of art to its ability to open up the experience of new relations to "life."[3] Hence in this chapter, I build on the ecological possibilities of critical theory by exploring Adorno's notion of "the shudder" of aesthetic experience and its connection to the concepts of life, nature, and violence.[4] This reading shows that "aesthetic experience" is perhaps better understood as a kind of "ecological experience," an experience that both destabilizes and reorients the subject in relationship to the objectivity of itself and the environment. This reorientation shines new light onto the deeply ecological character of Adorno's critical theory, and helps to detail further the connection between his aesthetics,

metaphysics, and politics. I begin by revisiting Cook's reading of the domination of nature in Adorno's work.

THE ECOLOGICAL DIMENSION OF ADORNO'S CRITIQUE OF NATURE

Cook begins her reading of Adorno by stating that the critique of natural
history, the notion that human history is inseparable from nature, informs "all
of Adorno's work."[5] "Philosophy is," for Adorno, "tasked with demonstrat-
ing that human history is linked inextricably to our own internal, instinctual
nature and non-human nature," while at the same moment, highlighting that
"nature is historical [and] profoundly—often negatively—affected by human
history."[6] Philosophy charts the way in which history is the result not of
conceptual development or abstract thought but of the material conditions of
the natural world and our instincts. The heart of this instinctual nature is, for
Adorno, the drive for self-preservation.

As he and Horkheimer argue in *Dialectic of Enlightenment*, it is the desire
for self-preservation that gives force to all our "ideas, prohibitions, religions,
and political creeds."[7] As Cook puts it, for Adorno "[o]ur history can be
interpreted as natural history because its trajectory can be traced in the vicis-
situdes of our instinctually driven domination of nature. Human history 'remains under the spell of blind nature' in the form of the unbridled instinct for
self-preservation."[8] The instinct to survive, our instinctual fear of death,
motivates our domination of nature and this domination leads to violence.

The fundamental ethical concern of Adorno's critique of the domination
of nature is that this domination tends to perpetuate violence both to the
external nature of the world and to the internal nature of human beings. The
control of nature does violence by treating natural things "instrumentally"
and "reducing them to their exchange value in the capitalist marketplace."[9]
The reduction of objects to the category of exchange creates a logic of
fungibility in which the value of the specificity of any object is sacrificed for
its exchangeability. The logic of exchange profoundly curtails the value of
individual object, as every object becomes just a placeholder for a unit of
exchange value, which can be equally satisfied by an array of like objects.
This is the heart of Adorno's and Horkheimer's critique of Enlightenment,
and it is what leads them to conclude that "[e]nlightenment is totalitarian."[10]
However, the logic of fungibility found in the Enlightenment impulse towards equivalence is perhaps most problematic for the objectivity of individual human beings.

Cook writes of the violent effect of the domination of nature on human
beings, for Adorno "[e]xchange relations damage human beings . . . by
expunging differences between them in order to make 'nonidentical individu-

als and performances become commensurable and identical.'"[11] At the heart of the domination of nature is the violence of identity inherent in exchange, in which the existence of objects and living beings risks being sacrificed to interchangeability. Just as in the case of all objects, the objective character of the human subject must, through the domination of nature, come to be given value only in the limited sphere of instrumentality. Hence, the motivating ethical force of Adorno's concern for the domination of nature is the possibility of violent fungibility, and specifically the violent fungibility of human life in the face of instrumental exchange. However, this concern for the violence done to life and subjectivity is not unique to Adorno's critique of natural history, as it is found across his work and, in particular, in his critique of dialectics and capitalism.

Negative Dialectics begins with a definition: "The name of dialectics says no more, to begin with, than that objects do not go into their concepts without leaving a remainder."[12] In its most elementary form, dialectics names the non-identity between objects and their concepts. It articulates the structural fact that concepts cannot fully capture their objects. This failure of thought ever to represent adequately its object is the first moment of violence within dialectics. Thought necessarily leaves behind or excludes those aspects of objects that cannot be taken up into the general categories of conceptualization. Hence, as Adorno argues in his lectures on metaphysics, it is the "special spatial and temporal position of the elements subsumed under the concept" that must be "disregarded."[13] The violence of dialectics is an exclusionary violence in which the unique time and space of objects is sacrificed to the generalizing force of the concept. This structural and violent intolerance of thought to anything that is other than thought has particularly profound consequences not just for objects, but also for the relationship of thought to its own objective moment.

The logical result of the violent relationship of thought to its object is that thought is driven to do violence to its own objectivity. Adorno writes:

> The ideological side of thinking shows its permanent failure to make good on the claim that the non-I is finally the I: the more the I thinks, the more perfectly will it find itself debased into an object. Identity becomes the authority for a doctrine of adjustment, in which the object—which the subject is supposed to go by—repay the subject for what the subject has done to it.[14]

Given the exclusionary violence entailed in the process of conceptualization—a violence Adorno associates with ideology—the subject, this living breathing human being here and now, must be devalued in order to allow it to fit into the abstract, universal schema of the "subject."[15] All the differences that separate one thinking subject from another, all the things that make one human being unlike the rest of its species, must be excluded and devalued, insofar as such differences cannot be the basis of any universal category. The ironic result of this exclusion is that the more the subject thinks about itself, the more it attempts to identify itself, the more surely it turns itself into an object of thought, and the more it eliminates the value of its material existence. Hence for Adorno, dialectics risks the very exclusion and domination one finds in his critique of natural history. However, this violence to life is also socially at work in capitalism through the "*Tauschprinzip*" or exchange principle.

For Adorno, exchange expresses socially the violent identifying logic of conceptualization:

> The exchange principle [*Tauschprinzip*], the reduction of human labor to the abstract universal concept of average working hours, is fundamentally akin to the principle of identification [*Identifikationsprinzip*]. Exchange [*Tausch*] is the social model of the principle . . . it is through exchange [*Tausch*] that non-identical individuals and performances become commensurable and identical.[16]

The exchange principle reduces all labor to the abstract category of "working hours" and ultimately to the notion of the hourly wage. Through the exchange system all individuals and their labor are made commensurable via the common denominator of wages. The systematic reduction of the value of work to wages comprises the practical expression of the reduction of all individuals to the concept of the *subject* or the "specimen" and all that is non-conceptual to the categories of the conceptual. Adorno connects explicitly the exclusionary violence of the process of conceptualization and his concern for the evacuation of the materiality and "life" of the subject to the practical and profoundly Marxist concern for the violence of the wage labor system under capitalism.

The notion of wage labor functions, like the categories of the concept, violently to exclude and reduce to differences of wage all the material differences separating workers and their labor. Exchange renders all qualitative differences as quantitative differences, which, in effect, reduces all difference. Speaking of the dominating system of exchange, Adorno writes:

> The universal domination of mankind by the exchange value [*Tauschwerts*]— a domination which a priori keeps the subjects from being subjects and degrades subjectivity itself to a mere object—makes an untruth of the general principle that claims to establish the subject's predominance. The surplus of the transcendental subject is the deficit of the utterly reduced empirical subject.[17]

In a world reduced to a system of exchange, the individual human being has value only insofar as it conforms to the standard of wage labor and is rendered identical to all other workers. This reduction undermines the subject's claim to any unique subjective specificity, effectively reducing the living, breathing subject to the "worker." The push to conform to the transcendental category of the wage-earning subject makes any claim to *empirical* subjectivity false, for Adorno. In a system of exchange, one can express one's *individuality* and *subjectivity*, "the surplus of the transcendental subject," only by earning a larger wage. One can be an individual only by conforming ever more fully to the concept of the wage earning subject, that is, by reducing one's empirical specificity. This system reduces the subject to a mere object, a node in the system of social value, a means rather than an end. Now there is much to say about Adorno's profound commitment to Marx. However, in terms of the role of life in Adorno's work, we see the central role this notion of life plays both in his critique of dialectics and capitalism.

The concern to resist violence is the guiding ethical imperative of Adorno's critical theory. Whether in his thoroughgoing critique of the identitarian relationship of thought to its object, his critique of the exchange principle in the logic of capitalism, or his investigation of the logic of fungibility in the dialectical relationship between subjectivity and objectivity, it is always the question of violence that takes center stage. Immanent critique is, after all, the form of analysis that best "lends a voice to suffering," a project that is, for Adorno, "a condition for all truth."[18] Adorno's work is centrally concerned not just with the domination of nature, but, more specifically, with the violence done to the living nature of human beings, a fact that underscores the absences of the notion of "life" from the work of thinkers concerned with the ecological possibilities of Adorno's work. However, this concern for violence and life is not limited to Adorno's critique of metaphysics, political economy, and natural history, as life is also at the very heart of aesthetic theory.

LIFE, THE SHUDDER, AND AESTHETIC COMPORTMENT

On the final page of *Aesthetic Theory*, summarizing the essence of his theory of aesthetics, Adorno writes:

> Ultimately, aesthetic comportment is to be defined as the capacity to shudder [*die Fähigkeit, irgend zu erschauern*]. . . . What later came to be called subjectivity, freeing itself from the blind anxiety of the shudder, is at the same time the shudder's own development; life in the subject is nothing but what shudders.[19]

The ability to shudder defines aesthetic comportment. There can be no aesthetic experience without the shudder, without the capacity for a certain involuntary and bodily reaction or receptivity, "as if goose bumps were the first aesthetic image."[20] However, the shudder is also the very "life" of the subject; it is what lives in subjectivity. The shudder maps the emergence of subjectivity as its own development, overcoming a certain fear in the face of this shudder of "life," a fear whose elimination, Adorno suggests, paradoxically makes subjectivity possible while remaining inseparable from it: "the reaction to the total spell that transcends the spell."[21] Here Adorno is rearticulating the paradoxical logic of Enlightenment, identity, and subjectivity, as it is only through the drive to disenchant, identify, and dominate external and internal nature, that is, disenchant, identity, and dominate "life," that the emergence of the living, human subject is possible. Or to paraphrase the epigraph of *Minima Moralia*, subjective life is possible only insofar as it does not live.[22] Adorno links this paradoxical emergence of "life" to the logic of "mimesis," as aesthetic comportment is "the process that mimesis sets in motion."[23] Thus for Adorno, life is at the heart of aesthetic theory and mimetic comportment, a claim that suggests that it is nothing less than human life that Adorno sees as at stake in aesthetics.[24] However in this passage, Adorno also links the shudder and the notion of aesthetic comportment to his concern, outlined above, for the violent relationship between subject and object, thought, and the world.

Having affirmed the shudder as the very life of subjectivity, Adorno goes on to relate this shudder of life to a resistance to "reified consciousness" and to "being touched by the other."[25] The shudder or living part of subjectivity is that within consciousness that resists thought's tendency to take itself as all there is or all that matters. It is the reminder of the objective essence of thought, a reminder that subjectivity is and remains dependent on objectivity. This resistance to reification opens up the possibility of an encounter with the other that "assimilates itself to that other rather than subordinating it," resisting thought's domination of objectivity and opening up a "relation of the subject to objectivity in aesthetic comportment" that "joins eros and knowledge," that brings together thought and the body.[26] Hence, the shudder resists precisely the violence of exchange and identity we explored in the first section by resisting subjectivity's tendency toward identity thinking. In *The Fate of Art*, J. M. Bernstein interprets this possibility for a new relationship between subject and object in terms of an "affective geometry" of "height and distance."[27] The shudder's resistance to the reification of consciousness is one that contests the identity of subject and object by both introducing a distance between them, and reorienting the objective as "above" the subjective. It is in this sense that, for Adorno, the shudder affirms "the primacy of the object," affirming what has been repressed, excluded, and damaged in thought's self-preservative tendency to position itself as superior or "above" the objective world.[28] There is, of course, much to say about the exact character of the shudder's resistance to subjectivity's domination of objectivity. However, Bernstein's analysis already suggests that whatever form this resistance takes, it will necessarily involve a spatial reorientation, a reconstitution of what lives in the subject through a change in the space in and around it. We see this emphasis on spatial reorientation, and particularly on a reorientation of "height," in the shudder's relationship to the domination of nature and demythologizing of the Enlightenment.

In the "Art Beauty" section of *Aesthetic Theory*, Adorno writes, "[i]f through the demythologization of the world consciousness freed itself from the ancient shudder, that shudder is permanently reproduced in the historical antagonism of subject and object."[29] Given that the shudder sits at the very heart of the antagonism between subject and object, it should come as no surprise that it has an essential relation to Adorno's and Horkheimer's critique of Enlightenment. One will recall that for them, the process of Enlightenment works to advance human control over the natural world through a process of demythologizing in which the world is made calculable, useful, and knowable precisely by excluding the threatening mystery of the natural world.[30] This threatening mystery is precisely the "ancient shudder," the reminder of a time when humans feared their powerlessness in the face of brute nature. The shudder is, thus, "a response, colored by the fear of the overwhelming [*Überwältigung*]."[31] Faced with the uncontrollable and seemingly random power of the natural world (storms, earthquakes, droughts, illnesses, eclipses, etc.), humans develop systems of myth, enlightenment, reason, and science to assist in their self-preservation, a development, which, as we saw in the first section, marks the need to understand history as natural history. History is the history of the domination of nature, and the shudder is the "recollection" or "afterimage" of that domination. Bernstein follows Adorno in articulating this fear of being "overwhelmed" in relation to the experience of the Kantian sublime, a certain experience of awe, wonder, and terror in the face of that which defies total conceptualization.[32] However, in this fear of being "overwhelmed," we see the figure of the "affective geometry" outlined above. In the experience of the shudder, the objectivity of the world is experienced as something that threatens to overpower, dominate, and crush subjectivity. In the shudder, the subject feels itself under siege by something that cannot quite be defined or identified, something that is experienced as over and above the subject such that it could be overwhelmed or swallowed by it. Hence in the shudder, the relationship of subject and object is reoriented such that the subject experiences itself as small in relation to an objectivity that stands threateningly over it. However, Adorno is careful to point out that this experience is not unmediated nor entirely direct.

Although the experience of the shudder is articulated in terms of a spatial reorientation between subject and object, Adorno emphasizes throughout *Aesthetic Theory* that the shudder is not an unmediated experience, describing it as variously an "afterimage," a memory, an "apparition," and "recollection."[33] In the shudder, the subject is not in danger of being literally over-

whelmed, swallowed, or crushed. One will not drown in the objective sublimity of Beethoven's 9th or collapse under the beauty of a painting on the
wall. Rather in the shudder, the subject experiences "a memento of the liquidation of the I, which, shaken, perceives its own limitedness and finitude."[34]
In the experience of the shudder, the subject perceives for a moment, and at
"one remove," the limits of its existence.[35] The subject perceives that it lives
in a world whose existence extends beyond it, a world that existed before it
and will continue existing after it. In the shudder, the subject experiences its
relation to the world, a world of which the subject is but a limited part and
upon which the subject's life depends, but which does not reciprocate this
dependence. It is in this sense that in the shudder the subject experiences "the
possibility of letting self-preservation fall away," letting go the illusion that
one was ever truly separate from the world or that one's subjectivity depends
necessarily on the domination of the objective world. Yet this realization of
the limits and finitude of subjectivity is, "not real; but delirium," since,
although the subject "becomes aware, in real terms, of the possibility of
letting self-preservation fall away, it does not actually succeed in realizing
this possibility."[36] This failure is the necessary result of the nature of subjectivity, since, were the "I" to truly accord itself with the object, the subject
would disappear leaving nothing to report. Hence, the spatial reorientation
introduced by the shudder might appear to be a merely metaphorical or
logical reorientation. Yet, Adorno insists that the experience of the shudder is
not merely speculative or conceptual.

Despite the mediated nature of the shudder it is, for Adorno, necessarily
something that happens in the world: "True, the annihilation of the I in the
face of art is to be taken no more literally than is art. Because, however, what
are called aesthetic experiences [*Erlebnisse*] are as such psychologically real,
it would be impossible to understand them if they were simply part and
parcel of the illusoriness of art. Experiences are not 'as if.'"[37] The experience
of the possible annihilation of the subject in the shudder is not a literal
annihilation, yet that hardly entails that it is not a real experience. In the
shudder, the shakenness of the subject is psychologically and physically real,
as, if this were not the case, one could not even talk about "aesthetic experiences" at all. The notion that there is a necessary materiality to all experiences and, therefore, to the categories of thought and subjectivity is a consistent theme across Adorno's work. For example, in his essay "On Subject and
Object: a Prolegomena," Adorno writes, "[n]o concept of the subject can
have the element of individual humanity . . . separated from it in thought;
without any reference to it, subject would lose all significance."[38] Subject
and subjectivity refer simultaneously to the logical, abstract, universal notion
of a *person* and to the particular human individual. For Adorno, any claims
concerning subjectivity always have concrete resonance. Hence, although the
challenge presented to the subject in the experience of the shudder is not an

entirely literal challenge, one must still understand it as "a speculative moment that is realized somatically, through a bodily reaction."[39] In the shudder, the subject experiences a glimpse of a different mode of being, a different life. I shall return in a moment to the precise character of this glimpse. However, insofar as the shudder is a real, bodily experience of a different or altered subjectivity, it must also involve a different or altered notion of the world.

In the section of *Aesthetic Theory* entitled "On the Categories of the Ugly, The Beautiful, and Techniques," Adorno takes up the relation between the shudder and images of beauty:

> The image of beauty as that of a single and differentiated something originates with the emancipation from the fear of the overpowering wholeness and undifferentiatedness of nature. The shudder in the face of this is rescued by beauty into itself by making itself impervious to the immediately existent; beauty establishes a sphere of untouchability; works become beautiful by the force of their opposition to what simply exists.[40]

Beauty arises precisely at the moment in which it becomes possible for things to be other than they appear. Beautiful objects are not possible in a world of undifferentiated nature, as the very difference between the beautiful and the ugly requires differentiation. Hence, beautiful objects only arise with the emergence of natural history and the domination of nature, which is to say that images of beauty co-arise with the shudder. In fact, the shudder is "rescued" by beauty, insofar as the notion of beauty makes space for a certain resistance to "what is." The beautiful is structurally opposed to "what is," as it shows us a glimpse of something beyond what merely exists. It shows us an excess, a possibility, or, as Adorno will write towards the end of *Aesthetic Theory*, an "anamnesis of the vanquished, of the repressed, and perhaps of the possible."[41] Hence for Adorno, the shudder is not only what lives in the subject, but is also a resistance to the existing world captured in artworks. Hence, the shudder is not merely a psychologically real reorientation of the subject but is a reorientation of the world.

For Adorno, the power and importance of art and of the experience of the shudder is that they open up resistance to the existing world or, more specifically, to the notion that the existing world is the only possible world. In the artwork, we see not some specific time or place but rather a forgotten time before the institution of the currently existing formations of life and the world. We see that this is not the only world that has been, nor the only one that could be. It is in this sense that the artwork "rises above human beings and is carried beyond their intentions and the world of things."[42] Art and the experience of the shudder changes us not by giving us a concrete object or making us totally new people, but by denaturalizing and demystifying the necessity, naturalness, and totality of what exists. Hence, the artwork and the experience of the shudder express at root the basic concerns of Adorno's critique of natural history and fundamental ontology, the concern that the desire to uncover the ontological structures of the world and human existence works to ontologize that history and its suffering, suggesting that "in a secret world of being all of this [violence] will have had some kind of purpose."[43] However, this notion of the shudder as resisting the suffering and necessity of the existing world returns us to the concern for life and subjectivity with which we began.

Although the shudder opens a resistance to the existing world insofar as the materiality of the artwork allows the experience of an altered notion of the world and of the subject, the "realness" of this experience has the pro-foundest consequence for the subjectivity of the subject. Having reiterated again the "real" concrete aspects of the experience of the shudder and of the artwork, Adorno writes: "The subject, convulsed by art, has real experiences; by the strength of insight into the artwork as artwork, these experiences are those in which the subject's petrification in his own subjectivity dissolves and the narrowness of his self-positedness is revealed."[44] In the experience of the shudder, the subject sees not only the possibility of a world beyond that which presently exists, the "insight into the artwork as artwork," but also the limits and narrowness of its own current existence. The shudder's challenge to the limits of the currently existing formations of the world entails a challenge to the currently existing formations of subjectivity and "life" as well. In the shudder, the subject sees that its life and the existing understanding of life are, like the existing world, limited. They are one possibility among others, neither necessary nor natural. Adorno associates this experience both with "true happiness" and "grief," as this insight confronts the subject with its "morality."

In the moment of the shudder, the subject experiences the happiness of seeing that its life, here and now, is not the only possible life, not the only possibility of what life can be. Yet, this happiness also reveals the limits of the subject's life, here and now, the limits of any sedimented form of life in the face of the possibility of a radically altered or radically new understanding of life. This interplay between actuality and possibility, happiness and grief, living and dying is the very experience of "life," for Adorno; it is what "lives in subjectivity." Life is the experience of the limits and possibility of living, the limits and possibility of a world beyond the suffering of the current state of things. This is the urgent question of "life" which metaphysics puts to us, the question of whether it is still possible to live, still possible to challenge the world as it exists, still possible for there to be more than this life, this world? This question is so urgent for Adorno because if the answer is no, then we are left, as he says in *Minima Moralia* with a totally administered society in which "life no longer lives." It is beyond the scope of this project to fully explore Adorno's answer to the question of whether it is still possible to live.[45] However, what this reading of the shudder reveals is that insofar as aesthetic comportment fundamentally redefines the relation and character of life and the world, it is, at root, not just an aesthetic experience but an ecological experience.

Given the necessary connection between the notion of the shudder, life, and the domination of nature in Adorno's aesthetic theory, one sees that at stake in aesthetic experience is the destabilizing and reorienting of the relationship between the subject and the objectivity of itself and the world. In the experience of the shudder, the subject confronts the limits of its "life" and of the world, it confronts its dependence on an environment that both came before it and upon which its existence depends, and it sees that "life" is nothing but this confrontation. The shudder of life opens up the realization that the subject has never been, in truth, above or superior to the objective world, an insight that challenges the naturalness and necessity of what is. Hence, the subject is led, through the experience of the shudder, to see that this world and this life is but one possibility among others, an insight that opens up the possibility of a radically altered, new, and potentially less violent relation between subject and object, human life and the world. Hence for Adorno, the shudder is as much an ecological experience as an aesthetic one, an experience of the relations, tensions, conflicts, and possibilities between life and the world. This fact both corroborates and extends the notion that Adorno's critical theory has much to offer environmental thinking.

Given Cook's argument that Adorno's critique of nature has something important to offer ecological thought, and given the fact that this critique shares an identical ethical imperative with his critique of dialectics, his analysis of subjectivity, his critique of capitalism, and his theory of aesthetics it is difficult to avoid the conclusion that all of these aspects of Adorno's thought have something to offer ecology. In particular, his relating of the logic of capitalism to the domination of nature seems particularly germane, as one can hardly approach a serious ecology without an equally serious critique of capitalism. However, based on the analysis of violence, the critique of capitalism would be but one of the critical tools Adorno's thought offers ecological thinking. As Cook points out, for example, Adorno's engagement with the complicated and ultimately paradoxical logic of universal and particular, unity and diversity offers direct assistance to the thinking of radical ecology, since "activism itself presupposes the unity—in the form of solidarity—of diverse individuals."[46] Similarly, Adorno's conception of aesthetics and particularly the shudder's insight into the non-necessary, non-natural fragility of "what is" offers direct assistance to the ecological and environmental insistence that we must fundamentally change the current formations of the world to avoid climate catastrophe. In fact, there is an important way in which this insight tells us something key about the nature of critical theory.

Given that Adorno takes the risk of violence to life to be the driving concern of immanent critique, one comes to see that, for him, truly critical analysis must take seriously the way in which violence to life is at the very heart of our thinking, our economics, our conception of subjectivity, and our aesthetics. This is not to suggest that critical theory must only talk about questions of life or that all art must be "environmental." The point is not to make critical theory ecology. Rather, Adorno insists that all critical analysis, which is to say, all immanent analysis, is necessarily a matter of life and death, a worry over subjects and objects, living and non-living, life and world. For Adorno, a critical theory that finds itself unable to speak to ecology, unable to speak to concerns for life and the world, would, in fact, be no critical theory at all. It is the concern for life that gives theory its critical focus, its ethical power, and its continued relevance to ethics and politics.

NOTES

1. Andrew Biro, "Adorno and Ecological Politics," in *Adorno and the Need in Thinking: New Critical Essays*, eds. Donald A. Burke, et al. (Toronto: University of Toronto Press, 2007), 345–62; Andrew Biro, ed., *Critical Ecologies: The Frankfurt School and Contemporary Environmental Crisis* (Toronto: University of Toronto Press, 2011); Deborah Cook9 *Adorno on Nature* (Durham, UK: Acumen, 2011); Harriet Johnson, "Undignified Thoughts After Nature: Adorno's Aesthetic Theory," *Critical Horizons*, Vol. 12, no. 3 (2011): 372–95.

2. T. W. Adorno, *Metaphysics: Concept and Problems*, ed. Rolf Tiedemann, transl. Edmund Jephcott (Stanford, CA: Stanford University Press, 2001), 112.

3. Alastair Morgan, *Adorno's Concept of Life* (New York: Continuum, 2007), 98.

4. For a concise overview of the role of "aesthetic experience" in both twentieth-century continental and analytic philosophy, see Richard Shusterman's "The End of Aesthetic Experience," *The Journal of Aesthetics and Art Criticism*, Vol. 55, no. 1 (1997): 29–41.

5. Cook, 1.

6. Ibid.

7. T. W. Adorno and Max Horkheimer, *Dialectic of Enlightenment: Philosophical Fragments*, ed. Gunzelin Schmid Noerr, transl. Edmund Jephcott (Stanford, CA: Stanford University Press, 2002), 184.

8. Cook, 2.

9. Ibid.

10. Adorno and Horkheimer, 4.

11. Cook, 2. Also see Adorno 1973, 146.

12. Adorno 1973, 5.

13. Adorno 2001, 70.

14. Adorno 1973, 148.

15. Adorno develops this idea in *Dialectic of Enlightenment* around the concept of "the specimen." See Adorno and Horkheimer, 6.

16. Adorno 1973, 146. Translation modified.

17. Ibid., 178.

18. Ibid., 15–16.

19. Theodor W. Adorno, *Aesthetic Theory*, ed. and transl. Robert Hullot-Kentor (Minneapolis: University of Minnesota Press, 1997), 331.

20. Ibid.

21. Ibid.

22. Theodor W. Adorno, *Minima Moralia: Reflections on a Damaged Life*, transl. E. F. N. Jephcott (London: Verso, 2005), 19.

23. Ibid.

24. Adorno develops the notion of "mimetic comportment" most clearly in the "Semblance and Expression" section of *Aesthetic Theory* (100–17). He associates mimesis with the "living subject" (169) and the primacy of the object (115) as well as with resistance to the administered world of bourgeois society (104). Hence, Adorno everywhere links mimesis with the logic and figures embodied in the experience of "the shudder," an association that suggests that the experience of the shudder is itself an experience of mimetic comportment.

25. Adorno 1997, 331.

26. Ibid.

27. J. M. Bernstein, *The Fate of Art: Aesthetic Alienation from Kant to Derrida and Adorno* (University Park, PA: The Pennsylvania State University Press, 1992), 223.

28. Adorno 1997, 259.

29. Ibid., 84.

30. For a clear and concise account of this logic, see Alison Stone's "Adorno and the Disenchantment of Nature," *Philosophy and Social Criticism*, Vol. 32, no. 2 (2006): 231–53.

31. Adorno 1997, 245.

32. Bernstein, 222.

33. Adorno 1997, 79, 88, 286.

34. Ibid., 245.

35. Bernstein, 220.

36. Adorno 1997, 245.

37. Ibid.

38. T. W. Adorno, *Critical Models: Interventions and Catchwords*, transl. Henry W. Pickford (New York: Columbia University Press, 2005), 245.

39. Alastair Morgan, *Adorno's Concept of Life* (New York: Continuum, 2007), 99.

40. Adorno 1997, 51.

41. Ibid., 259

42. Ibid., 80.

43. Adorno 2001, 104.

44. Adorno 1997, 269.

45. For a thorough account of the concept of "life" in Adorno's work, see Morgan 2007.

46. Cook, 6.

Chapter Eleven

Enigmaticalness as a Fundamental Category in Adorno's *Aesthetic Theory*

Andrea Sakoparnig

Whenever we encounter a poem, a film, a piece of music, or something of the kind, we become entangled in incessant procedures of interpretation. In contrast to other objects we encounter in our daily lives, artworks demand a more sophisticated and active engagement. If we merely classify or categorize them, as we normally do when faced with objects, then they evade us. To uncover them, we have to engross ourselves in them, open ourselves for them. Adorno is the philosopher who most prominently conceptualizes this experience as essentially being an experience of the enigmatic character of an artwork. According to him, all artworks are inherently enigmatic (*rätselhaft*). He even goes so far as to claim that whenever we do not experience something as enigmatic, we are actually not dealing with an artwork. Given these claims, enigmaticalness is not merely a peripheral aspect of an artwork, but rather characterizes its very being as an artwork. Adorno's notion of enigmaticalness is based upon the familiar experience that an artwork calls for comprehension yet resists it, thus creating a seductive tension "between a do-not-let-yourself-be-understood and a wanting-to-be-understood."[1] He elucidates this peculiar phenomenon as arising from a paradox. The artwork's constitution on the one hand accommodates the subject's conventional operation of determination, and on the other hand differs from it in disappointing its criteria and regularities. However, we would not even know anything of the artwork's unique logicality if it did not balk at our logical approaches, that is, appear negative, enigmatic in the face of them. From the refusal of our logical approaches some crucial questions arise, such as: Why is it that, in the course of determination, we experience the logicality of artworks as enigmatic, and what does this experience of enigmaticalness imply for our conception of ourselves as rational beings? Adorno's answers are quite astonishing. He argues that by experiencing artworks as enigmatic, we not only become aware of the existence of another kind of logicality, but even more, we are compelled to question our image of ourselves as subjects that constitute objects. Aesthetic experience is thus of enormous relevance. Theoretical reflection upon it can support a new, non-violent relation between subject and object, thereby contributing to mending the deficiencies in our rationality. It is thus a pivotal task for aesthetics to develop these far reaching implications fully, since doing so will prove the philosophical implications of this experience beyond the aesthetic sphere.

HOW IT IS THAT ARTWORKS APPEAR TO BE ENIGMATIC—THE LOGIC OF AESTHETIC EXPERIENCE

First of all, we have to get an idea of why it is that artworks appear to be enigmatic, before we examine why Adorno takes this experience to be both a negative and a crucial one. The most general explanation of aesthetic enigmaticalness that Adorno provides explains enigmaticalness as resulting from an inadequate approach to the artwork. According to this, we fail to understand the artwork's meaning when we try to determine it in a conventional way. We apply operations of determination that are based on concepts and categories, and that do not conform to the way the artwork is determined in its own distinctive way. Thus, the experience of enigmaticalness is essentially a negative one as it is the experience of a failure—the failure of our conventional practices of determination. To give an account of this process will require several points of explanation: of how an artwork's meaning is determined, of how our practices of determination are designed, and above all, why the former mode of determination does not fully conform to the latter.

We can better understand Adorno's account of how an artwork's meaning is constituted if we examine the sources from which it derives its decisive aspects. On the one hand, there is Leibniz's concept of monads as integral entities without "windows,"[2] and on the other hand, Walter Benjamin's concept of constellation, an epistemological method that describes the practice of bringing particular and dispersed elements into a legible figuration.[3] Whereas the former is exemplary for proposing a model of an entity that is integral, immanent, and yet dynamically determined, the latter is exemplary in proposing a methodology of constructing such a thoroughly determined coherence out of something that is per se, objectively non-meaningful.

Adorno is strongly inspired by Leibniz's essential conceptual innovation, which involves characterizing monads as individual, self-sufficient, logically determined entities that are nevertheless dynamic and in a constant process of becoming.[4] Adorno compares artworks to monads, firstly, because of their inherent logic, secondly, because of the therefrom stemming specificity in generating meaning, and finally, because of their reflective relation to what is external to them. In keeping with Leibniz, Adorno regards artworks as syntheses of empirical elements, such that their unity must not be considered as a composition of parts but rather as a dynamic interrelation of forces. This leads him to the ontological notion of artworks as "at once a force field and a thing."[5] As self-determining syntheses, they build—out of themselves—a processual coherence in which every element is conditioned by, as well as conditioning, other elements, even if these elements are actually irreconcilable and non-identical, thus bringing about an integral coherence, or more precisely, an individual identity. It is important to emphasize that this individual identity is produced in a processual manner, since it means that the identity that results is only a moment within the process of generation. Adorno points out that even as objects artworks are processes, or objectivations of an inherent process, they thus bring forth an objectivity that is almost inevitably mistaken by analysis.[6] This idea of artworks as objectified processes again rests upon another essential aspect of Leibniz's thought. By referring to monads as so-called entelechies, Leibniz characterizes monads as having their own purpose (*telos*) in themselves and as having a capacity to actualize inherent potentials.[7] With this concept, Leibniz expresses the way in which entities attempt to actualize themselves, and provides a counter to prevalent mechanistic and causal accounts of them. This provides an impetus to Adorno: In a sense, he considers artworks as well to be self-actualizing entities due to their immanent forces, or as Adorno puts it, their impulses.

Obviously, artworks do not actualize themselves, but need to be created by an artist. To hold on the idea of an identity that actualizes itself processually, Adorno makes use of Walter Benjamin's notions of *mimesis* and constellation,[8] according to which an integral aesthetic immanence is the result of a specific artistic activity: that of a mimetically accomplished constellation. Adorno's inaugural lecture "The Actuality of Philosophy" indicates how important the concept of constellation developed by Benjamin in his "Epistemo-Critical Prologue" of *The Origin of German Tragic Drama* is.[9] In his lecture, he values the practice of constellation as an epistemologically significant methodology. Challenging the idea that philosophy is capable of comprehending reality, he instead proposes to view philosophy as "interpretation" (*Deutung*) and models his conception of interpretation on the practice of riddle-solving. This again is based on the idea that legible figurations ultimately join together out of a constellation of particular and dispersed elements—a profoundly Benjaminean idea.[10] Similarly, he conceives of artworks as such constellations, which is to say, as experimental arrangements, set in a reality deprived of any meaningful totality. However, aesthetic constellation can be brought about in different ways: mimetically or constructively. Adorno clearly favors artworks that result from a constellation that is mimetically generated, since he argues that only in such cases is their unity justified. It is not imposed upon the elements in a manner so as to tendentiously violate their particularity; instead, their unity results out of the elements' own impulses, thus not only respecting their particularity, but moreover preserving and reasserting it. Within this, we must remember that this notion of mimesis inspired by Benjamin differs fundamentally from that of antiquity. Whereas the latter understands the way in which mimesis generates meaning as imitative or illusory, or representative, the former interprets it as a highly sensitive, careful, and responsive attitude, facilitating a non-violent relation between elements.[11] As a consequence, every element's meaning is functionally dependent upon the whole relational network and its position within that network. Adorno therefore assumes that the primary task of the artist is to make him- or herself into a medium for rendering the mimetic impulses that are inherent to the elements, whereby we have to consider mediation not only as a passive, responsive submission, but also as an active, engaged endeavor. We get a sense for how much importance Adorno ascribes to the kind of immanence that is accomplished by a mimetically organized constellation by looking at his critical comments about other forms of synthesis. Adorno argues that construction brings about a corrupted synthetic form of constitution, even though he points out that construction is the only form of synthesis possible at present. In contrast to a connection of elements that is achieved by mimesis, in construction the synthesis of the elements is carried out at the expense of the quality of the elements. Therefore, the synthesis cannot assert itself as an immanent connection of elements in the strict sense, since unity is enforced upon elements. The constructive constellation subordinates to itself both what is external to the artwork as well as what is internal to it; it is thus heteronomous by nature, whereas the mimetic construction is autonomous.

In addition to elucidating the logicality of the artwork, Adorno provides us with a critical reflection on the conventional ways in which recipients determine the meaning of artworks.[12] In his account, we usually determine something in an analytical manner, which implies that explaining something amounts to reducing it to what is already known.[13] We make use of universals, categories, and concepts that inevitably level out the qualities of the particular. Adorno calls this mode of determination identification.

It follows from this that the logicality belonging to the artwork corresponds in one sense to our discursive thought, but also disagrees with it in another sense. At first sight, artworks appear as thoroughly determinate and thus determinable, but when we determine them in our usual way, by defining them analytically, we find that they become indeterminable to us. Whenever we try to understand the meaning of an artwork by determining the determinateness of its elements, we fail. That is because in the process of identification, we isolate elements from the context to which they owe their determination, thus negating their determinateness. Adorno expresses this problem quite explicitly: "As soon as one imagines having a firm grasp on the details of an artwork, it dissolves into the indeterminate and undifferentiated, so mediated is it."[14] If we bring this crucial thought from *Aesthetic Theory* together with one of the crucial insights from "The Concept of Enlightenment," we can say: Artworks are "beings-in-themselves," "self-same, self-identical,"[15] whereas our procedures of identification function "at the cost that nothing can at the same time be identical to itself."[16] Artworks resist identification and become enigmatic when we address them in an identifying mode, thus asserting their self-identity and challenging our conventional approaches. Hence, whenever we do not do justice to their identity, whenever we mistake them for mere objects, whenever we fail to understand that we should rather consider them as in a process of becoming, they become closed off, reticent, which is to say that they become enigmatic.

However, the blame does not merely lie on our side, since it is just as much an inevitable effect of an antinomy that lies in the artworks' distinctive identity, or more precisely in its objectivity. This antinomy is brought about by the objectivation that artworks necessarily have to undergo in order to actualize themselves. Although their particular identity basically emerges through immanent dynamic processes, it only finds reality when it is objectified, which involves being fixed. With that, we arrive at the paradoxical ontological nature of artworks that I mentioned above, their being a thing and a force field at once,[17] or as Adorno noted: "The movement of artworks must be at a standstill and thereby become visible,"[18] or "(t)he artwork is both the result of the process and the process itself at a standstill."[19] Taking this into account, the consequences for the artwork's meaning become obvious: Since meaning is only produced in and through the processual relation of the elements, as soon as this process is objectified, thus, seemingly brought to a halt, it is, as Adorno puts it, "broken or veiled."[20] This gives rise to the effect that "the more insistently they are observed the more paradoxical they become: Each artwork is a system of irreconcilables."[21]

Since we experience artworks as enigmatic as soon as we try to understand them by identifying their meaning, we arrive at the conclusion that we have to revise the practices by which we determine them. As we already saw, artworks are in themselves determined, but in an unexpected way. So because they are actually determined, it must be the case that they are potentially determinable, although not, as we learn, in a conventional way. It follows from this that, if we are to comprehend them, then the only thing that remains to be done is to let ourselves experience their unique kind of logicality, their intrinsic determinateness. So once we have realized that our analytical approaches are unrewarding, we acknowledge that we are compelled to shift from our identifying mode of determination, which is analytical and reductive, to a synthetic mode, which is rather a processual and reconstitutive reenactment. Instead of analytically identifying elements, thus wrongly reducing them to fundamental elements,[22] we mimetically reenact the elements' dynamic interrelation "by way of all mediations."[23] In so doing, we regard the individual element as a functional junction within a complex network of determination and reproduce the artwork in its processual constitution. The processuality of the artwork—that before was brought to a halt through objectivation—is then reanimated. It is only by having such a "living experience"[24] that we come to regard artworks as being "*in actu*"[25] with their inner tension not terminating in a fixed identity. The capacity for reenactment is, according to Adorno, best embodied in the practice of artistic performance, which he understands as the "imitation of the dynamic curves of what is performed."[26] We may regard this immersive reenactment, in which we are both responsive and active, as a *being in the artwork*—a perspective from which "enigmaticalness makes itself invisible."[27]

Even if we find this elucidation of enigmaticalness plausible, we still have to confront the challenge of understanding why the enigmatic character of artworks is not dissoluble. Indeed, Adorno insists that the shift from an analytical approach to a synthetic one does not prevent us from experiencing this enigmaticalness. It only temporarily makes it disappear, and it seems to vanish, but as we soon realize, it is only hiding. As soon as we step out of the process of reenacting the immanent completion of the artwork, its enigmaticalness returns. Adorno's explanation is instructive: When the musician reenacts the musical work, for instance, he does in a sense understand the score, but doing this in a manner that involves following its impulses: "in a certain sense he does not know what he plays."[28] The musician is, so to speak, on "this side of the enigma."[29] The very moment the immanent reenactment ceases, the enigma shows up again, and is all the more obscure.

This describes the paradox of aesthetic comprehension: In contrast to conventional comprehension, aesthetic comprehension is infinitely processual and utterly inconsistent. Being both, it contradicts not only our conventional operations of comprehension, which seek stabilization and coherence, but also, more generally, it contradicts our very notion of comprehension. What we procedurally understand in the course of immersive reenactment does not settle to form a fixed comprehension that we could take hold of. Because of their processual and dynamic identity, artworks are not "being" but "becoming"[30]; as a result, aesthetic comprehension also only "is" in the course of immersive reenactment, in the process of making and not (in) being. As long as comprehension, like the identity of the artwork, is *in motion*, it is does not count as "real comprehension" according to the perspective of our conventional concept of comprehension, which is stable, *in stasis*. Being in motion, comprehension is, so to speak, in a state of flux. This implies that comprehension—being in constant, processual generation—necessarily undergoes continuous changes, which is to say that it is ephemeral. In the course of processually reenacting the artwork, we might learn for instance that all of the prior meanings of elements can change retroactively from the perspective of the meaning of another later element, with the consequence that interpretations developed so far are constantly shaken. When we are engaged with the enigma in the course of reenacting the artwork, we feel no real irritation about these rejections and dislocations. It is only from an external perspective that these continuous changes in meaning create confusion. Along with these rather temporal peculiarities come logical ones. Thus in the immersive process of reenacting the artwork, we come upon what can only be regarded as inconsistencies from the perspective of conventional logic. Since every element in the artwork is functionally determined by *all* of its relations, a variety of different possible modes of structuring these elements emerge. This means that two or more possible interpretations, resulting from different processes of structuring the elements, can potentially conflict with one another. Following a certain set of structural determinations, for instance, might lead to one interpretation that would not be consistent with another, equally justifiable and compelling interpretation that would result from another process of structuring.[31] Once a variety of potentially contradictory interpretations puts itself forward as equally legitimate, the necessity to choose one of these interpretations arises. As a result, a decision between different understandings is both necessary, especially when they are contradictory and mutually exclusive, and impossible, since they are both legitimate; the decision *must* be made, but it *cannot* be made. Therefore, enigmaticalness can result from the in-decidability between inconsistent and incompatible understandings—an in-decidability that necessitates a decision *and* at the same time renders it impossible. Another variation on this would be when we generate two or more interpretations and therefore have to take the same element into account. In this case, it is not different processes of structuring the elements that would provide us with different, perhaps contradictory, interpretations; in fact, one and the same process of structuring might allow for different interpretations. The very process that brings about a certain understanding rules out the generation of another understanding that would also paradoxically be justifiable, or even fitting. This is because opting for one element to play a functional, which is to say, a determinative role within an interpretation makes it logically impossible to invest it simultaneously within another interpretation. This would be the case even if both interpretations were compatible. A decision to make an element play a functional role in only one interpretation may be out of the question for the same reasons that it is not possible to decide between a variety of different syntactic structures: we lack the criteria on which to choose one of the functional roles (i.e., potential meanings, or, we recognize that the element is actually dynamically bound to different structural units).

To illustrate the issue in a less abstract manner, we can think for instance of our experience of reading poems. In reading a poem, we can relate a word or a column to different words, or columns, with the result that a variety of meanings are supportable at the same time. All too often, a conclusive decision for one of the possible meanings cannot or even should not be made. Moreover, even contradictory or exclusive meanings and interpretations can paradoxically affirm each other in their mutual relationship. What is valid for the syntactical structuring dimension elucidated so far also applies to the semantic dimension of the poem. In poems, a variety of meanings of a word can be valid at the same time, even if they mutually exclude each other or result in different interpretations. Quite often, poems live off of this syntactic and semantic ambiguity or vagueness, which cannot be overridden by a definitive decision. Within this process, the retroactive dimension of meaning plays a substantial role: Given, for instance, that a verse has three words, starting with the first, we can say that, taken as single unit, we cannot decide which of its semantic or syntactic possibilities will be actualized. It is only with the second word that the meaning of the first becomes nearly decidable. However, the second word's potential meaning is itself determined by the semantic horizon established by the first, but can be redefined by the occurrence of the third word. So being with the third word, in the course of our reading the meanings of all the previous words—seemingly fixed— can once again begin to totter. In addition to that, there might be closer connections between the first word and the third or the second and the third, and depending on which seems to be more informative, we decide what it might mean temporarily; anyway, all meanings generated by our structuring can begin to falter again with the next verse.

To be more specific: We decide in the course of our reading whether the word "bow," for instance, is meant as the noun "a wooden stick" or rather "a tied ribbon," or the verb "to bend forward," or even the district in London (in case the whole text is written in uppercase)—with respect to which semantic and syntactic structuring we carry out with regard to all the other words in the verse. Is the verse in need of a verb, we tend to interpret "bow" as a verb, consequentially as "to bend forward." However, if there shows up a verb in the next verse that might do the job as well or even better, we might feel inclined to re-interpret it as a noun. Nonetheless, our first interpretation of "bow" as verb might also be still up in the air, even if we discarded it, as in a sense it still can be informative. So, often, especially in poems, a meaning that seemed to be certain at a definite time can suddenly change from subsequent perspectives; what is more astonishing, even if we feel to have reason to re-interpret a meaning, is the one discarded can still be of a certain formative influence—which is it may determine the semantic horizon or the syntactic role of other elements. Therefore it is even possible that "bow" in a poem actually bears all of the semantically possible meanings, which in ordinary language is almost never the case. The same can happen with propositions. We may be inclined to refer "his/her" to a syntactical unit very early in the poem, while in the course of our reading we learn that it might also (or even better) refer to a later referent. As a result, the meaning of the syntactical unit before might retroactively change. The same can take place with homonyms. If we only hear, for instance "accept/except" during a performance, we cannot decide whether this means "receive" or "excluding." But whereas in normal, everyday life, the context indicates which meaning we should favor, in poetry an uncertainty, or even in-decidability, often remains.

We may be inclined to take these points—Adorno's elucidations of enigmaticalness as resulting from the determination of the artwork's elements— as a version of the well-known over-determination thesis. This thesis assumes, in keeping with Kant's theory of the sublime, that each element in the artwork is related to such a hyper-complex degree that the meaning of the single, particular element cannot be identified, at least not conclusively. However, the thesis explains over-determinacy in terms of being determined too much or in too many different ways, as being abundantly meaningful, which should not be confused with Adorno's claim that artworks are determined in a specific way, namely processually and dynamically.[32] According to the over-determination thesis, we can say that if we had enough time to reconstruct all of the determinative relations of an element we could ultimately determine each element's determinateness and dissolve its enigmaticalness. So we would gather partial understandings and join them together to form an overall comprehension. In other words, we would begin by understanding something and continuously enrich this understanding, until we reach a holistic, overall understanding. To keep hold of the insolubility of enigmaticalness, some representatives of the over-determinacy thesis argue that we are only able to understand fragments of the artwork's unique logic. However, we do not achieve a real, overall understanding as fragmented comprehensions cannot be combined to form a complete understanding. As a consequence, mere partial comprehensions as such, as long as they cannot be related, remain incomprehensible for us. However, contrary to this account of over-determinacy, Adorno holds that the problem of comprehension is not so much with the mere complexity of determinateness as with its processuality and the paradoxes that arise from it, that is, ephemerality, in-decidability of meaning, and so forth. He emphasizes that the particular moments "go over into their other, find continuance in it, want to be extinguished in it, and in their demise determine what follows them."[33] So even if we had enough time, we would never exhaust the determinateness of all elements out of their dynamic interrelation. Whenever we think that we have identified the determinateness of an element, it soon gets another, thus not only retroactively negating the identification we have already made, but prospectively re-determining the identification we are to made with respect to subsequent elements. So not only the determinateness of the singular element changes, but also that of all the other elements (before and thereafter) to which it is related. However, this understanding again should not be confounded with the indeterminacy thesis, according to which, for instance, we cannot identify significant material (in Paul Valéry's or Roman Jakobson's semiological reformulations), and thus non-aesthetic understanding gets "de-automatized," or even suspended.[34] This thesis assumes that we normally connect what is signified, that is, the meaning, with the signifier, the bearer of the meaning, in order to form a meaningful sign. The basis for this is that both the signifier and signified can be identified according to the rules within a code. These rules stipulate what is to count as a signifier and what this signifier means. So conventional understanding starts with an identification of both the signifier and its embodied meaning. In contrast, the artwork, with a logicality of its own, does not offer any rules that facilitate this identifying and signifying process, as it already hinders the selection of significant material. Therefore, the question of what something means is corrupted from its very beginning—the aesthetic understanding vacillates, or as Valéry puts it, is in a state of a "prolonged hesitation between sound and meaning."[35] Adorno would not agree that comprehension is interrupted from its very beginning. He would rather claim that comprehension is evoked and then challenged in its conventional regime—even when he seems pretty close to this position, as some phrases indicate, for instance, his comparison of artworks to "hieroglyphs for which the code has been lost."[36] What Adorno holds is that artworks actually *are*, even from our perspective, determined. They are not at all undetermined. They only become indeterminable by the way we try to determine them. Being indeterminable is not at all the same as being undetermined. Otherwise the tension "between a do-not-let-yourself-be-understood and a wanting-to-be-understood,"[37] which Adorno argues is characteristic for artworks, would be lacking in any rationality.

Beyond this, there is a further difference of which we should be aware. These accounts of both over- and in-/under-determinacy are strategically directed towards explaining how enigmaticalness shows up as *non*-understanding in a variety of ways—as delay, suspension, or as a break of our categorical and discursive operations—but they thereby fail to explain the transformation our understanding undergoes and fail to show how it results in a specific, processual aesthetic understanding as Adorno does. Whereas all the above-mentioned explanations declare that an understanding of the artwork is corrupted from the beginning, Adorno's description of the logic of enigmaticalness may be better conceived of as being two phased: We actually *can* structure given signs, and thus gain understanding, but at the same time there are several other, intervening, but equally valid and legitimate, possible ways of structuring given signs, and thus there are several other possible understandings. So the problem of understanding is not located in our categorical and discursive approach as such, as usually claimed, but in the totality of equally possible, but inconsistent and incompatible judgments that artworks evoke. It is this irresolvable, impossible totality of judgments that disagrees with our notion of logic—as above mentioned, the artwork as "a system of irreconcilables."[38]

In any case, what all these accounts share is that they understand the logicality of the artwork as challenging the demands of our power of judgment. It is contrary to our nature as logical beings to accept a set of contradictory interpretations. As a result, our conventional practice of determination does not remain unaffected. Most prominently, Kant described aesthetic experience as an infinite processualizing of our cognitive powers, making our power of judgment reflective, and in this regard Adorno found him exemplary.[39] However, whereas Kant takes the aesthetic experience as a reassuring affirmation of our cognitive capacities,[40] Adorno takes it as a critical intervention against them, an interference "by that which is not the thought itself."[41]

Regardless of whether it is syntactic structuring or semantic structuring that gives rise to enigmaticalness, whenever we encounter an artwork our normally finite comprehension is "processualized," caught in an infinite play. If we are to comprehend an artwork, we have to endure its inconclusiveness, and we have to face the challenge of reflecting on all equally possible, even incompatible, contradictory, or ephemeral, interpretations. This logicality of keeping in play different, even inconsistent meanings, or meanings that have vanished due to their ephemeral character is one of the main things that makes artworks different from other expressive forms, such as, for instance, propositions. They are able to express through their complex logicality what could never be expressed through decisive propositions and discursive thinking.

THE RELEVANCE OF AESTHETIC ENIGMATICALNESS

Both of these characteristics of aesthetic comprehension, its processuality and its inconsistency, made Adorno question the notion of comprehension (*Verstehen*). He proposes to replace the previously central category with the reflection on aesthetic enigmaticalness. It is especially its haunting character, its only seeming disappearance and its constant return, that should, according to him, attract our theoretical attention. Rather than explaining enigmaticalness away,[42] we should feel obliged to make its logic explicit, which means concretizing the reason for its insolubility[43] —Adorno's polemical sideswipe against hermeneutical approaches is unmistakable.[44] Accordingly, we have to face the paradox that artworks hide something that—in reference to Poe's letter—"is visible and is, by being visible, hidden."[45] This makes the handling of enigmaticalness fall apart into two distinct yet mutually related dimensions, an experiential and a reflective dimension. To grasp enigmaticalness we are required to experience it and also to reflect theoretically on the content and logic of this experience. Through reflection, we explicate what is blind to the experience itself, but can only be caught in the mode of experience. This involves making explicit the relevance of this very experience.

To clarify this point, we have to return to our initial observations. We started with the subject's failure to determine the artworks' identity. This experience of failure is essential. Following Adorno, we should understand this rather as a "shudder [*Erschütterung*], radically opposed to the conventional idea of experience [*Erlebnis*]"[46] since this is what reveals the subject's "limitness and finitude"[47] and thus its dependence on objectivity. By experiencing itself as limited, the subject experiences objectivity to be something beyond itself, not as something posited by itself. According to Adorno, this convulsing shudder exposes the fundamentally problematic conventional relation between subject and object, as well as its underlying prevailing conceptions—objectivity and subjectivity. He thus points to the deficiencies of modern rationality. Adorno laid down his critical assessment of modern rationality, pertaining mainly to epistemological practices, along with Max Horkheimer in the early essay *The Concept of Enlightenment*. In this, they criticized modern rationality for its self-sufficiency and errant internal dynamics, which ultimately led to it becoming a violent and oppressive form (impressively exemplified by its horrific climax at Auschwitz). Originally, the individual's most effective means for coping with its primordial fears, rationality gradually became so powerful that it deteriorated into its dialectical negation: it developed destructive traits by negating everything not commensurable to and identifiable with the subject's categorical and discursive framework. The aim of Adorno's and Horkheimer's critique is not to denigrate the achievements of rationality, but to secure its epistemic competence by bringing it into a critical relation with those aspects in which it forsakes itself. For this to happen, discursive rationality must become aware that it does not comply with its own standards. To initiate this reflective turn towards itself, the mechanical operations of identification in discursive rationality must be brought to a halt. We realize such a fundamental interference within aesthetic experience, according to Adorno, or rather, we undergo it as an experience of enigmaticalness.

We have already seen that artworks call on us to determine them as dynamic constellations, and this again in a mode of determination that is in itself constellational, and no longer identifying in a conventional manner. Artworks do not only necessitate a different, non-identifying approach to determine them, but they also—due to their insolvable enigmaticalness—provoke a reflection on this shift, its reasons and its merits in contrast to conventional practices of determination; this reflection demonstrates that the process of identification inherent to the constitution of artworks and that we experience in their reenactment is an alternative to our concepts of identity and identification. We discover the possibility to synthesize heterogeneous elements in ways that do not violate their individuality, but preserve it. Artworks thus render what is ineffably individual more approachable, while simultaneously insisting on its inexhaustibility, and are thus instructive for the kind of synthesis subjects perform: conceptual judgments. [18]

Thus, at the heart of aesthetic experience lies a fundamental revision of the prevailing subject-object-relation, and as a consequence, a redefinition of our notion of objectivity. In and through aesthetic experience, we are constrained to bid farewell to two prevalent ways of conceptualizing objectivity, one in which the subject is supposed to subtract its engagement, the other in which the subject is thought of as constitutive, or positioning. Both such a residual and such a positioning conception of objectivity are replaced by an account that takes the "subject as the agent (*agens*)." [49] Therefore, we have to understand that the corrective intervention that artworks provide to subjective practices happens foremost within the process of identification, not in a denial of a subjective involvement as such. Taking up Adorno's observations in "On Subject and Object," we would even have to say that the object given to us in an undiminished experience is much more objective than the "indeterminate substrate of reductionism." [50] This is because artworks make perfectly evident a certain connection that has been forsaken in the course of the development of rationality: An appropriate manner of determining objects consists in a practice of determination that lets itself be determined by the determinateness of what is to be determined.

It is important to note that this crucial point, according to Adorno, can only be brought about in and as experience, and not by reflection, as something non-reflexive, or as already mentioned above, something "which is not the thought itself" is needed to make our thinking turn towards that to which it is necessarily bound. [51] Such an experience is no longer reduced to being merely an "example of categories." [52] When taken in its full scope, it is rather exposed as the basis to which conceptual reflection is tied.

THE IMPORTANCE OF ENIGMATICALNESS IN ADORNO'S THINKING IN GENERAL

We will finally see another important contribution made by aesthetic experience by bringing together Adorno's late observations on enigmaticalness, as developed in his *Aesthetic Theory*, with his early ideas, as presented in his inaugural lecture "The Actuality of Philosophy." In both, he points out that the relevance of enigmaticalness lies in its "change-causing gesture," [53] which is once again mainly due to the prospect that it allows for another, less violent, conceptual practice to emerge. The way in which artworks perform a rescue of the concrete is something that philosophy, as a discipline inherently bound to the medium of conceptual thought, has to take seriously in conceptualizing itself. The reflection on aesthetic experience, its unique logic and urgent consequences, prompted Adorno to propose a new, interpretative, conception of philosophy. In his early career, Adorno already advocated for an interpretive turn in philosophy that would involve a critical view on the current state of philosophy. After the crisis of idealism and the dusk of humanity (Nazi Germany), according to Adorno, reason can no longer justify reality by rediscovering itself in it, since reality's "order and form suppresses every claim to reason."[54] The alleged "adequacy of thinking about being as totality"[55] has thus lost its validity. The negation of this prerequisite abrogates the traditional form of philosophy. Moreover, the very possibility of philosophy comes into question. By describing the actual state of philosophy in such a critical manner, Adorno prompts us to face the threat of the liquidation of philosophy, which he finds epitomized mainly in three tendencies: the scientification, aesthetization, and the increasing dissolution of philosophy. However, from this scenario arises an all the more concise idea for a new, alternative notion of philosophy, and how it differs from scientific, aesthetic, and other practices. If we follow Adorno, philosophy distinguishes itself from science though the concept of interpretation. Whereas the sciences "accept their findings,"[56] philosophy "perceives the first finding which it lights upon as a sign that needs unriddling."[57] The challenge for philosophy is to "proceed interpretatively without ever possessing a sure key to interpretation."[58] It seems that with this description Adorno is inspired by what he takes to be the logic of aesthetic experience. As this description brings Adorno dangerously close to phenomenological accounts, he emphasizes that his idea of interpretation is not to be confused with the problem of meaning (*Sinn*), since interpreting reality does not coincide with portraying it as meaningful, thus justifying it. This very justification, according to him, is out of question due to the fragmentation, incompleteness, and contradictoriness in being. Adorno's conception of a philosophical practice that is interpretative and riddle-solving is directly modeled on what we experience when faced with artworks.[59] In emphasizing that the process of interpretation does not aim at discovering a "second, secret world"[60] *behind* the appearances, he rejects approaches that conceive of interpretation as a reductive analysis of the question that proceeds from the given to the known. In contrast, neither interpretive philosophy nor aesthetic comprehension take the solution to the riddle as lying ready-made, waiting only to be uncovered, but as something that has to be actively brought to light. It is this very intervention against facticity as a given and illusive essence that gives the aesthetic mode of experience its dignity. The idea of the rebus thus primarily serves as a model for a methodology that critically intervenes against the "walls of sheer facticity"[61] and helps to "break the bonds of a logic which covers over the particular with the universal or merely abstracts the universal from the particular."[62] Consequently, philosophy informed by reflection on aesthetic experience is to be understood as a practice of mimetic constellation. It has to bring the elements of a fragmentary reality received from the particular sciences "into changing constellations" of "trial combinations, until they fall into a figure which can be read as an answer, while at the same time the question disappears"[63] —as is the case with artworks, which we see in their processual constitution and our immersive reenactment of them. Thus, philosophy is a tentative, seeking practice, without a leading, orientating key, a constant gyration between concepts and objects, which is in need of both activity and spontaneity as well as passivity and responsivity. Although the constellation we are compelled to construct is the action of a subject, it is not subjectivist, but "is determined by the unity of its object , together with that of theory and experience which have migrated into the object ."[64] We can finally say that in order, to re-conceptualize the recognition, or comprehension, of an object, Adorno shifts paradigms: from a deductive, syllogistic model following the principle of linear-hierarchical inference to the model of combinatoric, constellational disclosure. A conceptual practice informed by reflection on aesthetic experience is non-definitory, non-classifying; instead it weaves a conceptual net around the subject matter: "As a constellation, theoretical thought circles the concept it would like to unseal, hoping that it may fly open like the lock of a well-guarded safe-deposit box: in response, not to a single key or a single number, but to a combination of numbers."[65] It is only by way of constellation that the conceptual thought faces, and deals with its own aporia: it compensates for the problematic aspects of its violent tendencies, since concepts used in the constellational mode represent "from without what the concept has cut away within" (ND, 162), thus attaining what is usually excised from thought.

NOTES

1. Theodor W. Adorno, *Aesthetic Theory*, ed. and transl. Robert Hullot-Kentor (Minneapolis: University of Minnesota Press, 1997), 302.

2. Cf. Gottfried Leibniz, *Monadology*, transl. Llyod Strickland (Edinburgh: Edinburgh University Press, 2014).

3. See Theodor W. Adorno, "The Actuality of Philosophy," transl. Benjamin Snow, *Telos31* (Spring 1977): 113–33. Cf. here 127: "Just as riddle-solving is constituted, in that the singular dispersed elements of the question are brought into various groupings long enough for them to close together in a figure out of which the solution springs forth, while the question disappears"; Adorno hereby refers to Walter Benjamin, "Epistemo-Critical Prologue," *The Origin of German Tragic Drama* (London: Verso, 2003), 27–56.

4. Leibniz, mainly 1–19.

5. Adorno, *Aesthetic Theory*, 179.

6. Cf. ibid., 178.

7. Leibniz, 18.

8. For the concept of *mimesis*, see Walter Benjamin, "On the Mimetic Faculty," *Reflections*, Vol. 336 (1978): 333–36.

9. Cf. Adorno, "The Actuality of Philosophy," 127.

10. Interestingly, Adorno presented this idea in such a way that Benjamin felt obliged to remind Adorno that in case of a publication he should not forget to refer to his work from which the idea of a constellation as a practice of riddle-solving is originally borrowed. See the letter Benjamin wrote to Adorno from July 17, 1931. Henri Lonitz, *Theodor W. Adorno. Walter Benjamin. Briefwechsel 1928-1940* (Frankfurt/Main: Suhrkamp, 1994), 16–19. Adorno owes much to Benjamin's take on philosophy. As we will see it is exemplary also for being modeled by "rebus." See Adorno's famous characterization: "The rebus becomes the model of his philosophy." Theodor W. Adorno, "A Portrait of Walter Benjamin," in *Prisms*, transl. Samuel M. Weber (Cambridge: MIT Press, 1981), 239.

11. See for Adorno's conception of mimesis, as inspired by Josef Benjamin Früchtl, *Mimesis: Konstellation eines Zentralbegriffs bei Adorno* (Würzburg: Königshausen und Neumann, 1986), and the mimesis concept in a broader context: Gunter Gebauer and Christoph Wulf, *Mimesis: Culture, Art, Society* (Los Angeles: Berkeley University Press, 1995).

12. Adorno goes deeper into the problems of our practices of determination in his early essay, written together with Max Horkheimer, "The Concept of Enlightenment," in *Dialectic of Enlightenment: Philosophical Fragments*, ed. Gunzelin Schmid Noerr, transl. Edmund Jephcott (Stanford: Stanford University Press, 2002), 1–34.

13. Adorno, *Aesthetic Theory*, 180.

14. Ibid., 101.

15. Ibid., 86.

16. Adorno, Horkheimer, "The Concept of Enlightenment," 8.

17. Adorno, *Aesthetic Theory*, 179.

18. Ibid., 176.

19. Ibid., 179.

20. Ibid., 78.

21. Ibid.

22. Cf. ibid., 176.

23. Ibid., 124f.

24. Ibid., 175.

25. Ibid., 176.

26. Ibid., 125.

27. Ibid., 120.

28. Ibid., 125.

29. Ibid.

30. Cf. ibid., 176.

31. This elucidation draws on what Andrea Kern impressively developed. See Andrea Kern, *Schöne Lust* (Frankfurt/Main: Suhrkamp, 2000), esp. 190ff.

32. For a further discussion of these accounts, see the very sophisticated and influential monograph of Christoph Menke, *The Sovereignty of Art: Aesthetic Negativity in Adorno and Derrida*, transl. Neil Solomon (Cambridge: MIT Press, 1999), especially part I.

33. Adorno, *Aesthetic Theory*, 176.

34. Menke, *Sovereignty of Art*, 29ff.

35. Paul Valéry, *Oeuvres II* (Paris: Pléade, 1960), 636.

36. Adorno, *Aesthetic Theory*, 124.

37. Ibid., 302.

38. Ibid.

39. Cf. Immanuel Kant, *Critique of Judgment*, transl. Werner S. Pluhar (Cambridge: Hackett Publishing Company, 1984). For the influence Kant's elucidation of the logic of aesthetic experience had on Adorno, see Gunnar Hindrichs, "Scheitern als Rettung. Ästhetische Erfahrung nach Adorno," in *Deutsche Vierteljahrsschrift für Literaturwissenschaft und Geistesgeschichte*, Vol. 74, No. 1 (2000): 146–75.

40. Cf. Kant's *Reflection*, in which he prominently pointed out the affirmative character of aesthetic experience. Refl. 1820a: *"Die schönen Dinge zeigen an, dass der Mensch in die Welt passe"*; roughly translated: Beautiful things indicate that the human being fits into the world.

41. Theodor W. Adorno, "Notes on Philosophical Thinking" *Critical Models: Interventions and Catchwords* (2005): 132.

42. Cf. Adorno, *Aesthetic Theory*, 347.

43. Cf. ibid., 122.

44. See ibid., 118: "The task of aesthetics is not to comprehend artworks as hermeneutical objects; in the contemporary situation, it is their incomprehensibility that needs to be comprehended."

45. Ibid., 121.

46. Ibid., 245.

47. Ibid. See also Hindrichs, "Scheitern," 147.

48. Cf. Adorno , *Aesthetic Theory*, 123: "Artworks are, as synthesis, analogous to judgment; in artworks, however, synthesis does not result in judgment."

49. Theodor W. Adorno, "On Subject and Object," *Critical Models: Interventions and Catchwords* (2005): 254.

50. Ibid.

51. Adorno, "Notes on Philosophical Thinking," 132.

52. Theodor W. Adorno, *Negative Dialectics*, transl. Dennis Redmond (London: Continuum, 1981), 25.

53. Adorno, "The Actuality of Philosophy," 129.

54. Ibid., 120.

55. Ibid.

56. Ibid., 126.

57. Ibid.

58. Ibid.

59. In his inaugural lecture, Adorno speaks about enigmaticalness with a view to classical riddles, which he later, in his *Aesthetic Theory*, does not. Therefore I favor here, with respect to his early work, the translation "riddle" for *Rätsel*, and "enigma" with respect to the later work. Thereby we should keep in mind that Adorno speaks of either *Rätsel*, or of *Rätselhaftigkeit*, and as is the case with regard to artworks of *Rätselcharakter der Kunstwerke*. When it comes to Benjamin, he seems to prefer *Rebus*. It would be productive to go deeper into the question how Adorno developed the riddle/enigma/rebus model in the course of his thinking and what might have motivated him to use different terms, each of with different semantic aspects. Having not enough place here, I have to delay this task for another opportunity.

60. Ibid.

61. Theodor W. Adorno, "A Portrait of Walter Benjamin" in *Prisms*, transl. Samuel M. Weber (Cambridge: MIT Press, 1981), 230.

62. Ibid.

63. Adorno, "The Actuality of Philosophy," 127. Adorno's conceptualization of philosophy as interpretation, with interpretation being understood in analogy to the aesthetic practice of riddle-solving, strikingly seems to resemble strikingly the Wittgensteinian account. The difference is: Wittgenstein thought that riddles are self-made, unnecessary problems that can therapeutically be cured by dissolving them. The meaning of dissolving thereby differs from Adorno's account as dissolving in Wittgenstein means to make disappear the problem by debunking it as a pseudo problem. Consequently, in a strict sense, in Wittgenstein there *is* no riddle: "The riddle does not exist. If a question can be put at all, then it can also be answered." (See Ludwig Wittgenstein, *Tractatus Logico Philosophicus*, transl. D. F. Pears and B. F. McGuiness [London: Routledge and Kegan Paul, 1961].) Thus Wittgenstein conceives of the riddle rather as a curable puzzlement, or as a deception rather than an objective enigma, as Adorno does. With a new perspective, or a new way of thinking "(t)he problems are dissolved in the actual sense of the word—like a lump of sugar in water" (see Ludwig Wittgenstein, *Philosophical Occasions*, eds. and transl. J. Klagge and A. Nordmann [Indianapolis: Hackett, 1993], 183). Accordingly, in Wittgenstein a puzzlement can be disentangled, a deception can be debunked, whereas in Adorno the enigmaticalness can only be concretized.

64. Theodor W. Adorno, "The Essay as Form," *New German Critique*, Vol. 32 (Spring-Summer 1984): 165.

65. Adorno, *Negative Dialectics*, 163.

Chapter Twelve

Aesthetic Education, Human Capacity, Freedom

Tom Huhn

The most striking kinship between Schiller and Adorno lies in their shared concern with the fate of human capacity. More specifically, we find in Schiller's schema of the genesis of human faculties the precursor of Adorno's contention that each of our capacities comes first to be severed from us only later to be turned against each of us by an administered society. Adorno's claim arrives by way not only of Marx, but still more fruitfully by way of Schiller's scenario in which our capacities begin in, and as, opposition to one another. This contrariness of all capacities proceeds to expand to each of us as whole entities.[1] More pointedly, for Adorno and for Schiller, our capacities turn to oppose us because they have been called into existence not merely by a fallen condition or a polluted environment but rather our faculties are called forth from us precisely in the service of dismantling our integrity. We find this idea previously formulated in Rousseau's *Discourse on the Origin of Inequality*,[2] where every human tool and convenience is portrayed as a yoke which, by constraining our creaturely—and human—integrity, thereby erodes our essential unity, both as individual creatures and with and within our environment. Most famously, or infamously, Rousseau sees even our sociability as a most profound threat to the primal unity of the lone human being. By means of the progressive expansion of our capabilities a new, pseudo-integrity is cobbled together, indeed designed, for a purpose aligned precisely against the potential (incipient) wholeness of each of us.[3]

As evidence of the undermining, false unity of human life, consider the infinity of self-destruction in modern life, the plague of self-mutilation among the young, our rampant drug and alcohol abuse, not to mention the unavoidable anxieties and depression of modern life. We might say these ills

are not mere symptoms of the genesis of the modern self but rather a verita-
ble engine of self-destruction, a mimesis as well as a protest against the very
dynamic that brings our abilities into existence.

Kant, more even than Rousseau, is a touchstone for Schiller's thinking
about the character of human capacity. If Schiller finds in Rousseau the
thought of the fragile vulnerability of the integrity of the human being, he
finds in turn in Kant's aesthetic theory the specification of the integrity of
human capacity. What I have in mind is a speculation regarding how Kant's
idea of disinterest landed on Schiller. Though many read Kant's famous
specification of disinterest in aesthetic judgment as the attempt to police the
merely personal from the more properly aesthetic engagement of the faculties
in general, we might also interpret *disinterest* as the autonomy of the faculties *in general* from any determination whatsoever. And this understanding
of what lies at the heart of the third *Critique* touches directly the very foundation of the project in Kant's discovery of the existence of reflective judgment
in opposition to the seeming ubiquity of determinative judgment.[4] Reflective
judgment is of course demarcated as the *condition of capacity* without the
activation of capacity by anything extrinsic to capacity itself.

This is the true meaning of reflective judgment, and so too likewise is it a
boundary that limits our present ability (capacity) to declare the meaning—
that is, function—of capacity. This is, if you will, the "meaning" of aesthetic
judgment. And this likewise reveals the irony of the term 'education' in
Schiller's aesthetic education—for what education really denotes is not the
instruction of human beings (even, or especially, in how to be human, for
example) but rather our liberation. Our freedom is to be won, first and foremost, from the determinations, and the very determinability, of our own
capacities. The more properly aesthetic formulation would emphasize—instead of "first and foremost"—that education is the capacity to liberate ourselves *continuously* from the very faculties that, paradoxically, constitute us.

Let us, in response to just this paradox, therefore turn to consider Schiller's concern with balance, and perhaps include therewith the old aesthetic
idea of harmony. Indeed, we might locate in Plato one origin of harmony, of
this most fecund notion of beauty and of the aesthetic sphere in general.[5]
Ironically, it is Plato's anti-aesthetic assertions that led to the idea that harmony is the most thorough characteristic of beauty. By describing the success of the work of art as due to imbalance, intoxication, divinely inspired
madness, Plato thus set the stage for the positive ascription of order, balance,
and rule to the sphere of the aesthetic. However, the harmony most important
for Plato lies not in the object but the subject. One might hazard that regardless of whether Plato is a genuine source for the Kantian notion of the
aesthetic balance and harmony of the faculties with one another, it is key to
acknowledge that this is one of the most important ideas Schiller takes from
Kant. The harmony of the faculties in relation to one another is the most

influential Kantian idea in Schiller's characterization of aesthetic education. The harmony of the faculties, a profound *disinterest* of the faculties towards one another, is mimetically inspired by the disinterest of the faculty of sensation, or the faculty of understanding, towards an object. Important to note here is the continuity from Plato's *Republic*—in which the harmony of the parts of the soul in relation to one another not only mimics but more importantly produces the harmony of the polis—to Kant's assertion that the aesthetic sphere is the only one in which a subjective universality might reign— and from there to Schiller's return to an explicit image of the ideal state as product of the balance which only the cultivation of the capacity of the aesthetic might produce.[6]

There is perhaps no better image of the kind of harmony he takes the aesthetic alone to be able to provide than the one provided by Schiller himself in the contrast between athletic and beautiful bodies.[7] The former is the product of muscles working against one another, indeed working at all, rather than the beautiful body that results from the lack of conflict and differentiation among its parts. Schiller's idea also reflects the Rousseauvian notion of the perfectibility of human beings, that is, what Schiller calls our empty infinity, our ability to become determined and indeed over-determined by whatever capacity we develop. For Schiller, we are defined not so much by what we do with our capacities, as we are rather the *products* shaped by each capacity coming illicitly to constitute the whole of what we are. We are the *telos* then not of ourselves but of the inherent opposition between capacity and singularity, between, we might also say, capacity and capacity. In other words: our primal integrity comes to be disrupted, then usurped, by the monopoly of now one, and then another, faculty. Hegel found his solution to this dilemma in Schiller's *Aesthetic Education* by instead reading each successive capacity, sensuousness, consciousness, etc., as the recapitulation, expansion, transformation, as well as cancellation of the previous faculty. Our wholeness is compromised whenever our enhancement occurs by way of one capacity or another. Thus the Schillerian aesthetic, and the education within and toward it, can become anything *but* the development of *yet another capacity*.[8]

Our true—aesthetic—education is covered entirely by the distance we are able to place between ourselves and the alienation, shrinkage, and confinement inherent to capacity-ness. Here then is the dialectic of human becoming for Schiller: Each capacity, regardless of the distinct progress it represents for human development, is also inescapably a loss of potential, a loss precisely of the possibility that whatever is most human in us might be retained. Any and every capacity any human being develops is de facto a human capacity (hence Hegel's citation of Terrence in the lectures on aesthetics).[9] And yet, à la Rousseau, every human capacity is also a prosthetic expansion, an artificial extension and enhancement that carries us literally beyond ourselves. Thus the implicit message of the aesthetic sphere is that there is nothing distinctly human to be gained in the development of capacities. The Schillerian turn of all education toward the aesthetic—indeed of all human becoming—is to acknowledge the unavoidable destructiveness—what will later be called instrumental rationality—of the expansion of our capacities. This brings to mind Rousseau's great claim regarding the true aim and genuine scope of education: that we need do no more (as if we can do it at all) than teach ourselves how to be kind to one another.[10] After successfully teaching and learning this lesson: be humane, what might possibly remain to be learned?

Semblance (*der Schein*) is the key term that expands this notion of subjective disinterest into objectivity and around which there is much to compare Adorno and Schiller to one another. Semblance is the shape, or better: the very form, of a certain kind of freedom, the freedom from actuality, the freedom we might say from the final stage of determination and determinedness. As it declares itself to be only image and appearance, and not reality or even object, *semblance* reveals its liberation from actuality. Insofar as semblance is nonetheless also a fixed bounded image it thereby participates in, and betrays its commitment to, determination and thus limitation.

Semblance, we might say, provides an *allegory of capacity*. The sound *of* something, the image *of* something, even the Aristotelian drama *of* some action, appears *as* semblance. Semblance is thus pervaded not only by that which exists in relation to something else but so too is semblance thus constituted as the preliminary per se, by the appearance of that which (it) is not. It is thereby also the origin of the fragment—of the broken off part that nonetheless purports to reflect the whole, precisely in its incompleteness. Semblance thereby allegorically enacts a better fate for our faculties. To appear, but always only provisionally, demonstrates—for the sake of our existence as exclusively capacity—that capacity too might take place without absolute conviction or full actuality. Further, and the other way around, it might well be imagined that all semblance comes into existence as a mimesis of capacity itself. The endlessness of aesthetic education is Schiller's acknowledgment that the dynamic of even this education must not be allowed to entrench itself as yet another ossified capacity. Recall here Adorno's suggestion that fireworks might serve as a prototype for all art, which is to say, an example of a thing (image) that in its very appearing at once also declares its transitoriness and lack of fixed actuality.[11] In this way, fireworks mimic the dynamic of aesthetic judgment as that which in its own disinterestedness refuses actualization.

A balanced imbalance is what aesthetic education seeks, a not becoming anything new or more. The more (*das Mehr*) in Adorno's aesthetics is a mimetic ironizing of the ceaseless *more* of human capacity. The more (*das Mehr*) of beauty, in its utter gratuitousness, is more for its own sake, an autonomous more, if you will. We have instead somehow come to be *more* at odds with our own capacities. Does Schiller mean by this that we are at odds with any and every capacity or only those capacities which detract somehow from either our wholeness or our further becoming? As regards the wholeness criterion . . . every and any capacity is opposed to it. But the other criterion, against our further becoming, there perhaps not every capacity is automatically aligned against us. What then would be the way to judge between what limits and what advances us? The question is not so much what we are to become but whether we *continue* to become. Hence the theory of permanent revolution. How to then make sense of any and all moments of stasis? À la Hegel, I suppose, we can imagine each object or thing that we become is also the opportunity to become something else. Otherwise only just flux. Which thing is the real, the static moments or the motion away from them? Both, all, of course. A proper guide to life then would have to include the learning of the pleasure and necessity of both aspects. Schiller wants balance, the constant moving back and forth between stasis and dynamism. This movement shows that the aesthetic for Adorno and Schiller is about the provisionality of that which has already come into existence. The aesthetic then signals the reintroduction not of our wholeness but of the provisionality of each of our capacities and thus too the like provisionality of what we have become as exclusively capacity. Semblance then is the metaphysically most correct, or shall we say advanced, form of existence. Its top note and essence are provisionality, the provisionality of becoming rather than being. Artworks are existing things that paradoxically display themselves as fully formed and yet somehow also still on the side of becoming. They are ephemera . . . it is therefore a great disservice to call them finished or masterpieces, to insist upon their permanence, to conserve them. How ironic it seems then to conserve those things whose very existence is a rebuke to conservation.

Schiller and Adorno's concern with the fate of human capacity also manifests itself as a concern regarding the proper relationship to our own capacities. Both acknowledge that our capacities simultaneously constitute as well as exceed us. And both likewise wonder whether our capacities might also sometimes diminish us. So too do they both find an allegory of human capacity in the nature of semblance, which is at once both more than what strictly speaking is, and less than what might be. Both consider how semblance exceeds itself without causing harm, most obviously insofar as the very form of semblance is in contrast to the existence of finished things, of things completed with their meanings seemingly shining forth from them. Semblance provides an apparition of a thing, a view somewhat adjacent to the thing, regardless of however much we are inclined to assign the true meaning of this or that thing to its appearance *as* this or that. Balance, then, for Schiller comes to be presented as the proper relationship between all of what we have become—the sum of our capacities—and what might still

remain undetermined by and for us. The aesthetic for him then signals a
focus not on what model to follow, or what to become, but rather the aesthetic stands as a model for how to have an ambivalent relationship to one's own
becoming. This is the key aspect of Schiller's taking up the Kantian notion of
disinterest. Though it appears in Kant as a disinterest in regard to things,
especially things of beauty, it ramifies into a disinterest more powerfully
aimed against the interest in, and interests of, one's own capacities. We
might say it is as if Schiller wanted to bring to self-consciousness an awareness of the momentousness of our capacities, again, not the power of any
capacity in and of itself but the fact that in coming to acknowledge the
breadth and limitation of every capacity we ought then best be able to come
to mediate the relationship between the human being and its capacities, whatever they may be. Note here that the gist of so many early writings on the
sublime, from Burke, Kant, and Schiller, has to do with the fate of human
being *after* the collapse of one or more of its capacities.

   "Humanity has lost its dignity; but Art has rescued it and preserved it in
significant stone. Truth lives on in the illusion of Art, and it is from this copy,
or after-image, that the original image will once again be restored."[12] The
English translation fails to capture the strong association, and indeed repetition, between *Urbild* (original image) and *Nachbild* (after image), which is to
say between nature and art at the locus of the image. Dignity we might best
understand in this context as being the moral aspect of wholeness and integrity. Dignity, for Schiller, stands in place of the lost totality of all things
human. This is why the image, and indeed the formulation of art as the
afterimage, becomes so important. The image is a symbol for precisely the
human function that most pressingly presupposes the integrity of the whole.
Every image begins, every image is made possible, only by the view that sees
it as a single unified entity. Thus it is the *image* of art, regardless of its
content, reference, or significance, that carries the primary function of art,
which is to convey the reality of the wholeness of a thing. Recall too how
important for Adorno is the Nietzschean insistence upon the absolute destructiveness of the principle of individuation.[13] It is this principle that serves
as the greatest wedge into the wholeness—or might we say with Schiller—
the dignity of the human. Art is to provide, according to Schiller, not only a
restoration of the lost primal integrity within ourselves as well as a unity with
others, but still more importantly, art is to transfigure the fact of our having
lost that integrity.

   That transfiguration of our lost integrity is to represent—literally—the
means and method by which we achieve freedom from determination. Consider play, a central term in Schiller's *Letters*, especially as he notes a continuity between the animal kingdom and ourselves: "An animal may be said to
be at work, when the stimulus to activity is some lack; it may be said to be at
play, when the stimulus is sheer plenitude of vitality, when superabundance

of life is its own incentive to action. Even inanimate nature exhibits a similar luxuriance of forces, coupled with a laxity of determination which, in that material sense, might well be called play."[14] The key nexus here is between "laxity of determination" and "superabundance of life," the latter precisely what we earlier considered in Adorno's notion of the more (*das Mehr*). That idea has to do with the absolutely crucial contention that all determination, however much it might rightly and successfully respond to human need, is nonetheless inescapably also a limitation on human becoming. It is crucial here to delineate need from capacity. Capacity, we might say, is the *overdetermination* of need. To have a need requires a response in the hope of quenching or fulfilling it. But to develop a capacity in response to a need is to make the need into a permanent, persistent force that shapes an organism into a permanent, persistent readiness to respond to just such a need having become absolutized. Though one needs to respond to need, one need not thereby become the instrument of need-responsiveness. One might also remark that domination is a close cousin of the instrumentalization of neediness. This is the dialectic in Schiller's thinking here: To be determined by what we perceive that we are not yet, is the force that most powerfully cuts at the totality of what we have been thus far. This is exactly why need and interest and inclination, and all the rest, are just those things which disqualify us, not from satisfaction and pleasure and life, but more importantly, those things disqualify us from the aesthetic, which is thus the disqualification from just that which might make us free.

What, exactly, according to Adorno and Schiller, are we attempting to recover? Adorno describes it as the object; Schiller as sensation. Both are, on the face of it, misleading. Just as Adorno does not intend, by object, a return to things, so too does Schiller not prescribe a return to sensation pure and simple. Both instead are proclaiming the importance of recovering, on the one hand, the fully human, subject-infused object, and on the other sensation that has been fully traversed, and traversed again, by all that is human. Schiller wants a recovery of sensation—but call it now sensuousness—as a fully human capacity, rather than a capacity of an organism to absorb and reflect its environment.[15] Adorno wants the recovery of objects where object means a thing that exemplifies the entirety of what is human in tension with what is not.

And yet, this specification remains too static, because it imagines an image as an immovable thing, as a mere reflection of what is, even if it is also an uncovering of what it reflects. This leads us to Schiller's idea of the living image, of the image not simply of life, but the image which is itself alive.[16] It is an image, or better: a life, a proxy for that capacity of ours to be alive but which is nonetheless not yet fully alive. We are truly alive only in the freedom we gain from—and from within—each and every one of our determinations. Here is perhaps what we seek in our gazing at images, here is perhaps an explanation as to why images seem to hold so much for us: We somehow discern in them just this ability to be alive in ways that we are not yet. The image provides then a model of how to be, hence the mimetic character of all images, of these models of how to be alive. Every image, insofar as it is an image and not the thing itself, already demonstrates the capacity to be free of the objects it ostensibly reflects. Every image thus points out the way to be freed from matter and materiality, reference and repetition. This highlights the major conundrum regarding our freedom: It is not by means of yet another determination, not by dint of the development of yet another capacity that we might liberate ourselves from the history of our own development. [17] It is rather in adjusting our relations to our capacities, in freeing ourselves, at least in part, in relation to our history, that we have the most to gain.

What's important to recall here is that our freedom is not arrived at by way of jettisoning our history, determinations, and capacities. Our freedom is rather the result of our reclaiming our capacities *in* freedom. This is of course most powerfully shown in Schiller's characterization of the return of sensuousness, or we might say, our return to sensuousness as a free capacity rather than as a means of adjustment to the world and our environment. Sensuousness is a capacity that once (first?) took hold of us, and in taking hold of us shaped us in a very particular, indeed peculiar, way. [18] The famous Schillerian *Aufhebung* is the cancellation as well as the retaining of this capacity. [19]

This dynamic is in turn related to the question of form. If form means, in the first instance, the preference for the relations of things to one another over the content or meaning of a thing, then we might surmise that Schiller's particular brand of formalism is root and branch committed to the distancing of the connection to content and meaning. Or to put it as Kant has it: Appetite and inclination are what disqualify and thwart the human ability to put some distance between its hungers and its own capacities. [20] Again, the aesthetic cannot be formulated, at least in this tradition, as yet another capacity, even if it is the capacity to forsake the pull and influence of every other capacity. It is rather the case that the aesthetic is to be imagined as a thing that happens, so to speak, behind our backs, in disinterest, and realized in things not directly aimed for. It is not that we are to be indifferent towards our relations to our capacities, as rather it is that we cannot bring ourselves forward here by means of those capacities. Perhaps that is not a terrible metaphor to use here: the formulation according to how we bring ourselves forward, how we come into life and into particular ways of being alive—this has always happened in our past by means of, and in fact as an expression of, our capacities. Our capacities can only bring us so far, can only bring us forward as beings who realize themselves in one form or another as ability. But Schiller would instead have us step back from ourselves, which is to say from our abilities as well as from reality: "As soon as ever he starts preferring form to substance, and jeopardizing reality for the sake of semblance (which he must, however, recognize as such), a breach has been effected in the cycle of his animal behavior, and he finds himself set upon a path to which there is no end."[21]

Form appears in this passage in its purest, well, form. It is primarily the movement of negation, to wit here, the negation of substance. Form is denial, most poignantly the denial of the priority of substance. In Adorno's aesthetics, this manifests itself as the autonomy of art, as the achievement by art of an independence from the material and the circumstances that gave rise to it.[22] But we see the beginning of this same thought in Kant's aesthetics, in the formulation there of artistic beauty appearing only as if it were natural beauty. In other words, humanly produced beauty must distance itself from—can we say disavow?—the very material and occasion out of which it nonetheless arises.[23] Schiller, too, is quite explicit about this, especially as it forms the core of what he intends by an aesthetic education. It means the cultivation of the preference for semblance over reality, for the balance of the faculties in relation to one another rather than in contest with the environment or those of others. And yet, again, *Aufhebung*, the insistence that that which has been cancelled somehow must also be retained. This is in Schiller the balance between and among the faculties, impulses, drives, inclinations, etc., as Schiller variously names these contrasting dynamics. Put differently, the disavowal is just that which sets in motion not merely the denial of a certain inclination and capacity but more importantly the first step by means of which the capacity will become a candidate for being taken up by human subjectivity as a fully free and human capacity, rather than a mere product of need, historical circumstance, and determination.

We become free, and at the same time more properly human, not by jettisoning our capacities and determinations but by recovering them as something more than determinations, as, we might say, elective affinities in regard to our own possibilities. The most genuine freedom, from Schiller's perspective, is the freedom we ourselves might attain in relation to our own limitations. What is so novel about this idea—akin we might also see to Kant's famous essay on the meaning of Enlightenment—is that it marks a retreat from the idea of human progress as the acquisition of more capacity and knowledge.[24] Schiller in effect acknowledges the limits of human development; this is not to say there is a limit to whatever capacities we might gain but rather that the path of increasing capacity and knowledge is a kind of dead end.

More strongly put: The path of human increase has become dysfunctional insofar as it has damaged whatever integrity or dignity we might once have had. Each and every determination is not just a limitation of what we might possibly become, but more importantly, each determination sets the parameters for every subsequent determination. This is how Schiller describes what Hegel will later term the dialectic. Form, for example, is not so much the product of a singular human capacity as it is rather the movement away from the previous determination of sensuousness. Form is then not a freely chosen human capacity but instead the negation of the previous determination of sensuousness. Form was for Schiller the inevitable product of the contentful determination of sensuousness. As Schiller has it, "All other forms of perception divide man, because they are founded exclusively either upon the sensuous or upon the spiritual part of his being; only the aesthetic mode of perception makes of him a whole, because both his natures must be in harmony in order to achieve it."[25] In other words, it is not more of our nature, more of any capacity of ours that is required, but less. We need less, fewer of our capacities to be in charge of us, less of everything that we are to be in the forefront of what we are and how we are in the world, toward others as well as toward ourselves.

"The transition from a passive state of feeling [*Zustande des Empfindens*] to an active state of thinking and willing cannot, then, take place except *via* a middle state of aesthetic freedom. . . . In a word, there is no other way of making sensuous man rational except by first making him aesthetic."[26] This passage reveals that Schiller also sees the aesthetic as the means by which human beings might transition from being objects to becoming subjects. We are objects insofar as we are the products of the determinations that happen to us, which is to say we become that which our capacities have enabled. And one of the surprising implications of the passage above is the implied expansion of the meaning of aesthetic. The aesthetic becomes in this passage the name for the very movement away from the "passive state of feeling," which is to say, from the determination of sensuousness. More broadly then, the aesthetic denominates the beginning of our having created a distance away from our very capacity to be receptive [*Zustande des Empfindens*], to be the stuff out of which determinations are made. The aesthetic then is not so much the positive freedom to make and to do as one might please as it is instead the negative freedom from the fact and form of our determinations.

We are to become more truly ourselves to the extent to which we recover some place between what we have become and whatever else we are. One is even tempted to say: We recover ourselves in founding an ambivalence towards what we already are. Only there, and then, are we in some kind of possession of ourselves rather than remaining in the state of being the possessed by our determinations. The balance among our faculties, which Schiller describes as the most important goal of aesthetic education and which, of course, he takes up as a version of Kant's harmony of the faculties within successful aesthetic judgment, is to be achieved precisely by means of the lessening of the influence of any one faculty over another. This harmony does not proceed by the exercise of some harmonizing of one faculty towards others but is the result of our retreat from the dominance of any one faculty or another. The harmony is thus understood by Schiller as a return to something like our previous undetermined condition, the most salient feature of which was that no one capacity dominated who and what we were. Aesthetic education is to have its aim as the restoration of that harmony, and with it of course the harmony of ourselves with one another (shades of Kant's subjective universality of the aesthetic), harmony between ourselves and our environment, and perhaps most importantly, harmony and unity between what we have become and what we are to become, in other words, freedom to become.[27]

The freedom for human beings, for subjectivity, has what Schiller calls its sensible pledge within the experience of material life, and that is beauty. Beauty is thus not an image of attractiveness but rather one of freedom from inclination. Beauty, following Kant's specifications, is then not a thing which causes freedom or harmony among our faculties as it is rather a reflection, or better: an *occasion* for that balance and harmony. As we have no faculty that might absorb or perceive the harmony of our other faculties, beauty remains an elusive experience, the experience towards which, for Schiller, all education, which is to say all cultivation of human capacity, ought to tend.

Schiller's elaboration of Kantian aesthetics is most visible in how he takes the Kantian notion of beauty as the ideal form of the appearance of harmony and expands it to the idea of aesthetic appearance, semblance, in general (*der Schein*): "Semblance we love just because it is semblance, and not because we take it to be something better," and semblance is "the very essence of the fine arts."[28] Semblance, not only one of the most important concepts in Schiller's aesthetic theory, is also a genuine advance over the Kantian aesthetics of beauty insofar as it provides an explanation for the fact of aesthetic appearance in general, regardless of whether any aesthetic appearance achieves the ideal state of beauty. In other words, with semblance Schiller is able to devise an account of the *form* of aesthetic appearance rather than the Kantian focus on the ideal instance—beauty—of aesthetic appearance.

It should be noted as well that this retreat from beauty, this falling back into the ranks of aesthetic appearance in general—semblance—is itself an aesthetic move. That is, we might well see this Schillerian strategy of backing away from the idealized aesthetic appearance of beauty as precisely an aesthetic disavowal. Indeed, we might consider this an instance of aesthetic irony, of beauty coming to be considered insufficiently disinterested such that semblance comes to be presented as a more appropriately aesthetic form than beauty. This, by the way, would also reveal a kinship between semblance and the sublime. Both are the product of an inclination away from beauty's potential entanglements. Both share the premise that beauty might well be itself insufficiently aesthetic. And the germ of this thought can already be discerned in Kant's preference for natural beauty over artistic beauty. The limitation of the latter is that it is the issue of human intention, however accidental the final product in relation to some intention or another—indeed Kant will insist that truly successful works of art, beautiful ones that is, must be the products of their having overcome whatever intentions set their making in order. We witness this same dichotomy, and preference, ramify further in Kant's hierarchy within artistic beauty between free and so-called dependent beauty.[29] Free beauty, and no doubt this term came to have special significance for Schiller in his formulation of the centrality of semblance to aesthetic images, is beauty which relies upon no concept, and is therefore, we might say, pure semblance. Dependent beauty relies on a concept or we might say a figure in order to give shape to its image.

In sum, human freedom is the core concern that animates the aesthetic theories of Schiller, Adorno, and Kant. (How ironic that some take an interest in aesthetics or art to be instead a focus away from that which is most pressing for human existence, our freedom.) As we are not yet masters of our own destiny (indeed mastery might itself be a notion that thwarts our attempts at freedom), so, too, are we unable to directly encounter what remains unfree in and about us. The whole realm of the aesthetic then exists as both a symptom of our unfreedom as well as a potential "capacity" for encountering and addressing our continuing unfreedom. Perhaps the aesthetic is in fact the greatest possible symptom of our unfreedom insofar as it manifests in such myriad and robust shapes the dialectic of what limits as well as what liberates us. Schiller's great hope was that the aesthetic would prove to be the only means by which human freedom, whose very ground rests in human capacity, might encounter itself. He saw the long history of human development as the unfolding of the capacities to do things, as the construction of *homo faber*. So too was Schiller convinced that the history of being human had reached a most momentous moment: the potential to free itself from having been shackled to the development of its capacities. The alternative path of human development would disavow the further capacity to *do* something or other and instead take up the possibility of *becoming* something free from all exercise of capacity. The aesthetic is the place where, in the heart of our unfreedom—in the exercise of our capacities, we might nonetheless liberate ourselves from our servitude to those capacities. Likewise for Adorno, every successful work of art demonstrates the tension between constraint and freedom. We cannot yet find freedom within ourselves, at best we might hope to spy an image of it in something else.

NOTES

1. Friedrich Schiller, *On the Aesthetic Education of Man*, transl. Elizabeth M. Wilkinson and L. A. Willoughby (New York: Oxford University Press, 1982), 33. This ought not be confused with Heidegger's construction of a standing reserve, which suggests that capacities might be taken up for one end or another. This Heideggerian notion, I'd like to suggest, is akin to the weak version of ideology, which has it that ideas, opinions, etc., are somehow neutral

entities detachable from the context (or, as Schiller would say, unity) in which they arose and thereby deployable for one purpose or another.

2. Jean-Jacques Rousseau, *Discourse on the Origin of Inequality*, transl. Donald A. Cress (Indianapolis: Hackett Publishing Co., 1992), 2.

3. Most helpful here is Fred Neuhouser's *Rousseau's Theodicy of Self-Love: Evil, Rationality, and the Drive for Recognition* (New York: Oxford University Press, 2008).

4. Immanuel Kant, *Critique of Judgement*, transl. James Creed Meredith (New York: Oxford University Press, 1952), 37–38.

5. See Plato, *The Phaedrus*.

6. Schiller, *On the Aesthetic Education of Man*, 45.

7. Ibid., 44.

8. This marks his difference from Kant who saw the aesthetic as a capacity of the whole being, of the systematicity of the whole being, whereas Schiller is far more keen to keep this "capacity"—call it aesthetic judgment or taste—a capacity that never fully arrives.

9. Georg Wilhelm Friedrich Hegel, *Introductory Lectures on Aesthetics*, transl. Bernard Bosanquet (London: Penguin Books, 1886), 51.

10. Jean-Jacques Rousseau, *Emile*, transl. William H. Payne (New York: D. Appleton and Co., 1918), 45. "O men, be humane; it is your foremost duty. Be humane to all classes and to all ages, to everything not foreign to mankind. What wisdom is there for you outside of humanity?"

11. Theodor Adorno, *Aesthetic Theory*, transl. Robert Hullot-Kentor (New York: Continuum, 2002), 81.

12. Schiller, *On the Aesthetic Education of Man*, 57.

13. Arthur Schopenhauer, *The World as Will and Idea, Vol. I*, transl. E. F. J. Payne (New York: Dover Publications Inc., 2003), 352–53. "Just as the boatman sits in his small boat, trusting his frail craft in a stormy sea that is boundless in every direction, rising and falling with the howling, mountainous waves, so in the midst of a world full of suffering and misery the individual man calmly sits, supported by and trusting the *principium individuationis*, or the way in which the individual knows things as phenomenon." Quoted by Nietzsche in Friedrich Nietzsche, "The Birth of Tragedy out of the Spirit of Music," in *The Birth of Tragedy and Other Writings*, transl. Raymond Geuss (Cambridge, UK: Cambridge University Press, 1999), 16–17.

14. Schiller, *On the Aesthetic Education of Man*, 207.

15. Ibid., 79

16. Ibid., 121

17. Frantz Fanon, *Black Skin White Masks*, transl. Charles Lan Markmann (New York: Grove, 1967) 10. "Man's tragedy, Nietzsche said, is that he was once a child."

18. Schiller, *On the Aesthetic Education of Man*, 139.

19. Ibid., 124–25. "Since, however, both conditions remain everlastingly opposed to each other, there is no other way of uniting them except by destroying (*Aufgehoben*) them."

20. Immanuel Kant, *Critique of Judgement*, transl. James Creed Meredith (New York: Oxford University Press, 1952), 42.

21. Schiller, *On the Aesthetic Education of Man*, 207.

22. Adorno, *Aesthetic Theory*, 1–7.

23. Kant, *Critique of Judgement*, 140–41.

24. Immanuel Kant, "An Answer to the Question: 'What is Enlightenment?'" in *Kant: Political Writings* (Cambridge, UK: Cambridge University Press, 1784), 54–60. In Kant's essay, this is presented as the necessity to withdraw from all authority insofar as authority functions as that which limits one's own capacity to realize the self—regardless how misguided a self might be produced—as just that disavowal of the power of something or someone else over oneself.

25. Schiller, *On the Aesthetic Education of Man*, 215.

26. Ibid., 161.

27. Ibid., 173–81.

28. Ibid., 193.

29. Kant, *Critique of Judgement*, 39–42.

Bibliography

Adorno, Theodor W. "The Actuality of Philosophy." *The Adorno Reader*. Edited by Brian O'Conner. Malden: Blackwell Publishers, 2000.
———. "Adorno Seminar vom Sommersemester 1932." *Frankfurter Adorno Blätter IV*. München: edition text + kritik, 1995.
———. *Aesthetic Theory*. Translated by R.Hullot-Kentor. Minneapolis: University of Minnesota Press, 1997.
———. *Ästhetische Theorie*. Frankfurt am Main: Suhrkamp, 1970.
———. *Ästhetik (1958/59)*. Frankfurt: Suhrkamp, 2006.
———. "Commitment." *Notes to Literature*, vol. 2. Translated by S. Weber Nicholson. New York: Columbia University Press, 1992.
———. *The Complete Correspondence 1928-1940*. Edited by H. Lonitz. Translated by N. Walker. Cambridge: Harvard University Press, 1999.
———. *Critical Models: Interventions and Catchwords*. Translated by Henry W. Pickford. New York: Columbia University Press, 2005.
———. "Die Aktualität der Philosophie." *Gesammelte Shcriften*, vol. 1. Frankfurt am Main: Surkhamp, 2003.
———. "Der Begriff der Philosophie. Vorlesungen Wintersemester 1951/52." *Frankfurter Adorno Blätter II*. München: edition text + kritik, 1993.
———. "Drei Studien zu Hegel." *Gesammelte Scriften*, vol. 5. Frankfurt am Main: Suhrkamp, 2003.
———. *Hegel: Three Studies*. Translated by Shierry Weber Nicholsen. Cambridge: The MIT Press, 1993.
———. "The Idea of Natural History." Translated by Robert Hullot-Kentor. *Telos* 60 (Summer 1984): 111–24.
———. "Die Idee der Naturgeschichte." *Gesammelte Schriften*, vol. 1. Edited by Rolf Tiedemann. Frankfurt a.m.: Suhrkamp Verlag, 1972.
———. *The Jargon of Authenticity*. Translated by Knut Tarnowski and Frederic Will. London: Routledge & Kegan Paul Ltd., 1973.
———. *Kierkegaard: Construction of the Aesthetic*. Translated by Robert Hullot-Kentor. Minneapolis: University of Minnesota, 1989.
———. *Metaphysics: Concept and Problems*. Edited by Rolf Tiedemann. Translated by Edmund Jephcott. Stanford, CA: Stanford University Press, 2001.
———. "Minima Moralia." *Gesammelte Schriften*, vol. 4. Frankfurt am Main: Suhrkamp Verlag, 2003.
———. *Minima Moralia: Reflections from Damaged Life*. Translated by E. F. N. Jephcott. London: Verso, 1974.

————. *Negative Dialectics*. Translated by E. B. Ashton. London: Routledge, 2000.

————. *Negative Dialektik. Gesammelte Schriften*, vol. 6. Frankfurt: Suhrkamp Verlag, 1970.

————. *Notes to Literature*, vol. 1. Translated by Shierry Weber Nicholsen. New York: Columbia University Press, 1991.

————. "On Popular Music." *Essays on Music*. Edited by Richard Leppert. Los Angeles, CA: University of California Press, 2002.

————. "On the Use of Foreign Words." *Notes to Literature*, vol. 2. Translated by Shierry Weber Nicholsen. New York: Columbia University Press, 1992.

————. *Philosophische Terminologie. Zur Einleitung*, two volumes. Frankfurt am Main: Suhrkamp Verlag, 1973.

————. *Prisms*. Translated by Samuel M. Weber. Cambridge: MIT Press, 1981.

————. "Soziologie und empirische Forschung." *Gesammelte Schriften*, vol. 8, pt. 1. Frankfurt am Main: Suhrkamp Verlag, 2003.

————. "Spätkapitalismus oder Industriegesellschaft?" *Gesammelte Schriften*, vol. 8, pt. 1. Frankfurt am Main: Suhrkamp Verlag, 2003.

————. "Theses on the Language of the Philosopher." *Adorno and the Need in Thinking: New Critical Essays*. Edited by Donald A. Burke.Translated by Samir Gandensha and Michael K. Palamarek. London: University of Toronto Press, 2007.

————. "Vers une musique informelle." *Gesammelte Schriften*, vol. 16. Edited by Rolf Tiedemann. Frankfurt a.m.: Suhrkamp Verlag, 1972.

————. "Vers une musique informelle." *Quasi una Fantasia: Essays on Modern Music*. Translated by Rodney Livingstone. New York: Verso, 1998.

Adorno, Theodor W., and Max Horkheimer. *Dialectic of Enlightenment: Philosophical Fragments*. Edited by Gunzelin Schmid Noerr. Translated by Edmund Jephcott. Stanford: Stanford University Press, 2002: 1–34.

————. "Dialektik der Aufklärung." *Max Horkheimer: Gesammelte Schriften*, vol. 5. Frankfurt am Main: Fischer Taschenbuch Verlag, 1997.

———— and Walter Benjamin. *Adorno Benjamin Briefwechsel 1928-1940*. Edited by Henri Lonitz. Frankfurt am Main: Suhrkamp, 2004.

————. *The Complete Correspondence 1928-1940*. Cambridge: Polity Press and Blackwell, 1999.

Anzaldúa, Gloria. *Borderlands/La Frontera: The New Mestiza*, twenty-fifth anniversay edition, fourth edition. San Francisco: Aunt Laute Books, 2012.

Baudrillard, Jean. *Simulacra and Simulations*. Translated by Sheila Faria Glaser. Ann Arbor, MI: University of Michigan Press, 1995.

Benhabib, Seyla. *Critique, Norm, and Utopia: A Study of the Foundations of Critical Theory*. New York: Columbia University Press, 1986.

————. "Arendt and Adorno: The Elusiveness of the Particular and the Benjaminian Moment." *Arendt and Adorno: Political and Philosophical Investigations*. Edited by Lars Rensmann and Samir Gandesha. Stanford: Stanford University Press, 2012.

Benjamin, Walter. *The Arcades Project*. Translated by Howard Eiland and Kevin McLaughlin. Cambridge: Belknap Press, 1999.

————. *Gesammelte Schriften*, vols. I–III. Edited by Rolf Tiedemann and H. Hermann Schweppenhäuser. Suhrkamp: Frankfurt am Main, 1972–1989.

————. *The Origin of German Tragic Drama*. Translated by John Osborne. New York: Verso, 1998.

————. *Selected Writings, Volume 1: 1913-1926*. Edited by Marcus Bullock and Michael W. Jennings. Cambridge: The Belknap Press of Harvard University Press, 1996.

————. *Selected Writings, Volume 2: 1927-1934*. Edited by Michael W. Jennings, Howard Eiland, and Gary Smith. Translated by Rodney Livingstone, et al. Cambridge: The Belknap Press of Harvard University Press, 1999.

————. *Selected Writings, Volume 3: 1935-1938*. Edited by Howard Eiland and Michael W. Jennings. Translated by Edmund Jephcott, et al. Cambridge: The Belknap Press of Harvard University Press, 2002.

————. *Selected Writings, Volume 4: 1938-1940*. Edited by Howard Eiland and Michael W. Jennings. Cambridge: The Belknap Press of Harvard University Press, 2003.

Bernstein, David W. "John Cage, Arnold Schoenberg, and the Musical Idea." In *John Cage: Music, Philosophy, and Intention, 1933-1950*. Edited by David W. Patterson. New York: Routledge, 2002.

Bernstein, J. M. *The Fate of Art: Aesthetic Alienation from Kant to Derrida and Adorno*. University Park: Penn State Press, 1992.

———. *Adorno: Disenchantment and Ethics*. Cambridge: Cambridge University Press, 2001.

Bertram, G. W. "Metaphysik und Metaphysikkritik." *Adorno-Handbuch*. Edited by R. Klein. Stuttgart: Metzler Verlag, 2011.

———. "Das utopische Potential der Kunstnach Theodor W. Adorno: Eine Reaktualiseriung." *Ästhetik – Religion – Säkulurisierung II. Die klassischeModerne*. Edited by S. Prombka and S. Vietta. Munich: Fink Verlag, 2009.

Biro, Andrew. "Adorno and Ecological Politics." In *Adorno and the Need in Thinking: New Critical Essays*. Edited by Donald A. Burke et al. Toronto: University of Toronto Press, 2007, 345–62.

Biro, Andrew, ed. *Critical Ecologies: The Frankfurt School and Contemporary Environmental Crisis*. Toronto: University of Toronto Press, 2011.

Bloch, Ernst. *Erbschaf dieser Zeit, Erweiterte Ausgabe*. Frankfurt am Main: Suhrkamp, 1985.

Borges, Jorge Luis. *Selected Non-Fictions*. Edited by Eliot Weinberger. New York: Viking, 1999.

Bourdieu, Pierre. *Distinction: A Social Critique of the Judgment of Taste*. Translated by Richard Nice. Cambridge: Harvard University Press, 1984.

Bosteels, Bruno. *The Actuality of Communism*. New York: Verso, 2011.

Buck-Morss, Susan. "Aesthetics and Anaesthetics: Walter Benjamin's Artwork Essay Reconsidered." *October*, 62 (Autumn 1992).

———. *The Origin of Negative Dialectics*. New York: The Free Press, 1977.

Buchanan, Ian, and Marcel Swiboda. *Deleuze and Music*. Edinburgh: Edinburgh University Press, 2004.

Bürger, Peter. *Theory of the Avant-garde*. Translated by Michael Shaw. Minneapolis: University of Minnesota Press, 1984.

Cage, John. "Future of Music: Credo." *Silence*. Middletown: Wesleyan University Press, 1961.

———. "History of Experimental Music." *Silence*. Middletown: Wesleyan University Press, 1961.

———. "Experimental Music: Doctrine." *Silence*. Middletown: Wesleyan University Press, 1961.

———. "Counterpoint." *Writings about John Cage*. Edited by Richard Kostelanetz. Ann Arbor, MI: University of Michigan Press, 1993.

Caygill, Howard. *Walter Benjamin. The Colour of Experience*. London: Routledge, 1998.

Cook, Deborah. *Adorno on Nature*. Durham, UK: Acumen, 2011.

Coyle, Lauren. "The Spiritless Rose in the cross of the Present: Retracing Hegel in Adorno's *Negative Dialectics* and Related Lectures." *Telos* 155 (Summer 2011): 39–60.

Danto, Arthur C. "The Artworld." *Aesthetics and the Philosophy of Art: The Analytic Tradition*. Edited by Peter Lamargue, et al. Malden: Blackwell Publishing, 2004.

———. *After the End of Art: Contemporary Art and the Pale of History*. Princeton: Princeton University Press, 1997.

Deleuze, Gilles, and Felix Guattari. *A Thousand Plateaus: Capitalism and Schizophrenia*. Translated by Brian Massumi. Minneapolis: University of Minnesota Press, 1987.

———. *Anti-Oedipus: Capitalism and Schizophrenia*. Translated by Robert Hurley, et al. New York: Penguin Books, 1977.

Derrida, Jacques. "Des Tours de Babel." *Difference in Translation*. Translated and edited by Joseph F. Graham. Ithaca: Cornell University Press, 1985.

———. "Transfer ex Cathedra: Language and Institutions of Philosophy." *Eyes of the University. Right to Philosophy 2*. Translated by Jan Plug and Others. Stanford: Stanford University Press, 2004.

Eiland, Howard, and Michael Jennings. *Walter Benjamin: A Critical Life*. Cambridge: Harvard University Press, 2014.

Erjavec, Aleš. "Aesthetics and the Aesthetic Today: After Adorno." *Art and Aesthetics After Adorno*. Edited by J. M. Bernstein, et al. Berkeley: University of California Press, 2010.

Fanon, Frantz. *Black Skin White Masks*. Translated by Charles Lan Markmann. New York: Grove, 1967.

Ferris, David, ed. *The Cambridge Companion to Walter Benjamin*. Cambridge: Cambridge University Press, 2004.

Finlayson, Gordon. "Adorno: Modern Art, Metaphysics, and Radical Evil." *Modernism/Modernity* 10 (2003): 79.

Forster, Michael. *Hegel and Skepticism*. Cambridge: Harvard University Press, 1989.

Früchtl, Josef. *Mimesis: Konstellation eines Zentralbegriffs bei Adorno*. Würzburg: Königshausen und Neumann, 1986.

Gadamer, Hans-Georg. *Truth and Method*. Translated by Joel Weinsheimer and Donal G. Marshall. London: Continuum, 2004.

Gandesha, Samir. "The 'Aesthetic Dignity of Words': Adorno's Philosophy of Language." In *Adorno and the Need in Thinking: New Critical Essays*. Edited by Donald A. Burke, et al. Toronto: University of Toronto Press, 2007.

Gass, William H. *Life Sentences: Literary Judgments and Accounts*. New York: Alfred A. Knopf, 2012.

Gebauer, Gunter, and Christoph Wulf. *Mimesis: Culture, Art, Society*. Los Angeles: Berkeley University Press, 1995.

Geuss, Raymond. "Suffering and Knowledge in Adorno." In *Outside Ethics*. Princeton and Oxford: Princeton University Press, 2005.

Habermas, Jurgen. "Consciousness-Raising or Rescuing Critique."*Philosophical-Political Profiles*. Translated by F. Lawrence. Cambridge: MIT Press, 1983.

———. *The Philosophical Discourse of Modernity*. Cambridge, MA: The MIT Press, 1990.

———. *The Theory of Communicative Action: Reason and the Rationalization of Society*, vol. 1. Translated by Thomas McCarthy. Boston: Beacon Press, 1984.

———. "Zur Logik der Sozialwissenschaften." *Gesammelte Schriften*, vol. 8, pt.1. Frankfurt am Main: Suhrkamp Verlag, 2003.

Hammer, Espen. "The Touch of Art: Adorno and the Sublime." *SATS* 1, 2 (2000): 91–105.

Hammermeister, Kai. *The German Aesthetic Tradition*. Cambridge: Cambridge University Press, 2001.

Hansen, Miriam "Benjamin, Cinema and Experience: the Blue Flower in the Land of Technology." *New German Critique* 40, (1987): 179–224.

———. "Room for Play: Benjamin's Gamble with the Cinema." *October* 109 (Summer, 2004), 3–45.

Hegel, G. W. F. *The Encyclopaedia Logic*. Indianapolis: Hackett, 1991.

———. *Introductory Lectures on Aesthetics*. Translated by Bernard Bosanquet. London: Penguin Books, 1886.

———. *Hegel's Phenomenology of Spirit*. Translated by A. V. Miller. New York: Oxford University Press, 1977.

———. *Lectures on Fine Art*, vol. 1. Translated by T. M. Knox. Oxford: Oxford University Press, 1988.

Heidegger, Martin. "Letter on Humanism." *Basic Writings. From Being and Time (1927) to The Task of Thinking (1964)*. New York: HarperPerennial, 2008.

Hindrichs, Gunnar. "Scheitern als Rettung. Ästhetische Erfahrung nach Adorno." *Deutsche Vierteljahrsschrift für Literaturwissenschaft und Geistesgeschichte* 74, 1 (2000): 146–75.

Hohendahl, Peter Uwe. "Aesthetic Violence: The Concept of the Ugly in Adorno's *Aesthetic Theory*." *Cultural Critique* 60 (2005): 170–96.

———. "Adorno: The Discourse of Philosophy and the Problem of Language." *The Actuality of Adorno: Critical Essays on Adorno and the Postmodern*. Edited by Max Pensky. Albany: SUNY Press, 1997.

Horkheimer, Max. *Between Philosophy and Social Science: Selected Early Writings*. Translated by G. Frederick Hunter, Matthew S. Kramer, and John Torpey. Cambridge: The MIT Press, 1993.

Huhn, Tom, and Lambert Zuidervaart, eds. *The Semblance of Subjectivity*. Cambridge: MIT Press, 1998.

Husserl, Edmund. *The Crisis of European Sciences and Transcendental Phenomenology: An Introduction to Phenomenological Philosophy*. Translated by David Carr. Evanston: Northwestern University Press, 1970.

———. *Ideas: General Introduction to Pure Phenomenology*. Translated by W. R. Boyce Gibson. New York: Routledge, 2002.

Jameson, Fredric. *Aesthetics and Politics*. London: Verso, 2007.

———. *Late Marxism:Adorno , or, The Persistence of the Dialectic*. London: Verso, 1996.

Jay, Martin. *Songs of Experience: Modern American and European Variations on a Universal Theme*. Berkeley: University of California Press, 2005.

———. "Against Consolation: Walter Benjamin and the Refusal to Mourn." In *Refractions of Violence*. New York: Routledge, 2003, 11–24.

Johnson, Harriet. "Undignified Thoughts After Nature: Adorno's Aesthetic Theory." *Critical Horizons* 12, 3 (2011): 372–95.

Joseph, Branden W. "'A Therapeutic Value for City Dwellers': The Development of John Cage's Early Avant-Garde Aesthetic Position." In *John Cage: Music, Philosophy, and Intention, 1933-1950*. Edited by David W. Patterson. New York: Routledge, 2002.

Kant, Immanuel. *Critique of Judgment*. Translated by Werner S. Pluhar. Cambridge: Hackett Publishing Company, 1984.

———. *Critique of the Power of Judgment*. Translated by Paul Guyer and Eric Matthews. New York: Cambridge University Press, 2000.

———. "What is Enlightenment?" In *Kant: Political Writings*. Cambridge, UK: Cambridge University Press, 1784, 54–60.

Kern, Andrea. *Schöne Lust*. Frankfurt/Main: Suhrkamp, 2000.

Key, Susan. "John Cage's Imaginary Landscape No. 1: Through the Looking Glass." *John Cage: Music, Philosophy, and Intention*. Edited by David W. Patterson. New York: Routledge, 2002.

Kierkegaard, Søren. *Philosophical Fragments/Johannes Climacus*. Translated by Hong and Hong. Princeton: Princeton University Press, 1985.

Krakauer, Eric L. *Disposition of the Subject: Reading Adorno's Dialectic of Technology*. Evanston: Northwestern University Press, 1998.

Lacoue-Labarthe, Phillippe. "The Caesura of the Speculative." In *Typography: Mimesis, Philosophy, Politics*. Edited by Christopher Fynsk. Stanford: Stanford University Press, 1998, 208–35.

Lash, Scott. "Experience." *Theory, Culture & Society* 23 (2006): 335–40.

Latour, Bruno. *Pandora's Hope: Essays on the Reality of Science Studies*. Cambridge: Harvard University Press, 1999.

Leibniz, Gottfried. *Monadology*. Translated by Llyod Strickland. Edinburgh: Edinburgh University Press, 2014.

Lonitz, Henri. *Theodor W. Adorno. Walter Benjamin. Briefwechsel 1928-1940*. Frankfurt/Main: Suhrkamp, 1994, 16–19.

Lukács, Georg. "Reification and the Consciousness of the Proletariat." *History and Class Consciousness*. Cambridge: MIT Press, 1971.

MacDonald, Ian. "The Wounder Will Heal: Cognition and Reconciliation in Hegel and Adorno." *Philosophy Today* 44 (2000): 132–39.

Marcuse, Herbert. *One-Dimensional Man*. Boston: Beacon Press, 1964.

Marx, Karl, and Frederick Engels. "Contribution to the Critique of Hegel's *Philosophy of Law*. Introduction." *Collected Works*, vol. 3. Edited by James S. Allen, et al. New York: International Publishers, 1975.

———. "The German Ideology." *Collected Works*, vol. 5. Edited by James S. Allen, et al. New York: International Publishers, 1975.

———. "Die deutsche Ideologie." *Werke*, vol. 3. Berlin: Dietz Verlag, 1962.

———. "Zur Kritik der Hegelschen Rechtsphilosophie. Einleitun." *Werke*, vol. 1. Edited by Karl Dietz. Berlin: Verlag, 1976.

Marx, Karl. *Capital: A Critique of Political Economy*, vol. 2. Translated by David Fernbach. New York: Penguin Books, 1978.
———. *Das Kapital*, vol. 2. *Werke*, vol. 24. Edited by Karl Dietz. Berlin: Verlag, 1963.
———. *Selected Writings*. Edited by Lawrence H. Simon. Indianapolis: Hackett Publishing Company, Inc., 1994.
Menke, Christoph. *The Sovereignty of Art. Aesthetic Negativity in Adorno and Derrida*. Translated by Neil Solomon. Cambridge: MIT Press, 1999.
Miller, Elaine. "Negativity, Iconoclasm, Mimesis: Kristeva and Benjamin on Political Art." *Idealistic Studies* 38, 1-2 (2008): 55–74.
Morgan, Alastair. *Adorno's Concept of Life*. New York: Continuum, 2007.
Morgan, Marcia. *Kierkegaard and Critical Theory*. Lanham: Lexington Books, 2012.
———. "Adorno's Kierkegaard Reception: 1929-1933." *Kierkegaard and Critical Theory*. Lanham: Rowman & Littlefield/ Lexington Books, 2012.
Müller-Doohm, Stefan. *Adorno: A Biography*. Translated by Rodney Livingstone. Cambridge: Polity, 2009.
Neuhouser, Fredrick. *Rousseau's Theodicy of Self-Love: Evil, Rationality, and the Drive for Recognition*. New York: Oxford University Press, 2008.
Nicholsen, Shierry Weber. "Language: Its Murmurings, Its Darkness, and Its Silver Rib." *Exact Imagination, Late Work: On Adorno's Aesthetics*. Cambridge: The MIT Press, 1997.
Nietzsche, Friedrich. *The Birth of Tragedy and Other Writings*. Translated by Raymond Geuss. Cambridge, UK: Cambridge University Press, 1999.
———. *The Gay Science*. Translated by Walter Kaufmann. New York: Vintage Books, 1974.
O'Connor, Brian. "Adorno and the Problem of Givenness." *Revue Internationale de Pilosophie* 58, 227 (2004/1): 85–99.
Palamarek, Michael K. "Adorno's Dialectics of Language." In *Adorno and the Need in Thinking: New Critical Essays*. Edited by Donald A. Burke, et al. Toronto: University of Toronto Press, 2007.
Pensky, Max. *Melancholy Dialectics*. Amherst: University of Massachusetts Press, 1993.
Pizer, John. "Jameson's Adorno, or, the Persistence of the Utopian." *New German Critique* 58 (Winter 1993): 130–31.
Rancière, Jacques. *Aesthetics and its Discontents*. Translated by Steven Corcoran. Malden: Polity Press, 2004.
———. "The Aesthetic Revolution and Its Outcomes." *Dissensus*. Translated by Steven Corcoran. New York: Verso, 2010.
Richter, Gerhard, ed. *Language without Soil: Adorno and Late Philosophical Modernity*. New York: Fordham University Press, 2010.
Rosen, Michael. *Hegel's Dialectic and its Criticism*. Cambridge: Cambridge University Press, 1982.
———. *Voluntary Servitude: False Consciousness and the Theory of Ideology*. Cambridge: Harvard University Press, 1996.
Rousseau, Jean-Jacques. *Discourse on the Origin of Inequality*. Translated by Donald A. Cress. Indianapolis: Hackett Publishing Co., 1992.
———. *Emile*. Translated by William H. Payne. New York: D. Appleton and Co., 1918.
Schaeffer, Pierre. *In Search of Concrete Music*. Translated by Christine North and John Dack. Berkeley: University of California Press, 2012.
———. "Acousmatics." *Audio Culture*. Edited by Christoph Cox and Daniel Warner. New York: Continuum, 2010.
Schiller, Friedrich. *On the Aesthetic Education of Man*. Translated by Elizabeth M. Wilkinson and L. A. Willoughby. New York: Oxford University Press, 1982.
Schlegel, Friedrich. "Athenäumsfragmente." *Friedrich Schlegel: Kritische Schriften und Fragmente*. Edited by E. Behler and H. Eichner. Paderborn: Schöningh, 1988.
Schopenhauer, Arthur. *The World as Will and Idea*, vol. I. Translated by E. F. J. Payne. New York: Dover Publications Inc., 2003.
Seel, Martin. *Adornos Philosophie der Kontemplation*. Frankfurt: Suhrkamp, 2004.
Shusterman, Richard. "The End of Aesthetic Experience." *The Journal of Aesthetics and Art Criticism* 55, 1 (1997): 29–41.

Smith, Stephen Decatur. "Awakening Dead Time: Adorno on Husserl, Benjamin, and the Temporality of Music." *Contemporary Music Review* 31 (2012): 389–409.

Snyder, Joel. "Benjamin on Reproducibility and Aura: A Reading of 'The Work of Art in the Age of Technical Reproducibility." *Benjamin: Philosophy, Aesthetics, History.* Edited by G. Smith. Chicago: University of Chicago Press, 1989.

Steiner, Uwe. *Walter Benjamin: An Introduction to his Work and Thought.* Chicago: University of Chicago Press, 2010.

Stone, Alison. "Adorno and Logic." *Theodor Adorno: Key Concepts.* Edited by Deborah Cook. Stocksfield: Acumen, 2008.

Stone, Alison. "Adorno and the Disenchantment of Nature" *Philosophy and Social Criticism* 32, 2 (2006): 231–53.

Symons, Stéphane. "The Ability to Not-Shine. The Word "Unscheinbar" in the Writings of Walter Benjamin." *Angelaki: Journal of the Theoretical Humanities* 18, 4 (2013), 101–23.

Tone, Yasunao. "John Cage and Recording." *Leonardo Music Journal* 13 (2013): 11–15.

Valéry, Paul. *Oeuvres II.* Paris: Pléade, 1960.

Weber, Samuel. *Theatricality as Medium.* New York: Fordham University Press, 2004.

Wellmer, Albrecht. *Versuch über Musik und Sprache.* München: Diaphanes Verlag, 2009.

———. "Adorno, Modernity, and the Sublime." In *Endgames: The Irreconcilable Nature of Modernity.* Translated by David Midgley. Cambridge: MIT Press, 1998.

———. "Modernism and Postmodernism: The Critique of Reason Since Adorno." In *The Persistence of Modernity: Essays on Aesthetics, Ethics and Postmodernism.* Translated by David Midgley. Malden: Polity Press, 1991.

Williams, Alastair. "Cage and Postmodernism." *The Cambridge Companion to John Cage.* Edited by David Nicholls. New York: Cambridge University Press, 2002.

Wittgenstein, Ludwig. *Philosophical Occasions.* Edited and translated by J. Klagge and A. Nordmann. Indianapolis: Hackett, 1993.

———. *Tractatus Logico Philosophicus* . Translated by D. F. Pears and B. F. McGuiness. London: Routledge and Kegan Paul, 1961.

Wolin, Richard. *Walter Benjamin: An Aesthetic of Redemption.* Berkeley: University of California Press, 1994.

Wyllie, Robert. "Kierkegaard's Critique of the Public Sphere," *Telos*, 166 (2014): 57–79.

Zuckermann, Mosche, ed. *Theodor W. Adorno: Philosoph des beschädigten Lebens.* Göttingen: Wallstein Verlag, 2004.

Zuidervaart, Lambert. *Adorno's Aesthetic Theory: The Redemption of Illusion.* Cambrdige: MIT Press, 1993.

Index

aesthetic autonomy, xx, 4, 7–8, 15n5, 131–133, 134, 135, 138, 142n33, 178, 185

aesthetic comportment, xvi, xvii, 6–7, 28, 69, 77, 129, 131–132, 149–150, 154, 157n24

aesthetic education, 178–179, 180, 185, 186, 188n1

aesthetic experience, xi–xiii, xiv, xvi, xvii–xxiii, xxiiin7, xxivn8, 17, 26, 53, 67–69, 71, 73–75, 78, 79n3, 85, 86, 91, 95, 99, 129–130, 131–132, 134, 137–138, 139, 140–141, 142n15, 145, 149, 151–152, 153–155, 156n4, 157n24, 159–160, 163, 164, 169, 169–170, 171, 174n39, 175n40

aesthetic judgment, 26–28, 67, 81n49, 111, 137, 143n43, 168–169, 170, 178, 180, 186, 189n8

Adorno, Theodor W.: relation to Benjamin, xi–xii, xiii, xiii–xvi, xvii–xix, xx, xxii, xxiiin5, xxivn8, 1–9, 12–13, 14, 17–19, 20, 22, 23, 25, 26, 28, 29, 29n14, 31, 32–37, 38, 42, 45n22, 48, 49, 52, 53, 57–58, 58, 59, 60, 63n24, 67, 69, 74–75, 76, 78–79, 79n7, 83, 126n46, 127n70, 160, 161, 173n3, 174n10, 175n59; 'The Actuality of Philosophy', xxiiin1, xxiiin7, 29n14, 48, 54, 56, 161, 171, 175n63; *Aesthetic Theory* , xi, xiv, xvi, 15n28, 17, 26, 69–70, 74, 77, 79n2,

81n43, 81n46–81n49, 129, 130, 134, 138–139, 149, 151, 153, 153–149, 155, 157n24, 162, 171, 175n59; *Dialectic of Enlightenment*, xi, 56, 76–77, 80n16, 80n41, 81n42, 136, 139, 146, 156n15, 174n12; 'The Idea of Natural History', 48, 56; *The Jargon of Authenticity*, 56, 59; *Kierkegaard: Construction of the Aesthetic*, 20, 21, 25, 48; *Minima Moralia*, 43n4, 45n27, 62, 149, 154; *Negative Dialectics*, xviii, 43n1, 56, 147; *Notes to Literature*, 48, 59; 'On Subject and Object', 152, 171; 'On the Use of Foreign Words', 48, 60, 61; 'Theses on the Language of the Philosopher', 48, 59, 60–61

alienation, xx, 53, 73, 100, 103, 104, 107, 179

allegory, allegorical, xx, 48, 49, 57–58, 94, 100–101, 103, 109n10, 180, 181

art, xi–xiii, xiv, xvi, xvii, xx–xxii, xxivn20, 1–4, 5–14, 16n41, 26, 28, 59, 67–72, 73, 74–76, 77, 78–79, 79n7, 81n49, 84–88, 90–91, 95, 99–100, 103–104, 105–107, 111–113, 120, 124n1, 125n18, 127n70, 128n76, 129–136, 136–138, 139–141, 145, 152, 153–154, 156, 159–164, 167–169, 170–171, 175n44, 175n48, 175n59, 178, 180, 182, 185, 187–188

artifice, 105

199

Contributors

Georg W. Bertram is professor of philosophy at Freie Universität Berlin. He is the author of *Kunst als menschliche Praxis. Eine Ästhetik* (2014); *Die Sprache und das Ganze. Entwurf einer antireduktionistischen Sprachphilosophie* (2006); and *Hermeneutik und Dekonstruktion. Konturen einer Auseinandersetzung der Gegenwartsphilosophie* (2002). His research interests include Aesthetics, Philosophy of Language, Theory of Subjectivity, Social Ontology, Hegel, and contemporary philosophy of different traditions: Hermeneutics, Critical Theory, Postanalytic Philosophy, and Structuralism.

Marcia Morgan received her Ph.D. in philosophy from the New School for Social Research in New York City. She is currently Associate Professor of Philosophy and Director of the Women's and Gender Studies Program at Muhlenberg College in Pennsylvania. She is author of *Kierkegaard and Critical Theory* (Lexington Books, 2012), and editor and co-author with Agnes Heller of *The Concept of the Beautiful* (Lexington Books, 2012).

Natalia Baeza is a post-doctoral researcher at the University of Florence, after completing her Ph.D. at Notre Dame University. Her research interests include Hegel, Adorno, Critical Theory, and Psychoanalysis. She has written articles dealing with the problem of determinate negation in Hegel, dialectical method in Hegel and Adorno, and paranoid projection in Adorno.

Eduardo Mendieta is professor of philosophy and chair of the department of philosophy at the State University of New York, Stony Brook. He is the author of *The Adventures of Transcendental Philosophy* (Rowman & Littlefield, 2002) and *Global Fragments: Globalizations, Latinamericanisms, and Critical Theory* (SUNY Press, 2007). He is also co-editor with Jonathan

VanAntwerpen of *The Power of Religion in the Public Sphere* (Columbia University Press, 2011), and with Craig Calhoun and Jonathan Van Antwerpen of *Habermas and Religion* (Polity, 2013), and with Stuart Elden of *Reading Kant's Geography* (SUNY Press, 2011) He recently finished a book titled *The Philosophical Animal*, which will be published by SUNY Press in 2015.

Nathan Ross is associate professor of philosophy at Oklahoma City University. He is author of *On Mechanism in Hegel's Social and Political Philosophy* (Routledge, 2008), and articles on Hegel, German Romanticism, Schiller, Benjamin, and Adorno. He recently translated Georg W. Bertram's *Art as Human Practice: An Aesthetics* and is currently completing a book on aesthetic experience in classical German Philosophy and Critical Theory.

Alison Ross is an Australian Research Council Future Fellow in Philosophy at Monash University. Her research focuses on the History of Modern Philosophy, Aesthetics, and Critical Theory. She is the author of *Walter Benjamin's Concept of the Image* (Routledge, 2014) and *The Aesthetic Paths of Philosophy: Presentation in Kant, Heidegger, Lacoue-Labarthe and Nancy* (Stanford, 2007).

Stéphane Symons is assistant professor of Aesthetics and Philosophy of Art at the Institute of Philosophy at the KU Leuven, Belgium. His main research interests are twentieth-century French and German thought and literature.

Joseph Weiss is a lecturer at DePaul University in Chicago. His main research interests include Art Theory, Music Aesthetics, Marxism, and Critical Theory.

Surti Singh is an assistant professor of philosophy at The American University in Cairo. She specializes in Critical Theory, Aesthetics, Social and Political Philosophy, and Feminism.

Rick Elmore received his Ph.D. in Philosophy from DePaul University in 2012. He works primarily in the areas of contemporary French philosophy and Critical Theory with a focus on violence, ecology, and ethics. Rick is currently a Lecturer in Philosophy at Appalachian State University.

Andrea Sakoparnig is a PhD candidate at the Free University Berlin and a member of the International Research Training Group InterArt. She has worked with the Collaborative Research Centre 626 "Aesthetic Experience and the Dissolution of Artistic Limits" (Berlin). She has co-edited *Paradigmenwechsel. Wandel in den Künsten und Wissenschaften* and published several articles on Adorno's *Aesthetic Theory*. Her current research focuses on the concept of aesthetic objectivity. For ongoing projects and recent publications, see www.andrea-sakoparnig.de.

Tom Huhn is the chair of the Art History Department and the BFA Visual & Critical Studies Department at the School of Visual Arts in New York City. His books include *Imitation and Society: The Persistence of Mimesis in the Aesthetics of Burke, Hogarth, and Kant*; *The Cambridge Companion to Adorno*; and *The Semblance of Subjectivity: Essays in Adorno's Aesthetic Theory*.